Consultation within WTO Dispute Settlement:
A Chinese Perspective

Studies in Global Economic Law
Studien zum globalen Wirtschaftsrecht
Études en droit économique mondial

edited by Thomas Cottier

Volume 10

PETER LANG
Bern · Berlin · Bruxelles · Frankfurt am Main · New York · Oxford · Wien

Qi Zhang

Consultation within WTO Dispute Settlement: A Chinese Perspective

PETER LANG
Bern · Berlin · Bruxelles · Frankfurt am Main · New York · Oxford · Wien

Bibliographic information published by Die Deutsche Bibliothek
Die Deutsche Bibliothek lists this publication in the Deutsche Nationalbibliografie; detailed bibliographic data is available on the Internet at ‹http://dnb.ddb.de›.

British Library and Library of Congress Cataloguing-in-Publication Data:
A catalogue record for this book is available from *The British Library*, Great Britain, and from *The Library of Congress*, USA.

Published with a grant from the Faculty of Law, University of Bern, Switzerland.

ISSN 1423-9531
ISBN 978-3-03911-239-5
US-ISBN 978-0-8204-8043-5

Hochfeldstrasse 32, Postfach 746, CH-3000 Bern 9, Switzerland
info@peterlang.com, www.peterlang.com, www.peterlang.net

Acknowledgements

For permission to quote their views, I am grateful to the following Geneva-based WTO Mission representatives for sharing their experiences on the consultation procedure under the DSU of the WTO: Gustavo Nerio Lunazzi (Permanent Mission of Argentina), Cathy Raper (Permanent Mission of Australia), A. M. Badrul Hassan (Permanent Mission of Bangladesh), Celso de Tarso Pereira (Permanent Mission of Brazil), Rambod Behboodi (Permanent Mission of Canada), Mathias Francke (Permanent Mission of Chile), Liyong Jiang (Permanent Mission of China), Raimund Raith (Permanent Mission of the European Communities), Erika Koszegi (Permanent Mission of Hungary), Atul Kaushik (Permanent Mission of India), Keiichi Higuchi and Makiko Oshima (Permanent Mission of Japan), Hae Kwan Chung (Permanent Mission of Korea), Sr. Mateo Diego-Fernandez (Permanent Mission of Mexico), David Evans (Permanent Mission of New Zealand), Inger Gregersen (Permanent Mission of Norway), Mirko Zambelli (Permanent Mission of Switzerland), and Pornchai Danvivathana (Permanent Mission of Thailand).

The author would like to acknowledge the support of the following delegation diplomats in providing their data and sharing their opinions to fulfill the incomplete information on the WTO website: Claudia Uribe (Permanent Mission of Colombia), Johel Romero (Permanent Mission of Honduras), Krzysztof Januszek (Permanent Mission of Poland), and Mehmet Tan (Permanent Mission of Turkey).

I wish to thank Professor William Davey, Edwini Kessie of the WTO, Matthias Oesch of SECO, Fernando Pierola of Advisory Center on WTO Law and Professor Andreas R. Ziegler of Lausannne University for their invaluable suggestions and information.

Special thanks to Professor Thomas Cottier for academic supervision and moreover the support and encouragement throughout the whole process of writing, which is an enjoyable and rewarding experience.

Table of Contents

Part III
Consultation in WTO Dispute Settlement

Preface

Since the adoption of the WTO Agreements in 1995, considerable attention has been paid to the emerging and successful system of legal dispute settlement, undertaken by the panels and the new Appellate Body, under the auspices of the Dispute Settlement Body of the WTO. The system, however, is not limited to legal dispute settlement. It entails a mandatory phase of consultations to be held by the Parties prior to legal dispute settlement. More than fifty per cent of all disputes formally notified do not reach the panel stage and thus are either settled by consultation and negotiations, or dropped.

This phase of the dispute settlement process has so far received relatively little attention in scholarly work. Despite the lawyer's genuine interest – and sometimes even obsession – with legal procedures, there is a lack of evidence and empirical data on the consultations, which are conducted in a confidential manner between the Parties and from which the WTO Secretariat is excluded.

Dr Zhang Qi, undertook to fill this gap in her doctoral dissertation, which was submitted to the Faculty of Law of the University of Berne. During her research at the World Trade Institute from 2002 to 2005, she shed light on the practices of consultation in the WTO. She endeavoured to clarify the legal concept of consultation and its relationship to formal dispute settlement. The duty to consult is explored together with the question as to what extent panels should, or should not, review the process and content of consultations held, in preliminary rulings. To this end, she not only undertook an analysis of the case law and doctrine, but also gathered empirical information. She conducted a number of interviews with delegations in Geneva on the way consultations are led, the diverging practices and attitudes to the consultation process, and negotiations within the dispute settlement system. Her findings are reported in this book. Another interesting feature of the book is that the author looks at the problem from a Chinese perspective, taking into account the legal traditions of this emerging trading power. The book successfully combines legal and empirical work: it offers new insights into the consultation phase of dispute settlement.

Colleagues at the World Trade Institute will not only remember Dr Zhang Qi for her love of classical music and concerts in and around Berne. First and foremost, they will remember her as a friendly colleague, animatedly discussing her topic in workshops and seminars as she explored problems of interest to diplomats and lawyers, practitioners and scholars alike.

Berne, September 2006 Professor Thomas Cottier

Abbreviations

AB	Appellate Body
ACP	the African, Caribbean and Pacific States
ACWL	Advisory Center on WTO Law
AD	Antidumping
ADR	Alternative Dispute Resolution
AJIL	American Journal of International Law
APEC	Asian-Pacific Economic Co-operation
ARG	Argentina
ASEAN	the Association of Southeast Asian Nations
A.S.I.L.PROC	American Society of International Law Proceedings
ATC	Agreement on Textiles and Clothing
AUS	Australia
BAN	Bangladesh
BISD	Basic Instruments and Selected Documents
BRA	Brazil
CAN	Canada
CEFTA	Central European Free Trade Agreement
CH	Switzerland
CHI	Chile
CHN	China
C.M.L.Rev	Common Market Law Review
Com	Complainant
CPs	Contract Parties
CUP	Cambridge University Press
CVD	Countervailing duty
C.M.L.Rev	Common Market Law Review
DG	Director-General
DISC	Disc International Sales Corporation
DSB	Dispute Settlement Body
DSM	Dispute Settlement Mechanism
DSU	Understanding on Rules and Procedures Governing of the Disputes

EC	European Communities
ECJ	European Court of Justice
EEC	European Economic Community
EU	European Union
FDM.I.L.J.	Fordham International Law Journal
FSC	Foreign Sales Company
GATS	The General Agreement on Trade in Service
GATT	General Agreement on Tariffs and Trade
GATS	General Agreement on Trade in Services
GDP	Gross Domestic Product
GMO	Genetically Modified Organisms
GNI	Gross National Income
GNP	Gross National Product
GPA	Government Procurement Agreement
GSP	Generalized System of Preferences
HUN	Hungary
IC	integrated circuits
ICJ	International Court of Justice
ILM	International Legal Materials
ILR	International Law Report
IMF	International Monetary Fund
IND	India
INT' Law	International Lawyer
IPRs	Intellectual Property Rights
ITLOS	International Tribunal for the Law of the Sea
ITO	International Trade Organisation
IMF	International Monetary Fund
JAP	Japan
J.I.E.L.	Journal of International Economic Law
J.L.ECON.ORG	The Journal of Law, Economics & Organization
J.W.T	Journal of World Trade
KOR	Korea
LDCs	Least Developed Countries
LLDCs	Landlocked Developing Countries
L.P.I.B	Law and Policy in International Business
MAS	Mutually Agreed Solution
MERCOSUR	common market of the southern cone
MEX	Mexico

MFN	Most-Favoured-Nation
m/ina	Between Mutually Agreed Solution and Inactive
Minn. L. Rev.	Minnesota Law Review
MOFTEC	Ministry of Foreign Trade and Economic Cooperation
MTO	Multilateral Trade Organisation
NAFTA	North American Free Trade Agreement
NGO	Non-Governmental Organization
N or I	nullification or impairment
NOR	Norway
NT	National Treatment
NTB	non-tariffs barriers
NZ	New Zealand
OECD	Organization for Economic Co-operation and Development
PCIJ	Permanent Court of International Justice
Pep.D.R.L.J	Pepperdine Dispute Resolution Law Journal
Res	Respondent
RPT	Reasonable Period of Time
RTA	Regional Trade Agreement
SCM	Agreement on Subsidies and Countervailing Measures
S&D	Special and Deferential
SDT	Special and Deferential Treatment
SIDS	Small Island Developing States
SPS	Agreement on the Application of Sanitary and Phytosanitary Measures
TBT	Agreement on Technical Barriers to Trade
THA	Thailand
TMB	Textiles Monitoring Body
TRIM	Agreement on Trade-Related Investment Measure
TRIPS	Trade-Related Aspects of Intellectual Property Rights
TRQ	Tariff-rate Quota
U.N.	United Nations
UNCLOS	United Nations Convention on the Law of the Sea
UNCTAD	United Nations Conference on Trade and Development

U. Pa. J. Int'l Eco. L.	University of Pennsylvania Journal of International Economic Law
US	United States of America
USTR	Office of the United Sates Trade Representative
VAT	Value-added tax
VCLT	Vienna Convention on the Law of Treaties
WB	World Bank (International Bank for Reconstruction and Development)
WTO	World Trade Organization

Introduction

I. Scope of this Thesis

This study of the World Trade Organization (WTO) dispute settlement proceedings explores the consultation stage from a Chinese perspective. Dispute settlement procedures in the WTO require political and legal methods to settle disputes. The proceedings include consultations, the Panel, the Appellate Body (AB), and implementation. Consultations, under Article 4 of the Understanding on Rules and Procedures Governing the Settlement of Disputes (DSU), are a precondition for recourse to litigation procedures.

The procedure of consultations plays a significant role in general. During the General Agreement on Tariffs and Trade (GATT) period (since 1947), the political importance of consultations was particularly apparent. Consultations have continued to increase in number and efficiency as time has progressed. As of 31 January 2006, 335 consultation requests have been made, among them 186 (55%) disputes which ended before a Panel ruling, and 121 (36%) disputes which were settled after the Panel stage.[1]

From the statistics it would appear that a significant number of disputes have been resolved at the consultation stage. This suggests that the role of consultations in WTO dispute settlement proceedings is still vital. However, compared with later stages of the WTO dispute settlement procedures, this initial phase, has rarely received much attention. The research work described in this dissertation is intended to address a perceived paucity of structured views on the subject, and to provide insights into aspects of classical theory and present practice.

It is true that litigious procedures, in the WTO dispute settlement mechanism (DSM), have matured after over half a century of working experience, during which they have been applied by both developed and

1 See Annex II, the status of all disputes as of 31 January 2006.

developing WTO Member States.[2] Nevertheless, this does not mean the DSU encourages its Members to initiate the judicial mechanism to solve the disputes. Instead, the DSU aims to provide a forum for its Member States to reach mutually acceptable agreements. Judicial means for dispute settlement is not a goal, but a final method. Therefore, this study contributes to the debate on the balance of judicial and diplomatic proceedings.

As its name suggests, the DSM, which began with GATT and became the WTO's DSU, has more to do with settling disputes than seeking definitive answers for every case. What follows is an overview of the consultation process, including the separate roles of international law and WTO law, leading to diplomatic method in theory and practice.

For a better understanding of the so-called 'balance theory',[3] the study utilizes Chinese classical philosophy, which is embedded in the network of Chinese social behaviour patterns in legal practice. So in some respects this thesis is an interdisciplinary study involving negotiation theory, game theory and trade policy analysis of various countries, despite being mainly a legal work.

Within this context, it is argued that the importance of the consultation stage, particularly in the DSU, should be emphasized against a background of dispute escalation and against the domination of single definition of legitimacy.

The thesis examines consultations in public international law, mainly focusing on international dispute settlement theory and methods of international dispute settlement in everyday practice and historically.

Then, the study transposes the research to a historical analysis of the consultation process, from the GATT era, when the whole institution was marked by diplomatic domination, to the present day WTO. I draw insights and comparisons with the DSM in the GATT and the DSU in the WTO.

The final part of this dissertation ranges over the consultation part of the DSU, re-emphasizing its usefulness, and raising some suggestions for improving it.

2 See IV, the WTO Time, in Part II of this thesis.
3 See Part III of this research work.

The structure of this study is as follows:

The theory of negotiations and the Chinese approach to law are introduced.

Part I presents consultations against the background of international law. It includes an overview of international dispute settlement, the means of international dispute settlement, the relationship between negotiations and consultations, dispute prevention and Alternative Dispute Resolution (ADR), and the application of consultations in international law.

Part II considers the status of consultation during the time of the GATT, so providing a historical perspective and revealing the procedures' invaluable *raison d'être*.[4]

Part III includes current consultations under the WTO, highlighting the latest theory, arguments, research achievement, interview transcript, statistics and textual analysis with a supporting case study.

The final part puts forward recommendations for consideration.

II. Research Methodology

Research for this thesis on the means of dispute settlement is significant, as procedures are important as well as being a difficult aspect of the WTO. Analysis on consultations could be ineffectual in the absence of accurate data and sufficient materials.

For the sake of objectivity and impartiality in collecting data, the figures used stem either from quoted literature or WTO documents made available on-line. Some data cannot be found on the WTO website; these have, therefore, been obtained from some authoritative organizations which have been involved in research into WTO disputes. The purpose of this twofold approach is to maintain originality and faithfully disclose the facts, hence to avoid processing and reprocessing material or subjective assessment. All data from the disputes are shown in Annex II.

Any research is subjectively coloured in that it reflects researchers' arguments. In my view, this is because every coin has two sides. That is

4 Rational ground for existence.

to say, it depends on from which perspective the purpose of research is regarded, either in theory or in practice.

Researchers who have studied negotiations/consultations without taking into account the real-life experiences of practitioners, risk two things: failure to capture the essence of the process as it is actually practiced, and the consequential inability to communicate with negotiators because they failed to understand the process as negotiators perceive it.[5]

As the number of empirical studies within other disciplines including economics, politics, sociology and international relations grows, there is an increasingly pressing need to find a way to translate theoretical findings into language that practitioners understand and then to test the findings against the experience of practitioners.

Moreover, the central part of this thesis is built on interviews so as to solve some of the puzzles and to overcome the unavailability of official records kept by the WTO of consultations proceedings.

In this study seventeen Member States represent different continents including Africa, Asia, Australia, Europe, North America and South America.[6] In addition, Members have been selected to represent developed countries, developing countries and least-developed countries, most of which have frequently used the WTO dispute settlement mechanism.

These countries are Argentina, Australia, Bangladesh, Brazil, Canada, Chile, China, the European Union (EU), Hungary, India, Japan, Korea, Mexico, New Zealand, Norway, Switzerland and Thailand. A questionnaire was designed to make participation easier for the interviewees (see Annex I). A few representatives could not answer all the questions posed because of limited or no experience.[7]

5 Zartman, I. W. & Berman, M. R. The Practical Negotiator, New Haven and London: Yale University Press, 1982; xii.

6 There is no country on Antarctica.

7 According to author's statistics, fifteen countries have experience of the whole DSU proceedings both as a complainant and as a respondent. These fifteen countries are Argentina, Australia, Brazil, Canada, Chile, EU, Guatemala, India, Japan, Korea, Mexico, Philippines, Thailand, Turkey and United States. In this thesis, the top 12 disputants were interviewed with the exception of the US, the biggest player in the DSU, which declined to share its views. Nigeria, an African country, agreed to be interviewed, but as it had had no experience in this area, the representative offered his views merely as an observer. Because of concern about objectiveness and coherence, the results of this interview had to be excluded.

This thesis focuses on a large number of case analyses, given either the Panels' or Abs various factual and legal findings and treaty interpretation of the consultations. Background information related to any specific dispute was looked for online. Most of the documents scrutinized are from authoritative websites such as that of the WTO, as part of the requirement for first-hand and original research information wherever possible.

Many experts and scholars (including politicians, economists, lawyers, jurists, sociologists and the staff from various international organizations), have contributed much to the literature highlighting their insight in this field. Therefore, it seemed desirable to include a literature review section in this thesis.

In this thesis, a method of comparison permeates the interrelationships such as international public law and WTO law. The aim is to establish certain links vertically and horizontally in order to help understand the subject. This is facilitated by the use of tables, figures and flow charts.

III. Theory of Negotiations/Consultations

The consultation is always related to the concept of the negotiation that shapes its theoretical framework. This and other considerations in chapter III, requires a broad understanding in order to plan further research on negotiations/consultations in international law and in the DSU, as well as in the successful model of GATT.

A theoretical understanding of this subject is important. Therefore, I use a model to clarify the element of negotiations. The model identifies three stages in the process:[8]

1. Diagnose the situation and decide if negotiations are desirable;
2. Negotiate a formula or common definition of the conflict in terms amenable to a solution;
3. Negotiate the details to implement the formula on precise points of disputes.

8 See Zartman 1982; 9.

A process model is a more useful preparation for reality than a mere checklist because it is not a rigid construct.

There is no theory of negotiation that can encompass and explain the entire process, but there are a number of well-developed theoretical approaches that are distributed over different subjects, namely economics, international relations, law, management, politics, psychology and sociology.

It is easy to understand that there is no definitive winner or loser during the procedure of negotiations compared to judicial dispute resolution, although both parties might prefer to obtain an agreement, even if unbalanced. The winner is simply the one who gets closer to his objectives than the other, so that a successful negotiation/consultation means that ultimately both sides win.[9]

However, not all issues are negotiable at a given time. The parties in conflict may refuse to communicate, and, in that event, no negotiation is possible. Even if they are willing to communicate, directly or through other parties, the issue itself may still be non-negotiable. The reasons can be considered either objective or subjective, depending on one's view of perception and reality. After all, if every conflict could be resolved through negotiations, there would be no such thing as war.

When negotiation proves impossible, law has to be invoked, within the field of international dispute settlement, and *vice versa*.

A mutually acceptable resolution is certainly possible. These are two ways of arriving at an agreement: one is induction – to put the agreement together, building it primarily through mutual compromise or exchanged concessions on specific items; the other is deduction – to establish first the general principles, or formula, governing the issues susceptible to solution and then to work out the details of implementation.[10]

Figure 1 illustrates the course of normal negotiations:

9 See Saner, R. The Expert Negotiator, The Hague, London and Boston: Kluwer Law International, 2000; 39.

10 Zartman 1982; 89.

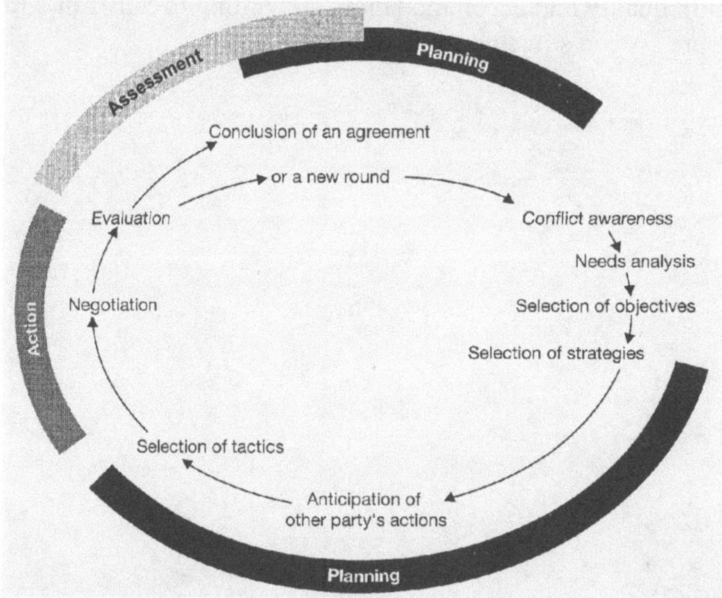

Figure 1. The cycle of negotiation
(Source: Saner, *The Expert Negotiator*)

Success in negotiation is often not a matter of chance, but the result of good planning and specialized skills. It could include the following procedures and elements:

Preparation: know yourself and your adversary. "If you know the enemy and know yourself, you need not fear the result of a hundred battles. If you know yourself but not the enemy, for every victory gained you will also suffer a defeat. If you know neither the enemy nor yourself, you will succumb in every battle."[11]

Making concessions: strategy and tactics. Strategy is an overall guideline that indicates the direction to take in order to achieve one's objectives. Elements of strategy include: positions in the conflict, competition, collaboration, compromise, avoidance, common interests, rela-

11 Sun Tsu, III. Attack by Stratagem in The Art of War (Original Title: Sun Zi Bing Fa, ca. 490 B.C.), London: Hodder & Stoughton, 1981, or http://www.chinapage.com/sunzi-e.html#03, last visited 12 August 2004.

tionship quality and accommodation. According to Sun Tsu's theory, there are sixteen strategic paths (Figure 2).

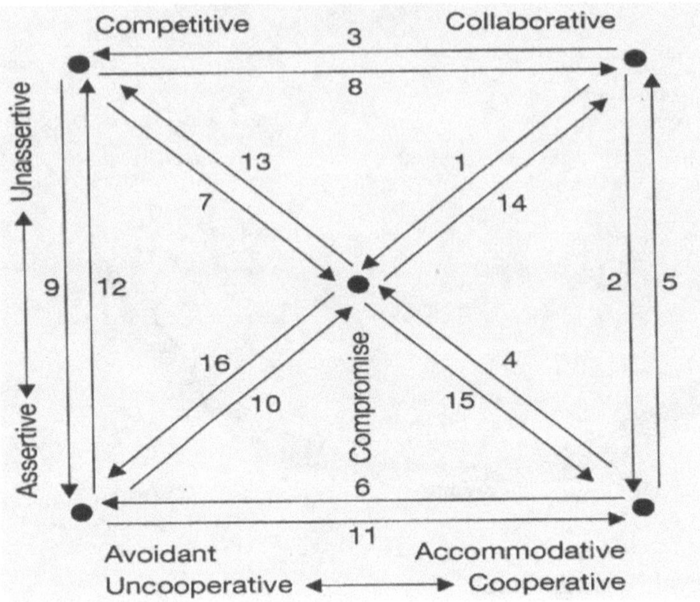

Figure 2. Sixteen strategic paths
(Source: Saner, *The Export Negotiator*)

All the options are open when it comes to deciding whether to pass from a confrontational stance to one of evasion or cooperation. Depending on the circumstances, any of the routes may constitute the optimum strategy.[12]

Tactics "always follow after strategy, fleshing it out with a concrete line of action".[13] It may not be directly oriented towards the objectives, but towards the strategy.

12 Saner 2000; 103–127.
13 *Ibid.*, p. 129.

IV. Chinese Approach to Law

Legalisation has an impact on the development of the WTO, and also influences the improvement of the DSU. Simultaneously, it presents challenges to the domestic legal systems, social life, cultures and beliefs of some Member States. China is a good example, where Confucianism has overwhelmingly influenced the country for thousands of years.

From the perspective of legal culture, the trend toward legalism within the WTO means the systemization of western ideologies, especially those of the United States. To the Chinese, the US has been characterized as a litigious society – one with too many lawyers and too much attention to legalism. However, the legal approach is the opposite of the Chinese tradition of solving disputes.[14]

Confucianism provides the basis for the norms of Chinese behaviour, emphasizing virtue, modal behaviour, reason, education and the rule of man. The 'bible' of Confucianism, named *Analects*, claims that the ultimate political goal is to create great harmony, where all people behave as brothers. Confucian values, identified as the foundation of China's great cultural tradition, have controlled the social order and regulated people in all their daily activities, including their legal consciousness, expectations of justice and trust in law.

Law in China appeared earlier than Confucianism, which emerged more than 2550 years ago.[15] The earliest law existed more than 4000 years ago, during the Xia Dynasty, the first dynasty in Chinese history. This legal tradition is distinct from the common law and civil law traditions of the West.[16] For the Chinese, law is for punishment rather than regulation. At that time Chinese law meant primarily criminal law. The

14 See Peng, S. Y. The WTO Legalistic Approach and East Asia: from the Legal Culture Perspective, in Asian-Pacific Law & Policy Journal 2000; 13:1; Keller, P. (ed.), Chinese Law and Legal Theory, Burlington: Ashgate, 2001; Yu, X. Z. Legal Pragmatism in the People's Republic of China. Journal of Chinese Law, 3 1989; 2: Wang, G. G. Chinese Law, The Hague: Kluwer Law International, 1999; Law and Punishment: the Western and the traditional Chinese 'Legal Mind', Oxford: Clarendon Press, 1986.

15 See Wang 1999; 11.

16 The legal system of China excludes the common law legal system of the Hong Kong Special Administrative Region and the civilian legal system of Taiwan.

emphasis on the penal code in Chinese law indicates that civil matters were either ignored entirely or included in the criminal codes. Ancient Chinese civil codes were few in number, and they were not independent of the criminal code.

To Confucius' followers, law is for uneducated people, and not for Confucians.[17] Traditional Chinese behave themselves properly and preserve social harmony. A well-known proverb describes law as something meant for an ordinary person, but not for a gentleman. A classic Confucius saying is, the gentleman understands righteousness; the educated man understands profit. For example, if a party was believed to be in the right position, it was better for him to be merciful to the wrong party and suffer a little. Forbearance was respected and such behaviour was highly praised by Confucius.

Confucians believe that education is the most essential and effective way to reach the goal of effective management.[18] They also follow the precept that education prevents what is going to happen, while law ameliorates what has already happened. Law is an instrument of last resort. The ancient Chinese considered an ideal society to be one that did not require extensive legislation or litigation because traditional Chinese morals were embodied in the ruler, who had responsibility for maintaining this harmony. The so-called 'a country of rite' is originally derived from this belief.

If disputes arose, mutual concessions were always encouraged, such as consultations or mediations. Disputes should be dissolved rather than resolved.[19] In China, failure to compromise resulted in a lawsuit, which caused both sides to lose and ruined one person's reputation in society. The winning party lost by bringing a lawsuit against the other party for his individual profit, as social harmony should prevail over individual profits. Law is viewed negatively, because it is not virtuous for one to challenge another's rights. This is in sharp contrast to Roman law, the foundation of modern Western law, which regulated the private and economic rights and duties of the individual.

17 See Wang 1999; 2–34.

18 In Analects, the first one is to learn. Everything is inferior, only good education is superior. This dominates the ideology of most Chinese people.

19 See Yu, X. Z. Legal Pragmatism in the People's Republic of China, Journal of Chinese Law 1989; 3:29.

Law meant evil in ancient Chinese.[20] Since ancient China only established 'criminal' law in people's minds, commoners feared law and legal institutions, which were used by their emperors solely to maintain the hierarchical order by punishing criminals and deterring common people from crime. In their view, when they violated law, they would be punished by this evil. They never thought law could protect their civil interests. Therefore, the modern attitude of subordination and deference to law were not considered in ancient China. From this point of view it might be easy to appreciate that society was ruled by law rather than existing under the rule of law.

Deep-rooted attitudes to the concept of law in China influenced attitudes towards dispute settlement. Where conflicts are treated as disruptive to social harmony, people prefer to resolve the disputes outside the formal justice system, where the disputants feel social harmony might be better achieved.

As a consequence, law was considered punitive and equivalent to crime, and litigation was regarded as a humiliating process. Because of this legal conditioning, most Chinese people still prefer to settle disputes through a flexible, informal, moderate and less-confrontational process, by which parties can maintain an amicable relationship.[21]

This unique phenomenon is at the heart of the great oriental civilization, which has existed for thousands of years. The Utopian-style society attracted many Asian countries and served as a standard model to shape oriental culture.

20 See Wang 1999; and Law and Punishment: the Western and the traditional Chinese 'Legal Mind' 1986; Oxford: Clarendon Press.

21 Chinese social order is known by its relationship-driven structure. Confucianism is keen on kinship and family. For example, the obligation to support aged or ill parents was a consideration in the decision to grant immunity or suspend a sentence in both capital and non-capital cases. An offender's execution could be suspended until after his parents' death if he was their only son. China has been a most family-oriented society throughout its history. Family constitutes the unit of the social and political community. In China, family supports the individual, and at the same time, the behaviour of individual family member determines the fate of the family. The family's obligations to the individual and the individual's obligations to his family rely on each other. These mutual obligations between the individual and the family serve as a social control agent.

Contemporary Chinese people still identify with a conflict-free, group-based social interrelationship.[22] Although social and economic changes have been a shock to traditional Chinese perceptions, the great wall of Chinese ideology has gained favour among Western countries, particularly after China's entry into the WTO and the dramatic improvement of the Chinese economy.

A. *China's Contribution to Interpretation of Strategy*

The Thirty-Six Strategies is a unique collection of ancient Chinese proverbs that describe some of the most cunning and subtle tactics ever devised. Whereas other Chinese military texts, such as *The Art of War,* focus on military organization, leadership and battlefield strategies, *The Thirty-Six Ji* is more suitably applied in the fields of politics, diplomacy and espionage. These proverbs describe, not only battlefield strategies, but also tactics used in psychological warfare to undermine both the enemy's will to fight – and his or her sanity. Tactics such as the 'double cross', the 'frame job', and the 'bait and switch', can be traced back through thousands of years of Chinese history to such proverbs as 'hide the dagger behind a smile', 'kill with a borrowed sword' and 'toss out a brick to attract jade'.[23]

Thirty-six strategies of China:

> Six multiplied by six equals thirty-six.
> Calculations produce tactics which in turn produces calculations.
> Each side depends upon the other.
> Based on this correlative relationship, ploys against the enemy are devised.
> Rigid application of military theory will only result in defeat on the battlefield.[24]

This original text of *The Art of War* is short, containing only 138 Chinese characters. It merely names each strategy followed by a brief explanation. The book was divided into six categories of six strategies each. The six categories are said to correspond to six situations. These include: stratagems when in a superior position; stratagems for confrontation;

22 See Keller, P. (ed.), Chinese Law and Legal Theory; 2001, Burlington: Ashgate.

23 The Thirty-Six Strategies in Ancient China (Original Title: *36* Ji, ca. 489–537BC). See http://www.chinastrategies.com/intro.htm

24 *Ibid.*

stratagems for attack; stratagems for confused situations; stratagems for gaining ground; stratagems for desperate situations. This division is based on the hexagrams of the I-Ching, which are groupings of six broken or unbroken lines. The first historical mention of *The Thirty-Six Strategies* dates back to the Southern Chi dynasty (AD 489–537).[25]

These strategies cover almost all tips for confronting tough situations. The ancient Chinese proverbs contribute many tips on military affairs that can be used to end war without resorting to force. Theoretically therefore, they could be a useful method to resolve conflicts without filing a case to the court within the area of international dispute settlement.

I posit that oriental tactics like these could prove useful for all parties to disputes in the WTO. My research and analysis reveal that the eastern ethos of dispute settlement and aversion to litigation may support the use of consultations within the WTO.

25 *Ibid.*

Part I

Consultation in International Law

In this part I introduce the concept of international dispute settlement and provide an overview. Second, I will discuss the relationship between consultations and negotiations. Third, I will focus on dispute avoidance and ADR, both relevant to consultations and international dispute settlement. Fourth, I examine the performance of consultations in international law. The final part will present some of the conclusions reached.

Chapter 1

Overview of Dispute Settlement in International Law

A consultation is defined as one, peaceful, method of settling international disputes. Logically, therefore, research should begin with the study of 'international dispute settlement'.

I. A Dispute

There are several definitions of a 'dispute'. One popular definition sees it as 'a disagreement on a point of law or fact, a conflict of legal views or interests between two persons'.[1] A dispute exists, 'when a claim based on a grievance is rejected in whole or in part'.[2] A dispute refers to, "a conflict between two parties (individuals or groups) which is asserted publicly – that is, before a third party".[3] A dispute takes place, "when the parties are unable to resolve their disagreement and one of them decides to take it into the public domain".[4]

An expanded definition that is applauded by most researchers is: "a dispute may be defined as a specific disagreement concerning a matter of fact, law or policy in which a claim or assertion of one party is met with refusal, counter-claim or denial by another".[5]

1 The Permanent Court of International Justice defined the concept of a dispute in the case of *Mavromattis Palestine Concessions (Greece v. U.K.)*, 1924 P.C.I.J. ser. A No. 2, at p. 11 (Judgment of Aug. 13).

2 Miller, R. E. & Sarat, A. Grievances, Claims and Disputes: Assessing the Adversary Culture, 15 Law & Society Review 1981; 527.

3 Mather, L. & Yngvesson, B. Language, Audience and the Transformation of Dispute, 15 Law & Society Review 1981; 776.

4 Gulliver, P. H. Disputes and Negotiations: A Cross-Cultural Perspective, New York: Academic Press, 1979, 75–76.

5 Merrills, J. G. International Dispute Settlement (3rd ed.), Cambridge: CUP, 1998, 1.

Furthermore, Merrills has interpreted a concept of international dispute in the broadest sense. "An international dispute can be said to exist whenever such a disagreement involves governments, institutions, juristic persons (corporations) or private individuals, in different parts of the world."[6]

The concept of a 'dispute' is important if methods of dispute resolution are to be established, as a disagreement may threaten the social order at a national level or may injure the relationship between or among countries at an international level.

If disputes are unavoidable, the purpose of law is to settle, 'by authority of the group various types of questions of concern to the group'.[7] The establishment of agreed ways of resolving a dispute is essential within any community particularly an international one.

II. Significance of Methods for the Settlement of International Disputes

If disputes fail to be settled at the national level, this could lead to a turbulent society. Failure to resolve international disputes may result in worldwide war. Effective dispute settlement must surely be the ultimate goal of international law, if peace is to be preserved. Sohn has said:

> The need to provide adequate means for the settlement of international disputes is related to two fundamental problems of international law – the necessity to prevent escalation of conflicts between states into breaches of the peace, and the requirement of providing proper procedures for the interpretation and application of rules of international law, both customary and conventional.[8]

Article 2(3) of the United Nations (UN) Charter requires that "[all] members shall settle their international disputes by peaceful means in such a

6 *Ibid.*, p. 1.
7 Hart, H. M. Jr. & Sacks, A. M. The Legal Process: Basic Problems in the Making and Application of Law, New York: Foundation, 1994; 1.
8 Sohn, L. The Future of Dispute Resolution, in MacDonald, R. St. J. & Johnston, D. M. (ed.), The Structure and Process of International Law: Essays in Legal Philosophy, Doctrine and Theory, Boston, MA: Nijhoff Publishers, 1983; 1121.

manner that international peace and security, and justice, are not endangered".[9]

This requirement has been cited in many decisions by international courts, and will be the basis of my Case Study to Consultation here as it is crucial for my research into international dispute settlement.

III. Methods of International Dispute Settlement

These methods have been included in the UN Charter, which makes certain treaty obligations mandatory almost all over the world. Article 33(1) states:

> The parties to any disputes, the continuance of which is likely to endanger the maintenance of international peace and security, shall, first of all, seek a solution by negotiation, enquiry, mediation, conciliation, arbitration, judicial settlement, resort to regional agencies or arrangements, or other peaceful means of their own choice.[10]

These methods are either diplomatic or legal. The diplomatic method includes negotiations (consultations), inquiry, good office, mediation and conciliation. The legal method consists of arbitration and judicial settlement. Diplomatic methods are generally labelled as non-binding outcomes, in contrast with legal methods, which are binding decisions on the basis of international law.

9 Article 2(3) of the UN Charter, under http://www.un.org/aboutun/charter/chapter1.htm last visited on 3 May 2005.

10 Article 33(1) of the U.N. Charter, under http://www.un.org/aboutun/charter/chapter6.htm, last visited on 3 May 2005.

Chapter 2

Controversial Legal Nature of Consultations and Negotiations

One of the arguments of international jurists and others is whether negotiation and consultation practices are legal proceedings or merely diplomatic devices.

Merrills argues that negotiation is a diplomatic method because the parties retain control of the dispute and they can accept or reject a proposed settlement.[1]

O'Connell wonders whether the negotiation should be considered a legal topic because of its informality. He acknowledges that negotiation is the 'antithesis of a legal procedure';[2] but he also points out that all other diplomatic means are subject to legal rules. He further observes that rules exist for the use of all the diplomatic means. Once countries consent to take up a dispute settlement mechanism, they are at the very least under an obligation to proceed in good faith, which is an important principle in international law.[3] In practice, the application of judicial means is more or less accompanied by the negotiation or consultation process.

It can be concluded from the observations and explanations of these two scholars that negotiation or consultation is a diplomatic procedure in any international dispute settlement. However, consultation or negotiation is a legal procedure, but not a compulsory one. Article 33(1) of the Charter of the UN states clearly that the parties are subject to a legally binding obligation to seek a peaceful solution. Even so, international

1 Merrills 1998, p. 88.

2 See O'Connell 2003, p. xv. He states that procedures of international dispute settlement range from negotiation to judicial settlement and claims that negotiation is one of the legal procedures. He implies in part that the negotiation is a compulsory procedure in any dispute.

3 The principle of good faith will be examined in section on good faith in consultation.

law, at least in theory, does not state that negotiation or consultation is a compulsory procedure in any dispute settlement system.[4]

However, this situation is changed by GATT/WTO regulations. In the WTO, the DSU provides proper procedures for consultation.[5] In practice, consultations are treated as a first step in the WTO dispute settlement mechanism. How consultation procedures are developed in the GATT/ WTO system is discussed below.

I. Relationship between Negotiation and Consultation

The words 'negotiations' and 'consultations' are often used interchangeably. The following will elaborate on the relationship between them by definition and a discussion of their similarities and differences.

A. *Definition of Negotiation*

When countries come into being, problems between them and others inevitably arise. To avoid 'mutually assured destruction', negotiation may be the only choice.[6] This is the oldest and the most fundamental method for resolving disputes amicably.

> Negotiation is a consensual bargaining process in which the parties attempt to reach agreement on a disputed or potentially disputed matter, usually involving

4 See Merrills 1998; O'Connell 2003; Sohn 1983.

5 Nevertheless, Article 4.3 of the DSU notes that if the Member does not respond within 10 days after the date of receipt of the request for consultations, or does not enter into consultations within a period of no more that 30 days, or a period otherwise mutually agreed, after the date of receipt of the request, then the Member that requested the holding of consultations may proceed directly to request the establishment of a Panel. In other words, under this provision, the DSU lists three possibilities that may allow consultations to be skipped. Theoretically the consultation is not a compulsory procedure. Whereas, practically the first procedure of WTO disputes is consultations on the whole without exception.

6 See Merrills 1998; p. 15.

complete autonomy for the parties involved without the intervention of third parties.[7]

Judge Moore has stated that negotiation is, "the legal and orderly administrative process by which governments, in the exercise of their unquestionable powers conduct their relations with another and discuss, adjust and settle their differences".[8]

These definitions of 'negotiation' confirm that it is a legal process through which parties bargain directly with each other. At the same time, a negotiation is a peaceful method to by which parties find solutions themselves and gain maximum control of the result.

B. *Definition of Consultation*

According to *Oppenheim's International Law*, the consultation usually "involves discussions specifically intended to impart or exchange information about the matter in question, or to seek or impart views about that matter".[9] Another definition of consultation is 'the interactive method by which states seek to prevent or resolve disputes'.[10] These two definitions are described from the angle of possible functions or results.

Kirgis writes that, the "consultation means something more than notification, but less than consent".[11]

As with the negotiation, the consultation serves both as a method which is responsible for preventing or settling a dispute and as a legal process for effectively achieving the desired goal. Consultations may also be of an explanatory nature.

7 Garner, B. A. (7th ed.), Black's Law Dictionary, St Paul, Minn: West Group, 1999; 1059.

8 *The Mavrommatis Palestine Concessions Case* (Judgment) PCIJ series A. No. 2. 1924; 62–63.

9 Jennings, R. & Watts, A. (ed.), Oppenheim's International Law (9th ed.), London: Longman, 1996; 1181.

10 Garner 1999; 311.

11 Kirgis, F. L. Jr. Prior Consultation in International Law: A Study of State Practice, Charlottesville: University Press of Virginia, 1983; 11.

C. *Similarities*

Definitions of negotiation and consultation establish that both are a means of dispute settlement as well as dispute avoidance.

Also, both of them are processes whereby parties communicate with each other with the purpose of reaching a mutual agreement.

Usually negotiation and consultation are the initial stage of a legal process. Nevertheless, they can be either the start of dispute settlement procedures or a terminator in the solving of disputes.

In such terms, negotiation and consultation are legal processes, but they are not legal methods because parties can agree to or refuse a proposed settlement at any time without it being binding.

D. *Differences*

With reference to the Organisation for Economic Co-operation and Development (OECD) document, the consultation may be a preliminary stage to a negotiation but differs from the latter when the country which initiates the consultation is merely seeking the opinions of those concerned on the proposed activities or measures.[12] To be more precise, the consultation is distinguished from the negotiation when consultation services are invoked for the purpose of seeking information. Negotiations contribute to a more intense form of contact than mere information exchange or consultations.

Considering the definition of consultations by Kirgis, the concept is closely related to a procedure "that is likely to inject external cost assessment into the decision-making process".[13] Hence, the particular value of consultation is the way it provides one chance, with the aid of some useful or related information, to reach agreement or to prepare for final decisions. Whether consultation settles disputes or not, the chance to resolve or avoid disputes does exist, although other factors can influence consultation acting as an initial or final stage.

12 OECD Doc. ENV (79) 23, at 6 (1979).
13 Kirgis 1983; 12.

It is generally accepted that consultations are a good way to avoid or prevent potential developments rather than settling actual disputes.[14] However, this does not mean that negotiation has no function in dispute avoidance. More precisely, compared with consultation, negotiation is more likely to serve the function of solving disputes. As negotiation takes place at the initial stage, it always provides an opportunity to avoid subsequent friction.

Of course, in practice, it is hard to draw a clear distinction between the stages of consultation and negotiation. Nevertheless, in theory, they are differentiated to a small degree.

Bilder has summarized some advantages of negotiation and consultation.

The merits of the negotiation process are:

1. It is the least risky way of trying to deal with disputes. Each country has maximum control over both the dispute settlement process and outcome, since it always has the option of simply walking away from the negotiation and *not* agreeing.
2. It places responsibility for resolving the dispute on the parties themselves, who are in the best position to develop a sensible, workable, and acceptable solution.
3. Since any settlement reached by negotiation is presumed to be agreed to by the parties to the dispute, rather than imposed on them by third parties, it is likely to have maximum acceptability and stability.
4. Negotiation favours compromise and accommodation between the parties – a 'give-and-take' rather than 'all-or-nothing' solution – which is most likely to preserve good long-term co-operative relations.

It is generally simpler and less costly than alternative dispute settlement methods and it can more easily be carried on secretly or without publicity. Moreover, the process of negotiation can develop attitudes, procedures and relationships which foster co-operation and dispute management between or among the parties more generally.[15]

Meanwhile, Kirgis concluded that consultation has the following advantages:

14 Most scholars conclude that consultation rather than negotiation is a technique for prevention. See Kirgis 1983, Prior consultation, part 2; Merrills 1998; 3; and O'Connell 2003; xix–xx.

15 Bilder, R. B. An Overview of International Dispute Settlement in O'Connell, M. E. (ed.). International Dispute Settlement, Ashgate: Dartmouth 2003; 24–25 note 36.

1. It permits nations to identify and try to resolve potential frictions and problems at any early stage, before positions become fixed and polarised and differences become more serious and intractable.
2. It may give the nation proposing action a better understanding of how its proposed policy may adversely affect the other nation, perhaps leading it to abandon the policy, or to vary it so as to avoid or limit harm to the other nation.
3. Even if consultation does not result in change of the acting nation's policy, it may provide opportunity for the nation affected to take measures of its own to avoid or reduce the harm.
4. Consultation shows an attitude of good will, good faith and good neighbourliness, thus helping to establish a climate favourable to dispute settlement and co-operation more generally.[16]

In most cases, the task of negotiation is clearly to settle disputes or to reach a mutual agreement in a friendly atmosphere. Moreover, negotiation is normally an essential component of any dispute settlement process. Even if other techniques are also used, the negotiation process usually accompanies them.

Consultation deals with disputes which might give rise to disagreement, but do not take place. This is one of its differences from negotiation which might adjust and solve existing disputes, although the boundary line is not that clear in practice. The operation of consultations is prior to dispute *stricto sensu,* and the operation of negotiations after the concretization of all the elements of a dispute. In the application of consultation in WTO disputes, it can be seen to perform quite well both in dispute avoidance and dispute settlement.

Not only are the two terms often correctly used interchangeably, but they may even have the same legal effect. Thus, where a consultation clause is designed to or operates to facilitate the settlement of an actual dispute, it becomes indistinguishable from the operation of a negotiation clause. Even when this is not so, the consultation and negotiation processes could be operated concurrently, with the consultation gradually merging into negotiation when discussions and conversations expose underlying differences of views between parties.[17]

16 *Ibid.*, pp. 31–32, see also Kirgis 1983.

17 See Lauterpacht H. (ed.), Oppenheim's International Law, Vol. II Dispute, War and Neutrality (7th ed.), London: Longman & Co, 1952; 8; Gould W. An Introduction to International Law, New York: Harper Brothers, 1957; 541; Serensen M. (ed.), Manual of Public International Law, London: Macmillan, 1968; 679.

Fundamentally, it can be assumed that the existence of a dispute is not a condition *sine qua non*,[18] nor an essential for the invocation of the consultation process generally, as it is for the negotiation process.[19]

In international law, negotiation and consultation are widely accepted as interchangeable concepts. Therefore, in theory or practice, there is no need to emphasize their differences too far.

18 Something that is absolutely essential.

19 See Fombad, C. M. Consultation and Negotiation in the Pacific Settlement of International Disputes, in O'Connell, M. E. (ed.), International Dispute Settlement, Ashgate: Dartmouth, 2003; 39.

Chapter 3

Two Concepts

Two concepts have recently emerged in the international dispute settlement field, namely: (1) dispute prevention, and (2) Alternative Dispute Resolution (ADR).

I. Dispute Prevention

Theoretically speaking, dispute avoidance is obviously different from dispute settlement, but the role and significance of dispute avoidance methods are highly relevant.

Against the background of globalization, international co-operation among states covers many areas. Many international agreements have emerged to regulate the behaviour of states and define their international relationships. As disputes are inevitable between individuals in domestic affairs, disputes are also unavoidable between nations; so dispute prevention has gradually but inevitably become a priority in many agreements.

This trend is particularly evident in many fields of international law. The agreements such as those of the International Monetary Fund (IMF)[1] and the WTO have as a key feature the obligation to consult.

There are a variety of procedures in dispute avoidance in addition to consultation. These include prior agreement on clear rules for dealing with problems which might give rise to disagreements or disputes; a practice of prior notification and consultation before taking unilateral

1 Article VIII of Agreement of the IMF lists general obligations of members. Section 6 includes consultation between members regarding existing international agreements. See http://www.imf.org/external/pubs/ft/aa/aa08.htm#6 last visited 10 November 2004.

action which could cause disputes; the establishment of *ad hoc* or permanent consultative bodies or joint commissions to resolve grievances, complaints or disagreements at an early stage.[2]

Despite the development of the role of consultations and various dispute prevention methods, international law does not necessarily impose any general obligation on states to avoid disputes or employ any particular methods to achieve this end. Nevertheless, there is some evidence that countries can act in accordance with the spirit of the declaration on the principle of international law concerning friendly international relationships and co-operation among states under the UN Charter, which requires states to seek an "early and just settlement of their international disputes".[3]

Kirgis observes that the use of consultations as a dispute avoidance device is growing. Through case studies and observations he offers his perspective that the rights to be consulted are increasingly employed by directly affected countries and are increasingly honoured by other countries in the same vein.[4]

In general, the end goal of dispute avoidance is an attempt by every state to recognize, understand and take into account other states' legitimate interests, views and concerns in order to reach agreement or compromise with each other and so solve disputes or calm down conflicts. Some case study examples are given below to indicate the significance of consultation in dispute prevention.

In China, the (Golden) Mean doctrine[5] is accepted by many Chinese people as one of the key moral principles; the concept that one should always try to put oneself in someone else's shoes remains valid for individuals as well as the country as a whole. Because of globalization, oriental theories and principles are increasingly being accepted by the west-

2 Bilder 2003; 31–32.
3 Fombad 2003; 43.
4 Kirgis 1983; 375.
5 One of the Confucian core philosophical thoughts is Zhong Yong (the Golden Mean). Confucius said: "the superior man embodies the course of the Mean; the mean man acts contrary to the course of the Mean. The superior man's embodying the course of the Mean is because he is a superior man, and so always maintains the Mean. The Mean man's acting contrary to the course of the Mean is because he is a mean man, and has no caution".

ern community, in the same way as western concepts are simultaneously shocking and influential to eastern societies.

II. Alternative Dispute Resolution

Since about the late 1970s, ADR processes have become fashionable in western jurisdictions such as Australia, the UK and the USA. The difference between ADR and international dispute settlement is hard to explain. O'Connell proposed that international dispute settlement as a subfield of international law existed long before the modern development of psychological practices and their connection with training people in how to prevent or resolve disputes. This includes modern ADR, in which developments in social psychology influence the outcome of negotiations or disputes between people.[6]

The forms of ADR include third-party assisted negotiation such as mediation and conciliation, independent expert investigation, appraisal and evaluation, combinations of the above methods, and others.[7] These are basically diplomatic methods which are part of the fabric of international dispute settlement. However, ADR processes emphasize solving disputes peacefully using the good offices of a third party. Freedom of choice with respect to third party facilitators allows disputants to draw upon appropriate technical, legal, cultural or other expertise, and even to bring together a balanced team of experts.[8]

ADR has been adopted into the Administrative and Institutional Provisions of the North American Free Trade Agreement (NAFTA).[9] Its processes work successfully in the USA[10] and are widely used in the UK.[11]

6 O'Connell 1993.

7 Chinkin, C. Alternative Dispute Resolution under International Law, in O'Connell, M. E. (ed.), International Dispute Settlement, Ashgate: Dartmouth, 2003; 501.

8 Chinkin 2003; 124.

9 Article 2022 of section C, chapter 20 under the NAFTA. This is a special provision of ADR.

10 In America, the popularity of ADR has manifested itself through the introduction of pilot schemes and legislative, administrative and voluntary programmes, within

ADR has not been applied by WTO Member states until recently. Although Article 5 of the DSU lists good offices, mediation and conciliation, there is no established recourse to methods leading to peaceful settlement by third-party intervention. It might be too early to say whether or not these methods are useful or not, since they were adopted into the DSU only in 1995, when WTO law came into force.

There are some systematic relationships between negotiation and consultation; dispute settlement, dispute prevention and ADR. The reason is that the consultation is not only a method of dispute settlement but also a means of dispute prevention.

---

the formal court structures and outside them, for the resolution of disputes in many areas of domestic law. Courses on ADR are run by most American law schools. These courses include the growing number of judicial decisions and statutes on ADR.

11 In Britain, ADR processes are promoted particularly for family matters and neighbourhood disputes, although there is a growing awareness of their potential use in commercial disputes.

Chapter 4

Use of Consultations in International Law

The Secretary-General of the United Nations, Boutros Boutros-Ghali in *An Agenda for Peace* advocated:

> [C]lose and continuous consultations between the Secretary-General and the Security Council as being essential to ensure full awareness of how the Council's influence can be best applied and to develop a common strategy for the peaceful settlement of specific disputes. Consultations between the United Nations and regional arrangements or agencies could do much to build international consensus on the nature of the problem and the measures required to address it.[1]

His summary of the case for consultation initiates the proposition that is the basis of my research. It is logical to consider consultation in terms of its history.

I. Historical Role of Consultation

The principle of consultation before action involving the interests of other States lies at the heart of the law of international economic relationships.[2] It needs to be carefully examined in any discussion of historical background.

Several books on this subject have been written by legal scholars. For instance, a former judge of the ICJ, Jessup, explored the role of consultations in maintaining or restoring international peace and security. He proposed three definitions of consultations:[3]

1 Boutros-Ghali, B. An Agenda for Peace, UN Pub.DPI/1247, 1997; 22 and 37.
2 Jenks, C. W. The Common Law of Mankind, London: Stevens, 1958; 156.
3 Jessup, P. C. International Security: The American Role in Collective Action for Peace, New York: Council on Foreign Relations, 1935; 64.

The broadest one states that consultation includes all exchanges of views between governments in addition to normal diplomatic intercourse. A narrower one is restricted to the conference method of conducting international affairs which is of interest to a number of governments. The third one regards consultation as applying particularly to an exchange of views relative to the solution of a controversy which is threatened or has already broken out, and which endangers the peace of the world. This last one is in the spirit of the UN Charter.

In 1933, at the London Disarmament Conference, American ambassador, Norman Davies stated that the US was contributing to the organization of peace and reduction of armaments. In particular, the US was willing to consult other states in case of a threat to peace, with a view to averting conflict.[4]

This proposal for a disarmament treaty was then incorporated in a revised British draft convention, part of which indicated:

> I. In the event of a breach or threat of breach of the Pact of Paris, either the Council or Assembly of the League of Nations or one of the parties to the present Convention who are not Members of the League of Nations may propose immediate consultation between the Council or the Assembly and any of the said parties to the present Convention.
>
> II. It shall be the object of such consultation, (a) in the event of a threat of a breach of the Pact to exchange views for the purpose of preserving the peace and averting a conflict; (b) in the event of a breach of the Pact to use good offices for the restoration of peace; and (c) in the event that it proves impossible thus to restore the peace, then to determine which party or parties to the dispute are to be held responsible.
>
> III. The provisions of the above article do not in any way prejudice the rights and obligations of the Members of the League, nor conflict with nor limit the powers and duties of the Assembly and Council under the Covenant.[5]

Although this treaty never came into force, Cooper concluded that consultations became an established feature of American foreign policy. He stressed that "consultation was an important aid to peace and the US may engage in it without any obligation for further action against its will".[6]

4 US Department of State, Press Release, 22 May 1933, p. 390; League of Nations, Conference on Disarmament, General Committee, Minutes, Vol. II, 475 (1933).

5 League of Nations, *Ibid.*, p. 494.

6 Cooper, R. M. American Consultation in World Affairs: For the Preservation of Peace, New York: MacMillan, 1934; 345–365.

Unfortunately, as the Second World War ended, the glorious history of consultation was gradually forgotten. The UN has constantly used consultation, but it has not systematized the process.

The United Nations Handbook on the Peaceful Settlement of Disputes between States was published, in 1991, as an Annex to a Report of the Special Committee on the Charter of the UN and on the Strengthening of the Role of the UN. It mentioned the instances of consultations only incidentally in a work of more than 400 paragraphs. It merely concluded that consultation may be considered as a variety of negotiation.[7]

Nevertheless, many international agreements, especially some regional ones, adopted the procedure of consultation as a crucial element.

II. Consultation under Treaties and Conventions

In Part V of Vienna Convention on Succession of States in Respect of State Property, Archives and Debts of April 8, 1983, Article 42 clearly provides:

> If a dispute regarding the interpretation or application of the present Convention arises between two or more Parties to the Convention, they shall, upon the request of any of them, seek or resolve it by a process of consultation and negotiation.[8]

Moreover, Article 33 of the UN Charter refers to negotiation as one of several means of settlement. Negotiation may encompass consultation. Therefore, consultation is a legal principle of dispute settlement.

7 See Handbook on the Settlement of Disputes between States, which was published as UN Pub.E.92.V.7. It was prepared by the Secretariat of the UN after seven years of work. The main references to consultations are in paragraphs 24–25, 51–52, 60 and 70.

8 Article 42, Part V of Vienna Convention on Succession of States in Respect of State Property, Archives and Debts, 8 April 1983.

A. *Regional Agreements*

Under the Treaty Establishing the European Community, the *chapeau* of Article 100 states:

> The Council shall, acting unanimously on a proposal from the Commission and after consulting the European Parliament and the Economic and Social Committee, issue directives for the approximation of such laws, regulations or administrative provisions of the Member States as directly affect the establishment or functioning of the common market.[9]

In the next stage, when the Commission of the Community finds that a difference between a Member State's law, regulation or administrative action distorts the conditions of competition in the common market and needs to be eliminated, it is obligated to consult that Member State. The Council and the Commission may take the appropriate measures provided for in the Treaty if no agreement can be reached to eliminate the distortion.[10] Another conflict may arise when a Member State anticipates that the adoption or amendment of provisions may cause distortion of the conditions of competition in the common market. It then has the obligation to consult the Commission. "After consulting the Member States, the Commission shall recommend to the States concerned such measures as may be appropriate to avoid the distortion in question".[11] The EC provisions on a duty to consultation are certainly connected with the purpose of dispute prevention.

In the NAFTA of December 8 and 17, 1992, Article 2006 specifies a time-frame for consultation. This Article is similar to Article XXII in the GATT and Article 4 of DSU in the WTO. However, a big difference is: in Article 4(7) of the DSU if the consultation fails to settle disputes within 60 days after the date of receipt of the request for consultations, the complaining party may request the establishment of a panel. With regard to consultations in the NAFTA, if the parties cannot solve conflicts within 30 days, they may request, in writing, the establishment of an arbitral panel according to Article 2008(1).

9 Article 100, Treaty Establishing the European Community, Consolidated version of the EC Treaty, from http://www.europa.eu.int/abc/obj/treaties/en/entoc05.htm last visited 15 November 2004.

10 *Ibid.*, Article 101.

11 *Ibid.*, Article 102.

The North Atlantic Treaty states that, "the Parties will consult together whenever in the opinion of any of them, the territorial integrity, political independence or security of any of the Parties is threatened".[12] Political consultation is a key feature in all-major NATO pronouncements on co-operation within the alliance. The fundamental reason is that a political alliance must reflect and generate mutual trust, which means that national decision makers shall take the interests of other members into account when they act on matters within the ambit of the Alliance.

> Consultation within an alliance means more than exchange of information, though that is necessary. It means more than letting the NATO Council know about national decisions that have already been taken; or trying to enlist support for those decisions. It means the discussion of problems collectively, in the early stages of policy formulation, and before national positions become fixed.[13]

Insofar as NATO consultation practice provides a model for member governments to consult the others before they make decisions in definable circumstances, the implication is that the consultation practice creates legal norms within the Alliance.[14]

In fact, NATO practice has established a norm requiring consultation within the Alliance, before a member state makes a final decision on a course of action. This norm can be supported, not only by the duty of parties to the North Atlantic Treaty to consult before any denunciation, but also by the regular defence-budget consultation procedure which involves the practice of consultation before undertaking arms control negotiations that are particularly likely to affect means of defence relied on by European allies.[15] The function of dispute avoidance in the process of consultation is overwhelming for its political particularity.

In Asia, the ASEAN refers to the WTO dispute settlement system as a model similar to the NAFTA, but according to Asian tradition it leaves the way open for an amicable settlement until the panel is established.

12 Article 4 of the North Atlantic Treaty.

13 Report of the Committee of Three on Non-military Co-operation in NATO, Dec. 13, 1956, in NATO Information Service, NATO Facts and Figures 308. 1976; 316.

14 Kirgis 1983; 201.

15 *Ibid.*, p. 201.

Consultations are central to the dispute settlement mechanism in the ASEAN.[16]

B. *Inter-state Agreements*

Another good example of the value of consultation comes from US and Canadian antitrust proceedings. The legislation requires cooperation and coordination between the litigants to avoid conflicts arising from the application of competition laws and to minimise the impact of differences between them and, in addition, to establish a framework for co-operation and co-ordination with respect to enforcement of marketing practices laws.[17] Then, it requires notification, enforcement co-operation, co-ordination in reference to related matters, avoidance of conflicts, consultation and other provisions.

The tone of this legislation is amicable and co-operative. It was put together following the long history of co-operation between two countries in matters relating to competition law, including the bilateral Understanding of 1959, 1969 and 1984, as well as the 1986 Recommendation of the Council of the OECD Concerning Co-operation Between Member Countries on Restrictive Business Practices Affecting International Trade. Member countries realised the importance of co-operation and co-ordination among their various competition authorities to further effective competition law enforcement in the free trade area. Any two contesting countries would need to give careful consideration to the other's important interests in the application of their competition laws.

> After consultation, it may be agreed to shape an indictment in a less offensive manner, to change the ground rules of an investigation so as to require only 'voluntary' testimony from witnesses, or those officials of the government initiating an investigation or action will keep their antitrust counterparts informed of progress in the case and allow them to voice their concern.[18]

16 See Article 2 of Protocol on Dispute Settlement Mechanism and Article 8 of Agreement on the Common Preferential Tariff.

17 Article I, Canada-United States: Agreement Regarding the Application of Their Competition and Deceptive Marketing Practices Laws, 35 ILM 1996; 309: 312.

18 See Campbell, B. R. The Canada-United States Antitrust Notification and Consultation Procedure. 56 Canada Bar Review 1978; 459:468.

This policy of co-operation developed through a series of bilateral understandings. The degree of co-operation indicates, not only that a consultation clause was adopted, but also an increasing shift in emphasis towards dispute prevention.

C. *General International Laws*

The prior agreements are regional or inter-state agreements; the following agreements are general international laws related to the consultation.

Countries contemplating or actually carrying out any activities which may threaten other countries' environmental interests now accept the need not only to give timely notice and information to the countries likely to be affected but also often to engage in consultations through which they seek in good faith to reach a compromise capable of avoiding or minimising any possible harmful effects.[19]

The international environmental law treats consultations as international recognition of an essential and basic principle. For instance, the 1972 Stockholm Action Plan for the Human Environment contains one particularly pertinent recommendation, calling upon governments to, "consult fully other interested States when activities carrying a risk of [climatic] effects are being contemplated or implemented".[20]

In 1979, the Geneva Convention on Long-Range Transboundary Air Pollution was signed under the auspices of the UN Economic Commission for Europe. The Convention provides that states are to develop policies and strategies by means of exchanges of information and consultation. Particularly, Article 5 notes that:

> Consultations shall be held, upon request, at an early stage between, on the one hand, Contracting Parties which are actually affected by or exposed to a significant risk of long-rang transboundary air pollution and, on the other hand, Contracting Parties within which and subject to whose jurisdiction a significant contribution to

19 Bilder, R. B. The Settlement of Disputes in the Field of the International Law of the Environment. Hague Recueil 1975; 139–240.

20 Action Plan for the Human Environment, Recommendation 70, U.N. Doc. A/CONF. 48/14 (1972), 11 ILM 1421 1972; 1449.

> long-range transboundary air pollution originates, or could originate, in connection with activities carried on or contemplated therein.[21]

Article 5 addresses the aims of consultations – both dispute settlement and dispute prevention.

Another important field for development of the means of consultations is the law of the sea. In the 1969 International Convention Relating to Intervention on the High Seas in Cases of Oil Pollution Casualties, the coastal party is allowed to prevent, mitigate or eliminate a grave and imminent danger to its coastline from oil pollution following a high seas maritime casualty. However, before acting, the coastal state must consult other states affected by the maritime casualty, particularly the flag state or states.[22]

Since most of disputes involve fishing activities, state practice requires consultation with interested parties in this field. This area contains rich sources to be researched; these will be elaborated in case studies below.

The Convention on the Law of the Sea requires prior consultation when proposed seabed activities might affect interests of a coastal state across whose jurisdiction seabed resources lie, and would require its prior consent when the activity may result in exploitation of resources within the coastal state's jurisdiction.[23] The principle is that, when seabed activities pose a risk to the special interest of a coastal state, there is a duty to consult it. The primary aim is to give the coastal state a voice in protecting its special fishery conservation interests in an area of the high seas adjacent to its territorial sea. The fishery conservation interest had been recognised in Article 6 of the 1958 Geneva Convention on Fishing and Conservation of the Living Resources of the High Seas. The consultation norm in the law of the sea also applies to other provisions, such as mineral exploitation within a coastal state's offshore jurisdiction.

It can be assumed that the practice of consultation is increasingly important worldwide, both in bilateral relations and in multilateral rela-

21 See Article 5, The 1979 Geneva Convention on Long-range Transboundary Air Pollution, http://www.unece.org/env/lrtap/lrtap_h1.htm last visited 30 November 2004.

22 Article 3, International Convention Relating to Invention on the High Seas in Cases of Oil Pollution Casualties, Nov. 29, 1969, 26 U.S.T. 765, T.I.A.S.No.8086.

23 Article 142(2), Convention on the Law of the Sea, UN Doc. A/CONF. 62/122 (1982).

tions. Moreover, it has permeated into many specific areas such as the sea and the environment, particularly in the field of international trade.

A benchmark for the use of consultation in the international community is undoubtedly the DSU of the WTO Agreements.

Chapter 5

A Duty to Consult

In an English case, the essence of consultation was said to be, "the communication of a genuine invitation, extended with a receptive mind, to give advice… if the invitation is once received, it matters not that it is not accepted and no advice is proffered".[1]

In a report to the Council of Europe in 1973, a group of legal experts observed after examining European practices relating to air pollution that, "there is no rule in ordinary international law that requires a state to consult another one before authorising potentially polluting plant to be set up close to a common border".[2]

So, a question arises whether there exists at all a duty to consult in the field of international law.

A review of the UN Charter shows that it does contain some provisions requiring the organisation to consult individual member states before taking certain steps affecting them. However, there is no such word as 'consultation' in these provisions. For example, Article 44 reflects the amicable principle that one member state shall be given prior notice before the organisation takes permissible action of peculiar sensitivity to that state.[3] But Article 106 clearly points out a duty to consult.[4]

1 *Agriculture Board v Aylesbury Mushrooms* [1974] 1 WLR 190, 194–195.

2 Report of Committee of Experts on Air Pollution, Procedures for Consultation at National and International Level Prior to the Setting Up of Polluting Plant in Border Areas, Council of Europe Doc. EXP/Air (73) 2, at 4 (1973).

3 The original provision of Article 44 states: When the Security Council has decided to use force it shall, before calling upon a Member not represented on it to provide armed forces in fulfilment of the obligations assumed under Article 43, invite that Member, if the Member so desires, to participate in the decisions of the Security Council concerning the employment of contingents of that Member's armed forces.

4 The original provision of Article 106 provides: [p]ending the coming into force of such special agreements referred to in Article 43 as in the opinion of the Security Council enable it to begin the exercise of its responsibilities under Article 42, the parties to the Four-Nation Declaration, signed at Moscow, 30 October 1943, and France, shall, in accordance with the provisions of paragraph 5 of that Declaration,

Kirgis acknowledged in his conclusion to *Prior Consultation in International Law*:

> Despite the growth of prior consultation norms, it is unlikely that there will be any all-encompassing prior consultation duty in the foreseeable future. Thus, to the extent that formal procedural structures for prior consultation may be desirable, they should be tailored to recurring, relatively well-defined, troublesome situations.[5]

However, he did not intend to give consultation a negative future, instead, he expected that his research could identify existing and developing prior consultation norms for the guidance of decision makers in the give-and-take of state practice. Moreover, he emphasised that the procedure of consultation should be practiced in international law. Its development will justify efforts to construct new or improved consultative mechanisms.[6]

Various facts support his claims. Some of the above-mentioned international agreements that followed publication of this book not only practice consultative mechanisms, but have also improved the procedures of consultation. As a significant part of the WTO, the DSU constructs an effective dispute settlement mechanism. Among those procedures, the consultation is the most important component, since the statistics disclose that over half of the disputes ended before the litigation stage(s). Consultations have been practiced for more than half a century – from the GATT era (from 1947) to the present WTO. From a common international agreement to a most influential organization, the evolution of the GATT/WTO has experienced the progress of globalisation.

Many scholars believe that there exists a duty on the parties to an agreement to consult. After carefully analysing the relevant cases, they conclude that a duty to consult may operate at three different levels depending on the nature of the issues involved.[7]

---

consult with one another and as occasion requires with other Members of the United Nations with a view to such joint action on behalf of the Organisation as may be necessary for the purpose of maintaining international peace and security.

5 Kirgis 1983; 375.

6 *Ibid*., p. 375.

7 Cheng, B. Dispute Settlement in Bilateral Air Transport Agreements', in Bockstiegel, K. (ed.), Settlement of Space Law Disputes: the Present State of the Law and Perspectives of Further Development, Proceedings of an International Colloquium, Munich 13 and 14 September 1979, Bonn: Carl Heymanns Verlag, 1980;

The first level contains a general obligation on the part of parties to undertake frequent and regular consultations. At this level, the main objective is usually to provide a regulatory framework to enable a continuous assessment and supervision of the implementation of the agreement.[8] This can be understood as a level for preventing disputes.

The second stage deals with consultations relating to specific issues which have arisen, and operates where the possibility of an actual dispute arising has become particularly acute.[9] Hence, the goal of this stage is to resolve disputes as well as to avoid conflicts.

The third level usually involves those circumstances where, in spite of the previous efforts under the consultation stage, disputes have arisen.[10] The target of this level is to attempt an amicable settlement.

Objectively speaking, the obligation to consult is likely to influence the actions of the states concerned in a direction acceptable to all.[11]

---

106. See also another article by Bin Cheng: The Role of Consultation in Bilateral International Air Services Agreements, as Exemplified by Bermuda I and II, 19. Columbia Journal of Transnational Law 1981; 183–195. Fombad 2003; 122–183.

8 Fombad 2003; 41.

9 *Ibid.*

10 *Ibid.*

11 Jennings 1996; 1182.

Chapter 6

Good Faith in Consultations

It has been debated whether the processes of consultations and negotiations should be subject to any strictly defined legal principles.[1] The consultation or negotiation, as contrasted with arbitral or judicial procedures, may be undermined by rigid adherence to rules or procedures. However, compliance and conformity with well-established principles of international law, in the conduct of consultations and negotiations, is still a vital factor, which determines the durability and effectiveness of any settlement reached by the parties.

Among them and perhaps the most fundamental principle that regulates the whole process, is that of good faith. This concept is termed *pacta sunt servanda*, and is arguably one of the oldest principles of international law. Expressions of good faith materialise in all three sources known to international law: treaties, custom and general principles of law.

Article 26 of the VCLT states that every treaty in force is binding upon the parties to it and must be performed by them in good faith.[2] Article 31(1) declares that "a treaty shall be interpreted in good faith in accordance with the ordinary meaning to be given to the terms of the treaty in their context and in the light of its object and purpose".[3] Article 46(2) explains that a violation will be regarded to have manifested if it would be objectively evident to any state conducting itself in the matter in accordance with normal practice and in good faith.[4]

1 Irvin J. The Role of Law in the Negotiated Settlement of International Disputes, 3 Vanderbilt International 1969; 58–73.

2 Article 26, Vienna Convention on the Law of Treaties, http://www.unog.ch/archives/vienna/ last visited 28 November of 2004.

3 Article 31(1), *Ibid.*

4 Article 46(2), *Ibid.*

The UN Charter states that all members shall fulfil, in good faith, in order to ensure rights and benefits resulting from membership.[5] The elaboration of this provision, in the Declaration on Principles of International Law Concerning Friendly Relations and Co-operation, among States adopted by the General Assembly in resolution 2625 (XXV), 1970, refers to obligations upon states to fulfil in good faith their obligations resulting from international law, including treaties.[6]

The importance of good faith is highlighted by Cheng: "the law of treaties is closely bound with the principle of good faith, if indeed not based on it, for this principle governs treaties from the time of their formation to the time of their extinction".[7]

Oppenheim's International Law, one of the most comprehensive and authoritative works on international law, notes that good faith is of overriding importance.[8]

According to Kelsen's international customary law theory, the prime rule of *pacta sunt servanda* recognises agreements to be carried out in good faith.[9]

Moreover, the ICJ in the *Nuclear Test* cases stressed its significance:

> One of the basic principles governing the creation and performance of legal obligations, whatever their source, is the principle of good faith. Trust and confidence are inherent in international cooperation, in particular in an age when this cooperation in many field is becoming increasingly essential. Just as the very rule of *pacta sunt servanda* in the law of treaties is based on good faith, so also is the binding character of an international obligation assumed by unilateral obligation.[10]

5 Article 2(2), Charter of the United Nations, http://www.un.org/aboutun/charter/ This Article lays down several principles of the Charter of the United Nations. Last visited 28 November 2004.

6 See Declaration on Principles of International Law Concerning Friendly Relations and Co-operation among States in General Assembly in resolution 2625 (XXV), 1970 http://www.jur.ku.dk/Folkeret/materialesamling/Kilde%202%20UN%20 GENERAL%20ASSEMBLY%20RESOLUTION%202625.doc last visited 28 March 2004.

7 Cheng, B. General Principles of Law as Applied by International Courts and Tribunals, London: Steven & Sons, 1953; 106.

8 Jennings 1996; 38.

9 Kelsen, H. *General Theory of Law and State*, Cambridge: CUP 1946; 369.

10 *The Nuclear Test Cases*, ICJ Reports 253. 1974; 253, 267.

It goes without saying that good faith is a basic principle in international law. Shaw, in his book, *International Law*, concludes that the principle of good faith is a background principle informing and shaping the observance of existing rules of international law and constrains the manner in which those rules may legitimately be exercised.[11] An obligation to consult in good faith was expressed in the *Nuclear Test* cases, as well.

To consult in good faith is to take into consideration the various interests involved, to seek to give them every satisfaction compatible with the pursuit of the consulting state's own interests, and to show that, in this regard, it is genuinely concerned to reconcile the interests of the other state with its own.[12]

Considering the provision related to consulting in negotiating in good faith of international law, one example is the 1961 Resolution on the Utilisation of Non-Maritime International Waters. In Article 7, it states:

> [D]uring the negotiation, every State must, in conformity with the principle of good faith, refrain from undertaking the works or utilizations which are the object of the dispute or from taking any other measures which might aggravate the dispute or render agreement more difficult.[13]

Here, the principle of good faith is treated as a norm in negotiations. The implied duty to consult or negotiate in good faith is to solve or prevent disputes or to prevent the dispute from escalating. That is to say, good faith is an excellent principle to utilise during negotiations and consultations.

This is affirmed in the *Lake Lanoux* case below. The tribunal observed that:

> International practice reflects the conviction that States ought to strive to conclude such agreements: there would thus appear to be an obligation to accept in good faith all communications and contacts which could, by a broad comparison of interests and by reciprocal good will, provide States with the best conditions for concluding agreements.[14]

11 Shaw, M. N. International Law (5th ed.), Cambridge: CUP 2003; 98.

12 *Ibid.*, p. 139.

13 Article 7, the 1961 Resolution on the Utilisation of Non-Maritime International Waters, 56 AJIL 737 1962; 738.

14 Kelson 1946; 130.

In this case, the arbitral tribunal found that there was an obligation to engage in a meaningful preliminary negotiation, but no duty to obtain the agreement of other interested states, if their consent proved unobtainable after a good faith effort.[15] The clear implication is that it is not a meaningful negotiation if it lacks a good faith component. A state could, in fact, be in breach of the requisite good faith if it tolerated an unjustified breaking off of discussions, abnormal delays, disregard of agreed procedures, or systematic refusals to take into consideration opposing proposals or interests.[16]

In short, the success of negotiations or consultations depends to a great extent on the good will of the parties and the issues at stake. A breach of good faith, like the breach of other international obligations, involves international responsibility for the guilty party. For instance, in the dispute between the UN and the US over the interpretation of Section 21 of the UN Headquarters Agreement of 1947 before the ICJ proceedings,[17] the UN claimed that the US was in breach of its duty of good faith when the US deliberately refused to engage in consultations and negotiations, as contemplated by the drafters of the dispute settlement procedures under Article 21 of that Agreement. Instead, the US restricted itself to informal contacts and consultations outside the dispute settlement procedure. The ICJ, in this case, pointed out that good faith not only applied to the conduct but also the invocation of, and implementation of solutions reached during the consultation and negotiation process.[18]

In some circumstances where both parties in a dispute are in breach of the law, a duty to negotiate in good faith is particularly significant, since a party may hesitate to comply with international obligations. The *Gabcíkovo Nagymaros Project* case is a good example.[19] Slovakia filed in the Registry of the ICJ a request for an additional Judgment in the

15 Chinkin 2003; 39.

16 Although there is no clear definition of good faith, non-good-faith performances were listed in the Lake Lanoux case, namely 'unjustified breaking off of discussions, abnormal delays, disregard of agreed procedures, or systematic refusals to take into consideration adverse proposals or interests'.

17 The Applicability of the Obligation to Arbitrate under Sect. 21 of the UN Headquarters Agreement case, ICJ Reports 1988.

18 *Ibid.*, p. 12.

19 ICJ Decision on *Gabcikovo – Nagymaros Project* (Hungary/Slovakia), 1994, last visited 28 November 2004, http://www.lawschool.cornell.edu/library/cijwww/icjwww/idocket/ihs/ihsframe.htm

case concerning Gabcíkovo-Nagymaros Project (Hungary/Slovakia), relating to the construction and operation of dams on the river Danube for the production of electricity, flood control and improvement of navigation. In its Judgment of 25 September 1997, the Court found that both Hungary and Slovakia had breached their legal obligations. It called on both States to negotiate in good faith in order to ensure the achievement of the objectives of the 1977 Budapest Treaty, which it declared was still in force, while taking account of the acutal situation that had developed since 1989. Owing to the ultimate purpose of compliance with international obligations in international law, the decision of the ICJ on both states to negotiate in good faith is not difficult to understand. In particular, a negotiation may be a way to remedy this case and also in international law.

Chapter 7

Case Studies of Consultations in International Law

The following five cases were examined for the purpose of understanding the above analysis, combined with several additional elements.

I. Lake Lanoux

In the *Lake Lanoux* case,[1] Spain argued that France was under an obligation to obtain Spain's consent to the execution of works for the utilisation of certain waters in the Pyrenees for a hydroelectric scheme. The tribunal held that France had a duty to consult with Spain over projects that were likely to affect Spanish interests. The nature of obligatory consultations is as follows:

> One speaks, although often inaccurately, of the obligation of negotiating an agreement. In reality, the engagements thus undertaken by States take very diverse forms and have a scope which varies according to the manner in which they are defined and according to the procedures intended for their execution; but the reality of the obligations thus undertaken is incontestable and sanctions can be applied in the event, for example, of an unjustified breaking off of the discussions, abnormal delays, disregard of the agreed procedures, systematic refusals to take into consideration adverse proposals or interests, and, more generally, in cases of violation of the rules of good faith.[2]

This was a case about an international watercourse system. There are additional studies on this subject of the existence of a duty to consult or negotiate. Interestingly, these studies have come to similar conclusions.

1 *Lake Lanoux Arbitration* (France v. Spain), (1957) 24 I.L.R 101, p. 127.
2 *Ibid.*, p. 128.

International law imposes, on a basin state, the obligation to consult and negotiate in good faith with co-basin states that object to a proposed work or utilisation of waters on the ground that it might cause them serious injury.[3] The implied duty to consult is: neither party might lawfully act unilaterally, without mutually co-operating with each other, in such a manner as to threaten significance in the area of an international watercourse system. In this case, the tribunal rejected Spain's argument, and said that "one can but admit that there does exist a duty of consultation and of bringing into harmony the respective actions of the two States when general interests are involved in matters concerning waters".[4]

As there is a close relationship between negotiations and consultations, some cases required a duty to negotiate. Specifically, the UN Charter contains few consultation provisions. The most prominent is Article 33, referring to negotiation, which may encompass consultation.

II. Air Transport Arbitration

In the *France/US Air Transport Arbitration* of 1978,[5] the US raised the issue of preliminary jurisdictional objections, concerning the application of Part 213 Order of the Economic Regulations; however, the US had not raised the issue during its preliminary negotiations with France. The tribunal therefore rejected the argument and pointed out that even if dis-

3 See Bourne, C. B. Procedure in the Development of International Drainage Basins: the Duty to Consult and to Negotiate, 212 Canada Year Book of International Law (1972), p. 233. More studies on international watercourse system of a duty to consult, see Schachter, O., Sharing the World's Resources, New York: Columbia University Press, 1977; 69–70. He states that recent trends suggest the eventual emergence of a prior consultation rule and notes the additional details that would have to be filled in if such a rule is to become fully effective. The members of the Institute of International Law Commission on pollution of rivers and lakes, divided on whether general custom requires notification and consultation when a pollution risk can be foreseen.

4 *Lake Lanoux Arbitration* (France v. Spain), 1957 24 I.L.R 101, p. 133.

5 *The France/US Air Transport* Arbitration Award of 1978, 54 ILR (1979).

cussions on the particular issues had not been specific or extensive, the two issues were in fact closely related.[6]

Although the relationship between consultation and negotiation should be carefully checked case-by-case, it is widely recognised and accepted that the distinction between these two concepts need not be stretched too far, insofar as there is no clear borderline between them, particularly when both of them serve as a method of dispute settlement.

III. North Sea Continental Shelf

In the *North Sea Continental Shelf* Cases, Denmark and the Netherlands tried to establish, against the Federal Republic of Germany, a continental shelf delineation based on equidistance. The ICJ noted that the negotiation principle is one which underlies all international relations, and is a dispute settlement method having "fundamental character in view of the restricted availability of international judicial or arbitral settlement".[7]

The Court then held that Denmark and the Netherlands could not simply maintain continental shelf rights out to the equidistance line with West Germany, which was not a party to the 1958 Continental Shelf Convention, but were instead obligated to enter into meaningful negotiations with the West German government. The Court explained that the duty to negotiate stemmed from the 1945 Truman Proclamation on the continental shelf, which recognised the need to agree on delimitation with adjacent states, and from the negotiation principle, as recognised in Article 33 of the UN Charter.[8]

Subsequently, Denmark, the Netherlands and West Germany did negotiate, and then ultimately agreed. Thereafter, the creation and adoption of two treaties was promoted.[9] Moreover, after this case other European

6 *Ibid.*, p. 303.

7 *North Sea Continental Shelf Cases*, 1969 ICJ Reports 3 (Judgment of 20 February 1969), p. 48.

8 *Ibid.*, pp. 47–48.

9 Treaty between the Federal Republic of Germany and Denmark, 10 ILM 603 (1971); Treaty between the Netherlands and the Federal Republic of Germany, 10 ILM 607 (1971).

countries, with continental shelf claims in confined areas, entered into intergovernmental negotiations rather than making potentially overlapping unilateral claims. This case illustrates the significance of negotiation and a duty to negotiate in international law.

IV. Fisheries Jurisdiction

Similarly, in the *Fisheries Jurisdiction* Cases,[10] the ICJ mentioned the obligation of States to undertake negotiations in good faith for an equitable solution of their differences. It also stated, "it is implicit in the concept of preferential right and that negotiations are required in order to define or delimit the extent of those rights. The obligation to negotiate thus flows from the very nature of the respective rights of the Parties".[11] It also pointed out that an obligation to negotiate may be inherent in the nature of the respective rights of parties to a dispute, and it may, therefore, be a proper exercise of judicial function to direct them to do so. In each case, the Court addressed the duty to negotiate or to consult with reference to Article 33 of the UN Charter.

It can be argued that the consultation is a compulsory procedure, although it does have a non-compulsory characteristic. If the consultation is to be compulsory, the circumstances in which the obligation arises, as well as its content, need to be carefully defined. Otherwise, one may experience allegation of failure to carry out the agreed procedure, which results in the consultation itself becoming a disputed issue.[12]

There is no established general rule governing the actual nature of compliance with the obligation to consult or negotiate. Actually, its flexibility and informality militates against stringent procedures. According to the *South West Africa* Cases, the ICJ argued that it remains a matter of fact to be determined objectively by an international tribunal whether there have been adequate consultations and negotiations to justify the conclusion that this precondition has been fulfilled. However, it

10 *Fisheries Jurisdiction Cases (Merits),* ICJ Reports (1974) 1, pp. 3, 32, 175 and 201.
11 *Ibid.*, pp. 32 and 201.
12 Merrills 1998; 6.

should be emphasised that it is not so much forms that such consultation and negotiation may have taken, as the attitude and views of the parties concerned on the substantive issues involved.[13]

V. Mavrommatis Palestine Concessions

The *Mavrommatis Palestine Concessions* case was said to indicate the significance of compliance with the obligation to consult or negotiate. Britain argued that there was no dispute, which could not be settled by negotiations under the terms of the mandate. In order to reject this argument, the court explained:

> Negotiation does not always of necessity presuppose a more or less lengthy series of notes and dispatches; it may suffice that a discussion should have been, and this discussion may have been very short; this will be the case if a deadlock is reached, or if finally a point is reached at which one of the parties definitely declares himself unable, or refuses, to give way and there can therefore be no doubt that the dispute cannot be settled by diplomatic negotiation.[14]

The Permanent Court not only tried to make it clear that negotiation is the beginning of settlement, but also considered some factors, which might block negotiation. It found that the question whether negotiations stood any chance of success or could be deadlocked, a relative one, which could not be determined without regard to, amongst other considerations, the views of states concerned, who are usually in the best position to judge as to the political or other reasons which could prevent a negotiated settlement.[15]

The words 'unable', 'refuse' and 'give away' are obviously against the principle of good faith. Under the circumstances, the court expressed its view that there is a binding international obligation to undertake preliminary negotiations, before the commencement of proceedings in front

13 *The South West Africa Cases* (Ethiopia v South Africa; Liberia v South Africa) (Preliminary Objections) ICJ Reports 1962; 319: 346.

14 *Mavrommatis Palestine Concessions* (Greece v. U.K.), 1924 P.C.I.J ser. A No. 2 (Judgment of Aug. 13), p. 13.

15 *Ibid.*, p. 15.

of an international tribunal. It seems the Court referred specifically to the precise wording of clauses in the mandate on which its jurisdiction was founded.

The judicial position was affirmed by the *German Interests in Polish Upper Silesia* case. The Court noted that, in the absence of specific stipulations in the jurisdictional clause rendering diplomatic negotiations a condition precedent, its jurisdiction could not be ousted on that ground.[16]

In most cases, international consultation and negotiation frequently commence with actors directly involved in the dispute before the issue is taken up at a high level between the protesting states, during which time no solution is reached. There is an obvious advantage in attempting to resolve issues at their lowest possible level and with the least possible publicity. Such a lower-level solution tends to be simpler, quicker and cheaper, and generally keeps a controversy from being enmeshed in broader political issues or engaging national sensitivities.[17]

VI. Conclusion

Part I of this thesis has identified the mechanism of consultations in international law under a variety of different circumstances. It focused on the function of dispute prevention in the consultation, other than dispute settlement. However, the ultimate target is to solve conflicts, either through dispute avoidance or dispute settlement. The emergence of research on dispute avoidance and ADR is to confirm the importance of this so-called 'diplomatic method', which shows in this thesis the effectiveness of consultation in the sphere of international law.

There is an argument about whether states must consult others as a duty in international law. According to Kirgis, there is no such duty in theory of international law whenever states contemplate taking or per-

16 *The German Interests in Polish Upper Silesia Case* (Jurisdiction), PCIJ series A. No. 6 1925; 14.

17 Bilder, R. B. The Settlement of Disputes in the field of the International Law of the Environment, Hague Recueil 1975; 224.

mitting a unilateral action that might adversely affect the interest of the international community as a whole. Nevertheless, he acknowledges that, in practice, it does establish a norm of consultations, or implication of a duty to consult and negotiate.

In other words, what he argues is that the strict rule of a duty to consult or negotiate is not clearly stated in any international treaty or convention, but merely 'implied' from them. This implication is particularly strong in the North Atlantic Treaty and the Law of the Sea.

However, in my view, a duty to consult is not just an implication. Through the elaboration of the consultation under international conventions, several treaties and conventions in the field of international law can support this observation, such as Article 42 of Vienna Convention on Succession of States in Respect of State Property, and Article 3 of the 1969 International Convention Relating to Intervention on the High Seas in Cases of Oil Pollution Casualties.

Moreover, in several treaties involving international organisation, a duty to consult is separately listed as a provision on its own (e.g. Article 4 of the North Atlantic Treaty, and Article 106 of the UN Charter).

Furthermore, the consultation is adopted as a legal procedure although it is not necessarily a compulsory proceeding. According to reports by international courts, there is a binding international obligation to undertake negotiations or consultations prior to the commencement of proceedings before an international tribunal. The typical examples are rulings of the *Mavrommatis Palestine Concessions* case and the *Fisheries Jurisdiction* cases.

Notwithstanding, both the consultation and the negotiation are diplomatic methods, because the parties retain control of the dispute and they can freely accept or reject a proposed settlement.

A duty to consult could not be adopted by international treaties and conventions as a compulsory provision. However, under the advocacy of customary international law, practice establishes the law. Case studies create a distinct impression that there exists a duty to consult. The *Lake Lanoux* case is a good example of a duty to consult requirement.

Thus, the consultation clause flourishes within international and regional organisations as part of their operating procedures. It propounds the duty to consult in international law. Through them, the DSU of the WTO interprets this phrase both theoretically and practically.

Part II

Consultation in the GATT and WTO

In Parts II and III, the concept of the consultation will be looked at in the specific context of international trade, and a unique forum: the World Trade Organisation. Part I showed that the consultation not only plays an important role in dispute settlement mechanism, but also demonstrates its dual concern with dispute prevention and dispute settlement.

This part consists of an introduction to the WTO as an international organisation; an overview of the dispute settlement mechanism (DSM) with consultations; an assessment of the consultations in the General Agreement on Tariffs and Trade (GATT). Present research on the role of consultation in the WTO will be elaborated in Part III.

My aims here are to exhibit the background of the consultation in the GATT/WTO and its evolution.

The interrelationship of consultation in the GATT, the so-called diplomatic-oriented procedure, and consultation in the DSU, a key Agreement under the WTO, shaped an integrated theory of consultations in the unique DSM under the WTO.

As the WTO is such a distinctive organisation, it provides a stage for consultations to play a positive role in dispute settlement.

Chapter 1

The WTO as an International Organisation

The WTO is a global international organisation dealing with the rules of trade between nations.[1] Its aim is to help link trade relationships among states. 148 countries had joined the WTO by the end of 2004. It was created from the GATT. However, the WTO is not just a simple extension of the GATT, and its importance is not merely restricted to trade.

1) The GATT was an organisation, which was administered through trade agreements. Whereas the WTO is a formal organisation, every Member must accept in its entirety a common set of rules and disciplines covering not only goods, but also services and intellectual property, which differ from the GATT – mainly goods agreements.
2) The WTO encourages Member states to compete under conditions of open, equal and fair trade.
3) One of the most significant achievements from the results of the Uruguay Round of Multilateral Trade Negotiations was the establishment of the dispute settlement mechanism under the framework of the WTO.
4) Another important improvement is that WTO committees and councils are open to all Member states. Decisions in the WTO are typically taken by consensus among all Member states and these decisions are ratified by Member states. To some extent, the risk of disputes spilling over into political or military conflict is reduced.

In general, these four special features make the WTO different from other international economic organisations. The following features are the main divergences from the GATT: formal organisation, context extension and dispute settlement system.

1 http: //www.wto.org/english/thewto_e/whatis_e/ last visited 16 November 2004.

I. As a Formal Organisation

As a formal organisation, the WTO has its own structure to carry out its mandate.

The flow chart is as follows:[2]

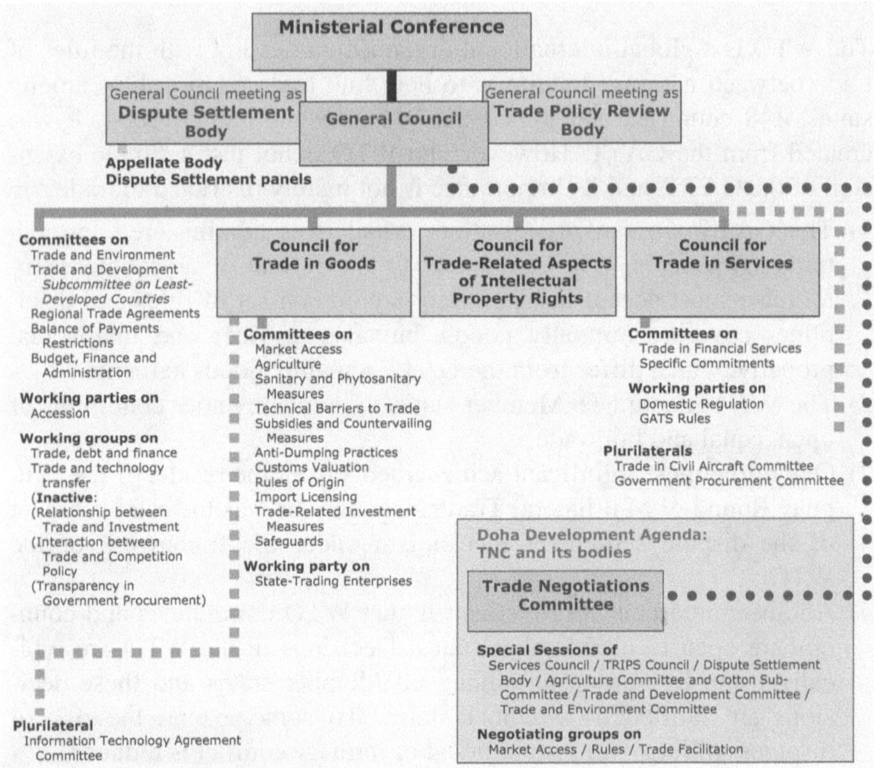

Figure 2.1. WTO organisation chart
Source: WTO web site
(http://www.wto.org/english/thewto_e/whatis_e/tif_e/org2_e.htm)

2 See WTO website, http://www.wto.org/english/thewto_e/whatis_e/tif_e/org2_e.htm last visited 16 November 2004.

The Ministerial Conference is the WTO's top decision-making body, which meets at least once every two years.

However, the real governing body is the General Council, which meets regularly in Geneva. The General Council meets in two forms. The first one is the DSB, which is mainly responsible for the dispute settlement procedure. The second one is the Trade Policy Review Body, which supervises regular reviews of WTO Members' trade policies and practices.

The main subsidiary bodies include: the Council for Trade in Goods, the Council for Trade-Related Aspects of Intellectual Property Rights, and the Council for Trade in Services (another one is the Plurilaterals), all of which should report to the General Council.

Under these councils are various committees. Each committee deals with specific agreements and prepares and adopts decisions for approval by the respective council.[3] The above tree structure (Figure 2.1) shows the differing responsibilities, which keeps the WTO on the right track.

II. Content Extension

The current rules of the WTO have emerged from the GATT. However, the WTO agreements are not limited to the GATT. "The GATT is the WTO's principle rulebook for trade in goods. The Uruguay Round also created new rules for dealing with trade in services, relevant aspects of intellectual property...".[4] On the whole, the GATT was generally about trade in goods, whereas, the WTO extends its agreements to services, and intellectual property rights as well as goods.

The volume of service trade rises each year. Services are invisible goods compared with physical products. Banks, insurance firms, telecommunications companies, tour operators, hotel chains and transport companies already permeate every aspect of social life.[5] The General

3 Article IV, Agreement Establishing the WTO.

4 See http://www.wto.org/english/thewto_e/whatis_e/inbrief_e/inbr03_e.htm last visited 16 November 2004.

5 Gallagher, P. Guide to the WTO and Developing Countries, The Hague: Kluwer Law International, 2000; 176.

Agreements on Trade and Services (GATS) provides a set of multilateral rules for trade in services. Members have rights to decide limitations on market access, as well as to decide national treatment commitments and limitations.[6] The Agreement creates an obligation to undertake successive rounds of further negotiations, usually starting no later than five years from its entry into force. It will be a permanent stimulus of efficiency, openness and growth in service trade:

> It is important, nonetheless, to recognise that, in theory and perhaps also in practice in at least some areas, important trade-offs may still exist between the gains from liberalised trade in services on the one hand and, on the other, the resultant sacrifice in regulatory diversity and innovation.[7]

The Uruguay Round brought Intellectual Property Rights (IPR) into the WTO system for the first time. This is an increasingly important area. The Agreement on Trade Related Aspects of International Property Rights (TRIPS) is a creative part of the WTO Agreements. This Agreement consists of copyright and related rights, trademarks, geographical indications, industrial designs, patents, and layout-designs of integrated circuits.

The use of inventions or creative works of other people, without their permission, is often labelled as piracy or theft. An intellectual property is a creation of the mind. Therefore, it should give adequate returns to the inventors so as to respect their efforts. In the same vein, intellectual property, like trade in services, has a close relationship with customers, and enters into sales channel as well.

Thus, an important element in the protection of IPR is to ensure that there is a balance between the interests of the innovator and of the user. Although the lack of intellectual property protection can deter international trade and investment, over-protection of those rights might lead to the same result. The TRIPS establishes a certain minimum of protection of IPR within Member states.[8] Meanwhile, the protection of IPR should contribute to the promotion of technological innovation, and assist in the transfer and dissemination of technology.[9]

6 *Ibid.*, p. 176.

7 Trebilcock, M. J. & Howse, R. The Regulation of International Trade, London: Routledge, 1995; 247.

8 TRIPS Agreement, Preamble.

9 TRIPS Agreement, Article 7.

Agreement on TRIPS incorporates and reinforces the provision of certain international conventions in the field of intellectual property such as the Paris Convention and the Berne Convention. Certain provisions from these conventions are required, and/or are encouraged to be adopted in national legislation. Each Member is to accord to the nationals of other Members treatment no less favourable than that accorded to its own nationals in relation to IPR.[10] The most complex and important parts among all those rights are implementation and operation. For example, the TRIPS Agreement requires states to ensure a more effective implementation process. Each Member is to accord the MFN treatment unconditionally to the nationals of all other Members.[11] Additionally, the TRIPS also sets out a framework for the enforcement of the IPR, which the Members are to introduce into their domestic system.[12]

III. Dispute Settlement Mechanism (DSM)[13]

One of the most significant achievements from the results of the Uruguay Round was the establishment of the dispute settlement mechanism under the framework of the WTO.

> The contribution of the WTO dispute settlement mechanism to the international trading system is amply demonstrated by the number of successfully resolved trade disputes that have taken place since its establishment, involving both developed and developing Members. Amongst its key features are its near automatic jurisdiction over trade disputes, its efficient and well-developed adjudicatory and appellate system and generally its rule-orientated approach.[14]

The WTO dispute settlement framework is set out principally in the Understanding on Rules and Procedures Governing the Settlement of Disputes (DSU). A Dispute Settlement Body (DSB) is established to admin-

10 TRIPS Agreement, Article 3.

11 *Ibid.*

12 Qureshi, A. H. International Economic Law, London: Sweet & Maxwell, 1999; 286.

13 The legal texts of Article XXII and XXIII under GATT will be examined in Part III.

14 *Ibid.*, pp. 288–289.

ister the rules and procedures under the Understanding. The WTO encourages states to settle their disputes through consultations. Following that stage, states can follow a carefully mapped out and stage-by-stage procedure, which includes the possibility of a ruling by a Panel, or the chances of appealing the ruling.

More trade means more scope for disputes to arise. The DSM aims to conform to the covered agreements and relieve the conflicts among Member states. Renato Ruggiero, former WTO Director General, calls the dispute settlement procedure as the WTO's most individual contribution to the stability of the global economy; without enforcement, the rule-based system would be worthless.[15]

The WTO, as an international organisation, increases its efforts in globalisation of economic activities. As an international organisation, it faces a number of challenges, including that of strengthening the DSM.

15 See http: //www.wto.org/english/thewto_e/whatis_e/tif_e/disp0_e.htm last visited 23 October 2001.

Chapter 2

DSM within the GATT/WTO

The DSM is the centre-piece of the WTO. Hence, it is necessary to research DSM's development to start. There are some debates within the dispute settlement system, especially between the legalistic model and anti-legalistic model. The former stresses adjudication and legitimacy, the latter addresses negotiation and diplomacy. The strong supporter of the legalistic approach is the United States. In order to understand the present position of the DSU, it is appropriate to begin with the Havana Charter from an historical point of view.

There follows a review of the literature, the assessment of the GATT, its relevant background, and the DSM in the GATT compared with the DSU in the WTO. A detailed analysis of consultation in the WTO, including its assessment, will be elaborated on in Part III.

I. The ITO Draft

Since the 'other' two pillars of the Bretton Woods agreement (the International Monetary Fund and the World Bank) were set up in succession, one would expect that the International Trade Organisation (ITO) should have also been established. Although the GATT was brought into being in 1948 before the ITO, many states hoped that such a formal organisation would emerge to regulate trade conduct.

The draft ITO Charter was ambitious. It extended beyond world trade disciplines to include rules on employment, commodity agreements, restrictive business practices, international investment, and services. Its scope was even broader than the present WTO's. Therefore, it was impossible to get it ratified at national level. Haste makes waste, so it failed.

Jackson and Hudec explained that the ITO never happened because the US Congress failed to approve it. Furthermore, Hudec pointed out that its failure was due to the increasing attractiveness of the informal structure that had grown up while everyone was waiting for something else.[1] For some governments, especially the US, the absence of a more formal structure had given GATT exactly the kind of institutional flexibility they had tried to build into the original ITO/GATT model.

The ITO was not established, but the GATT inherited invaluable elements from it.The Havana Charter establishing the ITO kept the nullification and impairment clause, which applied both to legal violations and to non-violation kinds of nullification and impairment.[2] It only provided a bilateral consultation procedure, followed by reference to the ITO, which could then investigate, give a ruling, or make recommendations, and authorise suspension of obligations in serious cases.[3]

The ITO did not consider establishing an expert tribunal to rule on legal questions at that time. After the destruction caused by two world wars, people longed for peace. This mindset made drafters consider using peaceful methods to solve disputes rather than non-peaceful decisions in court. In other words, the drafters hoped to trigger a diplomatic means to solve trade disputes.

II. Stages of the DSM in the GATT

The GATT lived although the ITO had become extinct. The remaining dispute settlement procedures contained in the final text of the GATT were the consultation as Article XXII and the nullification or impairment (N or I) provision as Article XXIII. The definition of N or I is "if any contracting party (CP) should consider that any benefit accruing to it directly or indirectly under this Agreement is being nullified or impaired or that the attainment of any objective of the Agreement is being im-

1 Hudec, R. E. The GATT Legal System and World Trade Diplomacy, London: Praeger, 1975; 21.

2 Hudec 1975; 27.

3 *Ibid.*, p. 28.

peded".[4] In other words, invoking the GATT dispute settlement mechanism does not determine actual breach of legal obligations. The N or I provision applied to any actions by a government. It is possible to bring a claim on the ground of N or I of benefits expected under the Agreement.

Since the world was focusing on re-establishing itself after the ruins of war, the trade volume climbed between 1953 and 1954, and the disputes also grew to become an important part of the GATT.

Jackson described the dispute settlement mechanism during the period of GATT as unique, but it was also flawed in part, by the troubled beginning of GATT.[5] Hudec has contributed many articles which reveal the facts behind the GATT dispute settlement. GATT law was unique because of its mix of legal and diplomatic strategies.[6] Since then, the argument on the approach of legal-orientation or diplomatic-orientation has been debated extensively.[7]

There are no definitions or procedural rules for consultations in the GATT legal text. Instead, GATT stresses, in Article XXII, the importance of consultation, which is a pre-requisite to invoking GATT procedures.[8] That is to say, it allowed for future interpretations to fill in textual gaps.

Hudec considered that the birth and improvement of the GATT were affected by the US, including, the N or I section.[9] In his books, the period of GATT was divided into several time sections, in which he reviewed, systematically, the spectrum of economic, political and social factors. Moreover, his research is conducted using a large number of case studies and empirical evidence. Statistical profiles extensively provide more

4 GATT XXIII: 1

5 Jackson, J. H. Restructuring the GATT System, London: Royal Institute of International Affairs, 1990; 31.

6 Hudec 1975; 65.

7 See part III.

8 In Article XXII:1, each contracting party shall accord sympathetic consideration to, and shall afford adequate opportunity for consultation regarding, such representations as may be made by another contracting party with respect to any matter affecting the operation of this Agreement.

9 For example, the US actively promoted the GATT instead of the ITO; many of the GATT Articles had evolved in the US bilateral trade agreements such as N or I. See Hudec 1975; 57.

elaborate information so as to decipher the GATT dispute settlement for future study.

There was a long and winding course from the ITO to the WTO. However, the WTO drew many lessons from some failures of the GATT, which were invaluable for the improvement of the WTO.

Human beings experience various kinds of difficulties from new-born baby toadult. No one anticipates troubles, even though they are inevitable during a lifetime. Nevertheless, these troubles can be helpful in order to gain more experience and to forge tenacious and independent character in human beings. A person without such experiences may not mature. Similarly, if there were no 'troubled' GATT from which to learn, the WTO would not have had the opportunity to improve to the point it is at present.

A. *Non-third Party Stage*[10]

Hudec overviewed the whole GATT dispute settlement chronologically. At the first stage, disputes were generally taken up through diplomatic procedures. This was because of the historical formation of the GATT. The aim of the GATT was to abolish tariffs and trade barriers. National governments cannot expect to abrogate trade protectionism in one day. Trade liberalisation must be implemented step-by-step.

Hudec proposed a two-step process: "first, governments should be required to collect all barriers to trade in one easily recognisable form the tariff. Second, they should then be encouraged to reduce tariffs by means of voluntary negotiation".[11] That is to say, because of its historical inheritance, from the start the GATT was evolved in the shape of diplomatic negotiation. For that reason, the stage of diplomatic procedures is an inevitable outcome.

In his opinion it was time to wait for the ITO and to lay a foundation of third-party adjudication. Hudec asserted that, at the initial stage, the GATT proceeding was more likely a rehearsed bit of 'stagecraft' designed to formalise the legal obligation.[12] It was, therefore, understand-

10 Hudec, R. E. Enforcing International Trade Law: The Evolution of the Modern GATT Legal System, New Hamshire: Butterworth, 1993; 6.

11 *Ibid.*

12 Hudec 1975; 85.

able why there was no third-party participation to adjudicate. However, involved CPs had to think about further procedure(s) to solve disputes as consultations were failing. A third party adjudication emerged in practice. When conditions are ripe, success is assured.

B. *Inter-sessional Committee of the Contract Parties (CPs)*

The emergence of the first case in the GATT was labelled as the second stage, during which time cases were brought to an inter-sessional committee of the CP. The first dispute took place in July 1948. The Netherlands complained that Cuba had levied a discriminatory consular tax.[13] Several consultations were unsuccessful. Finally, the Netherlands' delegation brought the dispute, indirectly, by requesting a ruling from the Chair. The key argument in this case was whether the MFN Treatment applied to consular taxes. The chairman replied yes, Article I of the MFN clearly applied to consular taxes. After that, there was no further discussion.[14] A few months later, Cuba reported that the discriminatory tax had been removed. In this case, the emergence of the chairman's ruling resolved the legal issue. There were three rulings during this period.[15]

C. *Working Parties*

The third stage was the working party stage when each CP sent a representative of its choice. To some extent, the working parties still wore the negotiating coat.

It was merely the beginning of improving the GATT dispute settlement mechanism. In fact, the composition of a panel considerably met

13 *The Netherlands v. Cuba Consular Tax*, GATT/CP.2/9 or BISD 11/12.

14 GATT/CP.2/SR.11 or BISD 11/12.

15 *Cuba – Consular Taxes* (BISD II/12), *India – Tax Rebates on Exports* (BISD II/12), and *United States – Restriction on Exports to Czechoslovakia* (BISD II/28).

the condition of fairness by acting by members acting in an individual capacity. Three rulings were filed by the working parties.[16]

D. *Panel Stage*

This stage follows Hudec's chronology and general assessment. In the meantime, in the absence of precise information about some disputes in the GATT, the case study is the basis of Hudec's research together with international affairs and some national laws (e.g. American law), as well as the GATT legal system. The rulings increased to 95.

1. *The 1950s*

In the 1950s, as a result of the influence of GATT Director-General Eric Wyndham-White, it became the practice to use the panel, which was recognised as the fourth stage, in dispute resolution. A panel was composed of individuals acting in their own capacity, not as national representatives. This was a significant difference as compared to the composition of the working party. Jackson noted, "this shift early on in GATT's history shows a desire in the GATT to emphasise adjudication by independent decision makers as opposed to negotiated settlements of differences by national representatives".[17]

The first case resolved by a panel was in September 1952. The United Kingdom argued that Greece had increased import duties.[18] The entire proceedings were informal, both judges and advocates acted as diplomats rather than lawyers. The panel report was drafted with an elusive diplomatic vagueness. Looking back at the cases of the 1950s, almost all legal rulings expressed an "intuitive sort of law based on shared experiences and unspoken assumptions".[19] In the first case of the panel, there was no ruling by the panel, but Greece acknowledged the violation.

16 *Brazilian Internal Taxes* (BISD II/181), *United States – Margins of Tariff Preferences to Cuba* (BISD II/11), and *Australia – Subsidy on Ammonium Sulphate* (BISD II/188).

17 Jackson, J. H., Davey, W. J. & Sykes, A. O. Legal Problems of International Economic Relations (3rd ed.), St Paul, Minn: West Publishing, 1995, p. 329.

18 *The UK v. Greece Increase on Import Duties on Products Included in Schedule XXV*, BISD 1S/51.

19 Hudec 1993, p. 12.

The 1950s was an infantile period of dispute settlement. The GATT needed more time to improve dispute settlement procedures.

2. *The 1960s*

In the 1960s, the total number of complaints was seven, and there were only five rulings.

The EEC took over the GATT Chairs of the then six European countries, shaping one superpower to contend with the US. The EEC was a strong supporter of solving disputes through diplomatic negotiation. At that time the other superpower, the US, also stayed with the EEC on the side of anti-legalism.

They both created a climate, in which legal claims were viewed as unfriendly actions. Nevertheless, it did not mean they would not use legal measures.

A case in point was *The Chicken War.*[20] The EEC imposed a fluctuating tariff on basic agricultural products. The US prevented the EEC from using the variable levy, rejected the alternative compensation from the EEC through several rounds of negotiations, and finally submitted the dispute to a panel. The panel came up with a figure of $26 million instead of the $44 million, claimed by the US, and the $19 million, claimed by the EEC.[21] The dispute was not solved during the stage of the negotiation, when disputants rode their particular high horses, but rather quickly after the panel procedure.

Regrettably, during the 1960s, the use of the GATT dispute settlement system declined. More active than the EEC and the US, the developing countries pushed through a proposal in the GATT designed to strengthen the dispute settlement procedures. These countries demanded greater freedom from the GATT and sought to increase the legal obligations of developed CPs. Nonetheless, as powerful CPs played important roles, objections overwhelmed the consensus. In spite of this, the dispute settlement procedures still continued to develop. Hudec averred that it was merely a pause in the progress of dispute activity.

20 *The US v. the EEC Panel on Poultry* in 1963, BISD 12S/65.

21 Hudec 1993, p. 220.

3. *The 1970s*

It was the US that created the GATT and the US which has always played a significant role in the GATT. In 1970, there were many export opportunities for American exporters and little import competition. As a result, American businesspeople, as well as politicians, actively promoted free trade development.

During 19701975, 13 complaints were filed, 11 of which involved America. The EEC provoked another two.

At that time, the EEC's primary objective was the conclusion of free trade agreements with the countries of the European Free Trade Association (EFTA). As the EEC worked on its regionalism, it had less interest in making the GATT powerful in the performance of these duties. Dam noted the contribution of the role of the EEC was "in triumphs of the Community perspective over national solutions".[22] In 1975, the EEC was renamed EC.

The EEC brought a successful community model. It promoted the atmosphere of free and equal competition in the community, and stressed regulation through legislation.

Jackson and Hudec marked the 1970s as a time of rebuilding the legal system. They believed the revival of activity was due to the US. In the 1970s, the US government became concerned about the loss of control in GATT legal affairs, and realised that GATT's existing legal machinery was almost useless, particularly after the Tokyo Round Negotiation.

For the history of the GATT, the Tokyo Round Negotiation (1973–79) was a milestone event. It was foreseen as a shift from tariff barriers to non-tariff barriers (NTB). The main task of the Tokyo Round Negotiation dealt with the NTB. Interestingly, the total text of all new codes was longer than the text of the GATT agreement itself.

As a means of removing the NTB, clear and strict rules were added to define what governments could or could not do with various non-tariff policy instruments. Obviously, a necessary component of the US's political strategy was to strengthen the legal framework of the GATT. The most visible enforcement tool would be the ability to bring lawsuits.[23] Hudec indicated that new code rules were required to strengthen the

22 Dam, K. W. The GATT Law and International Economic Organisation, Chicago: University of Chicago Press, 1970; 375.

23 Hudec 1993; 25.

dispute settlement procedure and to make them credible. Each code contained its own, somewhat advanced, dispute settlement procedure for this purpose.[24]

He further summarised some advantages to legal claims: firstly, legal actions could "become a normal and accepted part of GATT activity of a leading country like the US simply punctured the anti-confrontation balloon";[25] secondly, legal actions could provide useful results if properly managed; thirdly, legal actions would be a diplomatic justification for certain economic pressure such as unilateral trade retaliation, even if the GATT would not rule on such claims.[26]

The appearance of Section 301 of the Trade Act of 1974 of America verified his precise observations. The feature of unilateral sanctions ran in the opposite direction from that of the GATT, and threatened the GATT dispute settlement mechanism.

As the number of legal actions steadily increased, some legal problems arose, accordingly. In 1973, the EEC filed a lawsuit, arguing that the American Domestic International Sales Corporation (DISC) legislation was a GATT-illegal export subsidy.[27] The key defense was a well-founded argument that, from a functional tax policy perspective, there was no relevant difference between DISC and the three European laws as far as their reported subsidy effects were concerned.

During early GATT days, the dispute settlement procedures much relied upon strong consensus and no strict deadline on CPs involvement. The panelists were diplomats, who had rich political experience rather than legal knowledge. Moreover, there was no legal office to assist. At this point, it was difficult for panelists to explain their reasoning through legal analysis.

Because of numerous difficulties at almost every stage, the DISC case incredibly lasted 12 years. At the very beginning, the US refused to discuss the DISC law in the GATT. Then, it refused to conduct bilateral discussions, unless its three counter-complaints were discussed simultaneously.[28] After that, it refused to co-operate, unless the composition of the panel included two tax experts and would handle both the EC claim

24 *Ibid.*, p. 156.
25 *Ibid.*, p. 230.
26 *Ibid.*, p. 231.
27 *The EC v. the US Income Tax Legislation* (DISC), BISD 23S/98.
28 See BISD 23S/114, BISD 23S/127, and BISD 23S/137.

and the US counter-complaints at the same time, after the EC asked for a panel decision. Thereafter, through two and a half years of a seesaw battle, the panel finally was in place.

After conducting hearings and meetings, the DISC panel issued its findings in November 1976. The panel reports were written in the opaque decision-making style of the early GATT panel decisions. The panel found that the US DISC law violated Article XVI:4, which prohibits export subsidies on 'nonprimary' products. The report did not specify the extent and exact conditions of the violation. The panel reports on the three European laws came to the same conclusion, repeating almost exactly the same vague verbal formula used to express the ruling on DISC.

The three European defendants were of the view that the panel decision was wrong in finding their laws in violation, but right as to the conclusion that DISC violated GATT. They blocked adoption of the three reports against them. All other GATT delegations, who participated in the discussion, supported the European view.

The US took the position that it would accept the finding of violation against the DISC law only if the three European defendants accepted the findings against themselves. The case remained in deadlock for another five years. Except for one rather minor case in 1956, this was the first time in approximately 20 third-party legal rulings where parties had blocked adoption of a ruling.

Most GATT parties believed that the panel had made a serious mistake with regard to the applied European law. Since the EC Members were familiar with the rules of the GATT, they easily blocked the panel rulings by disrupting the consensus. Hudec summarised two weaknesses in that period of dispute settlement mechanism: one was the lack of any institutionalised sources of high-quality legal analysis. The other was the absence of a procedure to deal with legal errors in panel rulings.[29]

In the DISC case, America posed the tax policy problem. The panel dealt with it opaquely, and used vague words during the key debate. The second weakness Hudec considered led one to think about the necessity of the future Appellate Body, which at least gave another chance to correct legal errors in panel rulings to some extent.[30]

29 Hudec 1993; 45.
30 *Ibid*., p. 47.

These two consequences can be challenged in the following Foreign Sales Corporation (FSC) case, which inherited from the DISC case, by invoking the same legal issues. There was an institutionalised source of high-quality legal analysis in the DSU and a complete set of procedures to deal with legal errors in the Panel's and the AB's rulings in the WTO, but it had been pending during the implementation stage.

Although this case might be regarded as a flaw in the history of the GATT, it directly encouraged CPs, especially leading CPs, to reform the dispute settlement mechanism. Both Jackson and Hudec examined a document in 1979 entitled *Understanding regarding Notification, Consultation, Dispute Settlement and Surveillance*, which formed a sort of code of procedures for the dispute settlement practice in the GATT. This Understanding's salient features were as follows:[31]

1) Requirement of consultation as the first step;
2) Provision for panels with some words about whether a complainant has a right to a panel;
3) Reinforcement of the *prima facie* N or I concepts;
4) Outline of the work of a panel, including oral and written advocacy;
5) Permission to use non-governmental persons on panels, though with a preference for government persons;
6) Recognition of the practice of issuing a panel report with statement of facts and rationale;
7) Understanding that the report is then submitted to the CPs for final approval.

Although some codes needed further deliberation, most of them provided guidance on how to finalise the GATT dispute settlement system. Hudec concluded that dispute settlement had regained a central place in GATT affairs and would continue to increase in importance by the end of the 1970s.

The Tokyo Round began to stress a number of NTBs that restrained and influenced international trade flows. As mentioned before, it led to an increase in the activity and subject jurisdiction of the GATT system. It was proved by the statistics of the 1980s complaints after the Tokyo Round.

31 See Jackson 1990; 52 and Hudec 1993; 178.

4. *The 1980s*

In this decade, the DSM played an extremely important role in GATT. There were 115 complaints in the 1980s, while there had been only 92 complaints in the previous 30 years; there were 47 legal rulings produced by panels, whereas, there were 41 decisions from panels before the 1980s.[32]

The central role of the dispute settlement was confirmed in the 1980s. From available statistics, one may infer the strong desire of CP countries to settle increasing disputes during this period. In addition, the GATT Secretariat finally created a legal office in 1981. It demonstratedits attention to legal issues and also tried to improve the DSM in terms of its legitimacy. Of course, it worked in parallel with the new rules of the Tokyo Round. The CP countries were increasingly concerned that the dispute settlement procedure could supply a credible enforcement mechanism.

America, from the 1970s, strengthened legalisation of the GATT dispute settlement from its standpoint. A series of US complaints focused on the value of the Tokyo Round agreements. The EC, as usual, opposed this point.

In the meantime, complaints were also brought by other CPs apart from the US and EC. They increased the general visibility of dispute settlement work by raising the volume of activities. In addition, each positive result accumulated the experience and the reputation of the procedure for the GATT.

Another fact was the rise of developing countries, although they played a minor role in the GATT dispute settlement procedure. Many developing countries would place their great hopes on the GATT, solidifying market-oriented policies through joining the GATT.

Developing countries, especially from their governments' perspective, acknowledged that being CPs could increase the weight of international obligations in their local markets, with the help of international policies to regulate their trade conduct.

Simultaneously, the developing CPs never stopped fighting for their rights. The legalisation of GATT dispute settlement weakens, theoretically, the power differences between developed and developing CPs, and provides comparatively predictable results for involved parties, either in developed or developing countries.

32 Hudec 1993; 289.

The course of improvement does not always go smoothly. The steadily increasing number of disputes eventually brought an increased number of failings. For example, in 1981 the US claimed that EC export subsidies on wheat flour violated the Subsidies Code.[33] The panel found no subsidy code violation of the EC. Then, the US blocked approval of the panel ruling. Although the Committee made many efforts, at the end of 1992, the Wheat Flour panel report remained on the GATT's list of unfinished panel business.

During this period, the US granted an, export subsidy to allow American exporters to take the whole Egyptian market, which led to the filing of a complaint by the EC. Moreover, the US adopted more aggressive export subsidies for exports of wheat and flour unilaterally, and prolonged the export subsidy war. In this case, the consensus was a barrier rather than an act of good faith. This concern did not merely belong to the EC. Other CPs had the same worries, since the losing parties to the disputes could easily prevent the consequences of their loss through raising objections to the consensus.

Hudec pointed out that GATT law was not effectively protecting national interests, with the emergence of a massive US trade deficit during the mid-1980s. That view grew much stronger. Political leaders, who shared that view, began advocating a policy that had come to be called unilateralist, such as Section 301 of the 1974 Act. In 1984, the EC adopted a New Commercial Instrument No. 2641/84. This regulation could be considered the duplication of Section 301, which intensified the atmosphere of unilateral retaliation.

5. *General Assessment*

Looking back, the GATT dispute settlement system's shortcomings may be summarised as follows:

1) no strict timetable leads to prolongation of some cases;[34]
2) difficult to find appropriate panelists;[35]

33 Hudec 1993; 491.

34 *Brazilian Internal Taxes* case lasted almost ten years to be solved (BISD 7th Supp. 68–79 1961).

35 *The DISC Case* in 1973 was short of tax experts in the panel (BISD 23rd Supp. 98–114 1977).

3) a losing party may block adoption of a panel report by the council because of the consensus rule;[36]
4) some panels write imprecise reports instead of making sound and reasoned findings;[37]
5) some CPs take a long time to implement changes in their law necessary in order to make them consistent with GATT, as interpreted by the panel;[38]
6) there are debates about which procedure (GATT or a code) must be pursued.[39]

Some of the flaws became more and more sharp and were criticised by most CPs. A reform had to be undertaken. The dispute settlement system was one of the agendas during the 1986–1994 Uruguay Round.

Every researcher in the dispute settlement field sets aside room to discuss the history of the GATT/WTO. The assessment of past history is desirable, and the literature survey of key authors is essential, because these researches focused on understanding the past the better to direct the future.

Jackson proposed that the GATT dispute settlement system was not complete, but it was fairly successful.[40] His analysis was based on international law, and from this perspective, he found the panel findings contained rules interpreting the GATT application in a particular dispute. However, the Vienna Convention suggests practice establishes the

36 *The Subsidies of Wheat Flour Case* between the US and EC was an example (Hudec 1993).

37 In *the MIPS Case* between the EC and US, the panel concluded the administrative fee was permitted under Article VIII and II because it was limited to "the cost of services rendered", despite the fact that the costs were neither charged by a government nor had any relation to any governmental service (BISD 25th Supp. 68–109 1979).

38 In *the Screwdriver Assembly Case* although the EC agreed to adopt the panel report, it would be deferred until implementation of the result of Uruguay Round negotiation on the Antidumping Code, where the issue of circumvention measures was in fact still under negotiation. Meanwhile, the EC continued applying its existing circumvention regulation (BISD 37th Supp. 132–199 1991).

39 After Tokyo Round negotiation its Annex shaped a sort of codes of procedure for the dispute settlement practice. It therefore left a gap between Article XXII, XXIII and these codes.

40 See Jackson 1990; 83.

agreement.[41] In light of the Vienna Convention's codification of customary international law, and over four decades of GATT experiences, the practice of the GATT truly established a unique interpretation.

In Jackson's comments, either GATT or WTO law is in line with public international law, especially section three of the Vienna Convention addressing the interpretation of treaties.[42] He disclosed that complication of the dispute itself is on economic, political and social grounds. He supported, under the doctrine of international law, *stare decisis,* or that the common-law concept of precedents does not apply. Yet in practice, the GATT dispute settlement system was very much influenced by precedents, a fact which was often mentioned in GATT deliberations as well as in formal panel findings.[43] It might be possible that, in practice, one performance is efficient, but in theory, it is ineffective, such as the concept of precedents in the GATT.

The fluctuations in GATT dispute settlement were under the shadow of American domination. Jackson, Hudec and other researchers simultaneously criticised its troubled beginnings.

Nonetheless, the GATT law paid a price in reputation, for the benefit of leaving-by-doing experience. The failure could be considered a lesson to remember. Thus, the tortuous experiences of the GATT could help the later WTO to mature. Many GATT obligations had been enacted into some domestic laws in order to avoid conflict.

Behind the dispute settlement process and the margins of the legal text of the GATT, the new round of negotiation embarked on a political venture. Since the GATT had no well-crafted dispute settlement procedure, the issue needed to be addressed during the Uruguay Round.

41 Article 31.3, under the Vienna Convention on the Law of Treaties.

42 See Jackson 1990; 84.

43 The *Alcoholic Beverages* case between the EC and Japan as a precedent gave a good example of the "like product" classification (BISD 34th Supp. 83–135 1988).

III. The Uruguay Round – Birth of the WTO

Some described the trade policy as a reflection of bicycle theory, which means that without forward movement, the bicycle will fall.[44] With the development of society, politics and economies, trade policy must improve and reform. Historical development is closely linked to revolutions and new ideas. The political world structure and social framework become increasingly complex and economic and technical innovation is occurring at great speed. In response to this so-called New Economic Time, a requirement on reforming current trade policies is not a surprise.

In order to strengthen the credibility of the GATT legal system, it was particularly necessary to create a new agreement on dispute settlement. Hudec noted that while the US tried to justify its unilateral approach by arguing that GATT dispute settlement was too slow and too easily blocked by defendant governments, the other CPs decided to offerrevised and strengthened GATT dispute settlement procedures to eliminate this objection. Although their ultimate targets were similar, they reached the same goal, which encouraged the emergence of the DSU.

The DSU absorbed and consolidated all of the earlier GATT agreements on dispute settlement procedures, including the 1979 Tokyo Round Understanding with its Agreed Description of Customary Practice, the 1982 Ministerial Declaration, the 1984 Agreement on Panel Selection and the Procedural Reforms Adopted at the 1988 Montreal Midterm.[45]

Although the GATT changed to be more rule-oriented, the result did not satisfy some CPs, who argued it improved too slowly. Among them, the US strongly pushed for quickening the reform initiatives. In September 1986, a large ministerial meeting was held to construct the framework for a new trade round negotiation in Uruguay. The outstanding items in the Uruguay Round Negotiation were negotiations on some new subjects including services, intellectual property and trade-related investment measures.[46]

44 Jackson, J. H. The World Organisation, London: Royal Institute of International Affairs, 1998; 24.

45 Hudec 1993; 153.

46 Jackson 1998; 24–25.

In 1988, a Montreal ministerial meeting considered some substantial issues: (1) it made clear that a complaining party had a right to a panel proceeding; (2) it established a new optional arbitration procedure, under which disputing CPs could agree to abide by the arbitration award; (3) it confirmed that once the consultation of disputing CPs broke down, the Director-General had authority to step in and form a panel; (4) it firmed up the timetable for a panel procedure, allowing for the completion of an active procedure within nine months.[47]

Montreal made some progress in the dispute settlement process. Nevertheless, it did not reach agreement on the basis of draft texts prepared by each of the negotiation committees. Jackson argued that this was due to the political upheaval in the two largest trading blocs – the American presidential election, the replacement of an EC Commissioner with aides and important staff.[48]

Interestingly, the original agenda for the Uruguay Round did not mention the establishment of a new organisation to replace the GATT. In 1989, an informal and partly academic meeting was held in Geneva to discuss the idea of the WTO. Then, Canadian government officials and negotiators began working on a more specific and constructed proposal, which was discussed at a special meeting in 1990 between the US, the EC, Japan and Canada.

At the end of 1991, the Secretariat formally put forward the first full draft for a new organisation, the Multilateral Trade Organisation (MTO), whose name came from the EC. At that time, the US refused to establish a new organisation. Ironically, in the last few hours of the day preceding the 15 December 1993 deadline for completion of the Uruguay Round, the US indicated that it would accept the name of the World Trade Organisation (WTO) rather than the MTO. Further refinements were made at Marrakesh in 1994 when the Agreement was signed in most cases subject to subsequent national ratification procedures.[49] The WTO was thereby founded.

History is a mirror, reflecting itself, from the ITO, the GATT and the MTO to the final WTO and a revolution in trade policies and political negotiations. It is an inevitable outcome of historical improvement. The US played and is still playing a leading role in the progress of this revolution.

47 Jackson 1990; 65.
48 *Ibid.*, p. 39.
49 Jackson 1995; 27–29.

IV. The DSM in the WTO

Petersmann considered the new dispute settlement system of the 1994 Agreement as establishing the WTO.[50] It was pointed out that it was not by accident that the Uruguay Round ended two weeks after there was agreement on the DSU. The legal text of the DSU asserts the dispute settlement system of the WTO as a central element in providing security and predictability to the multilateral trading system.[51]

A. *Improvement of DSM in the WTO*

First, there are strict time-limitations for parties to follow dispute settlement in the DSU. For instance, in the consultation stage, "if the consultations fail to settle a dispute 60 days after the date of receipt of the request for consultations, the complaining party may request the establishment of a panel";[52] during the panel stage, "panels shall be composed of three panelists unless the parties to the dispute disagree, within 10 days from the establishment of the panel";[53] at the stage of Appellate Review, "as a general rule, the proceedings shall not exceed 60 days from the date a party to the dispute formally notifies its decision to appeal to the date the Appellate Body circulates its report".[54]

Second, the DSB is established to administer the operation of the DSU. The DSB is established to administer these rules and procedures and the consultation and dispute settlement provisions of the covered agreements.[55]

50 Petersmann, E. U. The Dispute Settlement System of the World Trade Organisation and the Evolution of the GATT Dispute Settlement System Since 1994 C.M.L.Rev. 1948; 31(6):1205.

51 Article 3.2 of the DSU.

52 Article 4.7 of the DSU.

53 Article 8.5 of the DSU.

54 Article 17.5 of the DSU.

55 Article 2.1 of the DSU.

Third, the procedure for good offices, conciliation and mediation are codified as voluntary choices. "Good offices, conciliation or mediation may be requested at any time by any party to a dispute".[56]

Fourth, the outstanding innovation is quasi-automatic decision-making through establishing panels, adopting the Panel and Appellate Body (AB) reports and granting of requests for suspension of concessions in case of non-implementing dispute settlement rulings. The establishment of the panel in the GATT period was an unsolved problem as it could only be established on the basis of consensus. Therefore, the defendant CPs could easily block its establishment.

The key improvement was the proposal to remove the veto power of losing parties. Instead of requiring a consensus decision of the GATT Council for each step of the process (a consensus which could be blocked by the defendant), all steps are taken quasi-automatically, subject to a consensus decision not to do so.[57] For example, panel rulings would be given legal effect, without the losing party's consent, subject to appellate review, which is final and binding.

Cross-retaliation[58] could take place if the injured party considers that same sector retaliation would not be practicable or effective, and where circumstances are serious enough.[59] It could be argued that, because of the quasi-automatic consensus of the retaliation, dispute settlement proceedings worsen a situation like trade wars, and the process may be easily abused, since words like 'practicable' or 'effective' and 'serious enough' are not precise enough to be interpreted.

Under the DSU, the right of a party to have a panel established is clearly set out under Article 6. If consultations fail to resolve a dispute within 60 days, the complaining Member can require the establishment of a Panel. The DSB shall establish the panel, unless there is a consensus in the DSB not to do so. This is opposite from panel establishment proceedings in the GATT. The change provided positive evidence for legalisation of the WTO dispute settlement system.

Fifth, the AB was considered a fantastic idea. As mentioned before, the complaining Member's decision to appeal will automatically be to

56 Article 5.3 of the DSU.
57 See Article 6.1, 7.1, 8.7, 16.4, and 17.14 of the DSU.
58 Retaliation is sought in another sector instead of the same sector.
59 DSU, Article 22.3.

proceed to appellate review. The establishment of the AB confirmed the legitimate trend of the WTO dispute settlement system.

Jackson argued that: "an appellate progress that has increased the rigor and careful reasoning of panel and appellate reports that are grappling with a very sophisticated system governing questions of the international trade system".[60] Palmeter stated that with the establishment of an AB, the legal system of the WTO "possessed an important characteristic of all mature legal systems: the separation of the judicial power from the other organs of the government".[61]

There is not an AB in the International Commission of Jurists (ICJ), or in the ECJ nor other similar institutions in the international community. The AB is a standing body, whereas, the panel is an *ad hoc* institution. The person serving in the AB should demonstrate expertise in law, international trade and the subject matter of the covered agreements generally.[62] The composition of the AB goes further than the panelists' requirement, which requires a sufficiently diverse background and a wide spectrum of experience.[63] Obviously, the AB is more concerned about jurisdiction than in choosing persons serving on the AB.

In addition, the DSU limits the power of the AB. The appeal "shall be limited to issues of law covered in the panel report and legal interpretations developed by the panel".[64] However, there are some debates regarding this limitation: if the DSB authorises too much power to them, it may give legalisation too much pressure; if no limitation to the AB, in practice, it may increase the time frame. Nevertheless, the AB has the authority to uphold, modify or reverse the legal findings and conclusions of the panel.[65]

Many effects have been made by the AB. Significant issues include the status of prior panel reports; the right of a Member to bring a claim under the GATT 1994; the specificity of a request for establishment of a panel; the terms of reference of panels; judicial economy; burden of proof; the scope of application of the GATT 1994 and the GATS; nulli-

60 Jackson, J. H. International Economic Law in Times That Are Interesting. J.I.E.L. 2000; 3(1): 7.

61 Palmeter, D. The WTO Appellate Body Needs Remand Authority. J.W.T. 1998; 32(1): 41.

62 DSU, Article 17.3.

63 DSU, Article 8.2.

64 DSU, Article 17.6.

65 DSU, Article 17.13.

fication or impairment; the scope of appeal; representation of governments by private lawyers in AB proceedings.[66]

Hudec examined the important function of the AB. In addition to closing off easy escaped routes, such as a CP veto from the enforcement process, the Uruguay Round reforms addressed concerns regarding the reliability of high-quality legal decisions, which have been contributed by the appellate tribunal.

Sixth, arbitration is one of the legal means of dispute settlement adopted by the DSU, although, in practice, only few of the WTO Members have utilised the arbitration process under Article 25 of the DSU.[67]

Seventh, the DSU is not an isolated agreement, but extended to other agreements as Appendix One,[68] some special or additional rules and procedures contained in Appendix Two.[69]

In general, these differences send a strong signal that the development from the GATT to the WTO is a progress of jurisdictionalisation on the aspects of time-framework, institution, means, procedures and judicial system.

B. *Assessment*

Hudec and Jackson emphasised three great improvements, namely time framework, quasi-automatic consensus and the creation of the AB.

Petersmann raised the issue of coexistence between the GATT Agreements and the WTO Agreements. If these multilateral agreements overlapped, they might produce a large number of legal and political issues in operation.[70] He put forward the argument that the innovations of the dispute settlement procedures should pass the test of dispute settlement practice, a view which was also shared by Hudec. Furthermore, he claims that GATT/WTO law cannot effectively protect their citizens in

66 WTO Appellate Body Report on *EC – Regime for the Importation, Sale and Distribution of Bananas*, Sept. 9 1997, WT/DS 27 AB/R, para. 142.

67 According to the statistics as of 30 April 2005, the only case resorted to the Arbitration is *US – Section 110.5 of the Copyright Act*, WT/DS160.ARB25/1.

68 It includes: Agreement Establishing the WTO, Multilateral Trade Agreements (Goods, Services, TRIPS and DSU) and Plurilateral Trade Agreements.

69 See Appendix 2, the DSU.

70 See Petersmann 1994; 1212.

strict compliance with its guarantees of freedom, non-discrimination and transparent policy-making as it excluded the right of individuals to directly invoke and apply GATT/WTO law before the courts.

The GATT/WTO dispute settlement procedures tend to be more sophisticated according to 'experience in practice' of the Vienna Convention. Key authors such as Jackson, Hudec and Petersmann overviewed the course of improvement of the GATT dispute settlement mechanism. The DSU legal text provides clear rules. These works lay a good theoretical foundation for later researchers.

V. Shift or Balance

A general impression of the DSM of the GATT/WTO is a change from diplomacy to legitimacy. Nevertheless, it does not mean we should merely rely on legal means and set aside diplomatic methods.

Sophisticated legitimacy is desirable, but efficient diplomacy carries the same weight. That is why the consultation Article of the GATT remains in the WTO. The DSU elaborates procedures and regulations on the consultation. It stresses that the consultation is the first step of dispute settlement.

None of the Member states had recourse to good offices, conciliation and mediation. Considering the WTO has only been established for ten years and Article 5 of the DSU is the first to adopt it, these diplomatic means are likely to improve through practice, because there is no detailed legal text.[71]

The point has to be addressed that if we focus too much on legalisation, the legal framework will impede the development of the WTO and excessively take part in every aspect of social life. We need diplomacy as the *détente.*

Everything needs balance. The United States needs the EC. Globalisation needs regionalisation, as legitimacy needs diplomacy.

71 Mediation was carried out by the Director-General, which was in the WT/GC/66 and Add.1, and WT/GC/71.

Chapter 3

General Assessment of the Role of Consultation in the GATT

The process of globalisation is a fact instead of a policy option. The WTO has had and will continue to have a central role in meeting the challenge of the globalisation process. The integration of globalisation is driven by various factors such as politics, economies, technology, law and society. The challenge now is to design a trading system in response. However, the key task is to resolve disputes. This lends weight to Mike Moore's words that settlement is the key principle.[1]

There has been a debate about whether the orientation of the DSM should be judicial or political (diplomatic). The typical method of diplomacy is the consultation, and of judicial methods the Panel, Arbitration and the AB in the DSU. Whichever means Member states choose, they untie a knot; the ultimate goal of the WTO is to enable free trade to flow in an undistorted and competitive market.

The Havana Charter provided a single procedure, bilateral consultations, followed by reference to the ITO, which could then investigate, give a ruling, or make recommendations and authorise suspension of obligations in serious cases.[2] At that time, the ITO did not consider establishing the tribunal to rule on legal questions. During the post war, people were eager to have stability and peace. Legal settlement in court might have appeared non-peaceful. The pursuance of peace dominated the whole of society. Apart from that, bilateral consultation is a good way to settle and prevent disputes in international law.[3]

One of the flaws of the GATT was not having a procedural framework for dispute settlement. The CPs had to improve procedures through

1 Mike Moore, WTO's Unique System of Settling Dispute Nears 200 Cases in 2000, Press Release (June 5, 2000), http://www.wto.org/english/news_e/pres00_e/pr180_e.htm

2 Hudec 1975; 27.

3 See Part I.

practice over years. Each CP shall accord sympathetic consideration to and shall afford adequate opportunity for consultations.[4] The Consultation part of the ITO was incorporated into the GATT.

Article XXII states that one CP may consult with other CPs with "the Economic and Social Council of the United Nations and with any appropriate inter-governmental organisation in cases where they consider such consultation necessary".[5] Although this procedure is not elaborated enough, the importance of consultations remains.

At the beginning of GATT's history, disputes were generally taken up through diplomatic procedures, such as consultation and conciliation. Diplomatic methods were the only means under the GATT. Meanwhile, judicial methods gradually developed from working parties to the panel. The GATT used the name of 'the panel' instead of a court or tribunal institution. One initiative was to encourage CPs to have recourse to mild ways of solving conflicts. When the dispute was referred to the panel, the panel would give sympathetic consideration and careful examination. Only the CPs were authorised by a majority vote to suspend concessions, not the panel itself. Judicial means mixed with diplomatic character.

In fact, the GATT law is a "rather unique blend of legal and diplomatic strategies".[6] At the time of the improvement of the judicial proceedings, the GATT stressed the requirement of consultations as the initial step. Statistics drew a remarkable picture: 67.2% (207/308) of those disputes which ended prior to a ruling (whether before or after the establishment of a panel) showed full or partial concessions by the defendant during 1948–1994.[7] Meanwhile, statistics also disclosed that the full satisfaction of those settled disputes in 139 valid complaints was 60%, partial satisfaction was 29%.[8] The consultation, a diplomatic means, played an important role and was highly valued by CPs.

4 Article XXII:1, GATT 1947.
5 Article XXII:2, GATT 1947.
6 Hudec 1975; 27.
7 Busch, M. L. & Reinhardt, E. Bargaining in the Shadow of the Law: Early Settlement in GATT/WTO Disputes, 24 FDM.I.L.J; 158:162, from WESTLAW.
8 *Ibid.*

Conclusion

This section has provided an overview of the WTO as an international organisation. Two possible relationships were introduced, namely the GATT and the WTO.

The GATT was the predecessor of the WTO, which inherited some characters from the GATT. An analysis of this relationship could help in understanding the present WTO system.

However, both legitimacy and diplomacy are subject to a party's preference and are determined by the purpose of dispute settlement. As a matter of fact, these two domains always interact, rather than replacing each other.

This section was about the transformation of the GATT/WTO, from an agreement to an international organisation, and about the dispute settlement system, from diplomacy to legitimacy. The purpose of this study of the GATT and the DSM in the GATT was to illustrate the historical status of the consultation.

Furthermore, this historical overview of consultation was to support the significance and efficiency of an old methodology in the GATT/WTO. It is fair to say that the DSM in the GATT slowly earned modest successes, and the DSU under the WTO earned major successes through its more efficient and organised continuum.

If the GATT was valued as a victory Agreement, it could attribute its success to consultations. If the GATT was criticised as an ineffective system, it was due to a lack of a formalised DSM.

Part III

Consultation in WTO Dispute Settlement

During the time of the GATT, the consultation proceeding played a role of some importance, as was discussed in Part II. The vitality of consultations should not be diminished. The DSM has been transformed from diplomacy during the GATT era to legitimacy in the WTO era.[1] Therefore, a question arises whether it is necessary to include the consultation into the DSU due to its nature as a diplomatic method and due to the legitimacy of the DSU.

Up to this point, research on the consultation in WTO dispute settlement consists of four sections as follows:

First, this section represents the main part of this study and is based on interviews. The exploratory research interviews are undertaken in order to supplement the limited literature on the subject, to present a clear picture of current practice and to identify deficiencies in the system. Many first-hand tables and statistics are introduced to solidify consultation/negotiation theory from the practical perspective.

The second considers the operation of the consultation, on a provision-by-provision basis, with consideration of the relationship between the negotiation and consultation, and with particular emphasis on good faith of the consultation under the DSU and the duty to consult.

Third, due to the importance of international trade, legal scholars and practitioners contribute significant amount of literature on the WTO, particularly the DSU. Their far-reaching analysis enriches not only WTO law, but also international law. Therefore, it is better to access these contributions in order to find out the different schools of thought.

The fourth identifies the linkages between consultations and the subsequent proceedings, the panel phase, with case study and some observations.

Finally, I draw a conclusion about the consultation procedure in light of its present operation under the DSU.

1 See Part II.

Chapter 1

Present Practice of the Delegations

The role of consultations is an area which traditionally is hardly studied by international lawyers, as it is generally treated as a diplomatic means of resolving disputes. At the same time, modern approaches to dispute prevention and settlement show that consultations play an important role in international economic relations, particularly, in legal proceedings under the DSU in the WTO. In order to supplement the limited literature on this subject and the unavailability of official records kept by the WTO of consultations proceedings due to the confidentiality requirement, interviews were conducted to gather opinions and experiences from various WTO Missions in Geneva.

The general picture of these 17 selected delegations is as follows as at 30 September 2004:

Table 3.1. The frequency use by interviewee Members of the DSU proceedings

Countries	*Consultations (1): as C*[1]	*Consultations (2): as R*	*C in P/Ds*[2]	*R in P/Ds*	*Join Consultations*	*3rd Party in P/Ds*
EC	64	53	33/35	21/28	53	21/28
CAN	26	12	16	8/10	47	36/53
BRA	22	12	12	2	10	20/31
IND	15	16	7	4/5	18	33/42
KOR	11	13	8	4/6	14	16/28
JAP	11	13	7	4/6	52	52/64
MEX	13	12	7	3	22	23/34
ARG	9	15	3	6	7	8/12
AUS	7	9	5	5	28	25/30
CHI	9	10	2	3/4	7	15/18
THA	10	1	4	1	6	13/23

1 As complainants (C), as respondents (R).
2 Panels/Disputes (P/Ds).

Countries	*Consultations (1): as C*[1]	*Consultations (2): as R*	*C in P/Ds*[2]	*R in P/Ds*	*Join Consultations*	*3rd Party in P/Ds*
NZ	6	/	3	/	22	11/22
HUN	5	2	/	/	3	2
CH	4	/	1	/	14	3/8
CHN	1	1	1	/	3	21/31
NOR	1	/	1	/	7	14/22
BAN	1	/	/	/	1	/

These 17 delegations are Argentina (ARG), Australia (AUS), Bangladesh (BAN), Brazil (BRA), Canada (CAN), Chile (CHI), China (CHN), EC, Hungary (HUN), India (IND), Japan (JAP), Korea (KOR), Mexico (MEX), New Zealand (NZ), Norway (NOR), Switzerland (CH), and Thailand (THA).

The questionnaire comprising twelve questions covers five major spheres on the research of consultations: views on usefulness of the consultation due to its controversial functions; the conduct of consultations by examining the present practice and emerging problems (pre-consultations, some influencing factors, etc); the Panel and the consultation to disclose their relationship; third parties during consultations concerning the issue ofsubstantial rights; and suggestions and reform for better operation according to the context of reform proposals from interviewed delegations.[3]

I. Views on Usefulness of the Consultation

Those interviewed (developing and developed countries) were most active in their participation in filing complaints under the DSU, offered differing views. All shared the opinion that the consultation phase is useful, but not all agreed on its value. In addition, what they consider the usefulness of consultations varies to some extent.

3 See Annex I.

Table 5.2. Usefulness of consultations

Evaluation	*Number of countries*
Agreed strongly	7: THA, MEX, BRA, EC, HUN, NZ, AUS
Agreed, but depends on different situations	6: CHN, CAN, ARG, NOR, CH, JAP
Pre-consultations are more useful	2: BAN, IND
Agreed slightly	2: KOR, CHI

Seven out of the total seventeen representatives highly agreed that the consultation is valuable and cannot be replaced. Six of them replied that, it depended on different situations. Two countries from the same culture shared the opinion that informal negotiation is more useful than formal consultations.

Another two countries considered that consultation proceedings might be an extra burden. Nonetheless, they recognised that it is generally useful. Chile noted that it could help to clarify some pending points and exchange information. Korea offered its view that consultations do not work for resolving trade remedy disputes, but are useful at information exchange, view exchange and the efficiency of future Panel work. With respect to the other cases, the parties have more chances to resolve disputes through consultation.[4]

The functions that the consultation serves are clarification, evidence collection, awareness of seriousness, deepening understanding, helping to discuss some particular issues and sending strong political signals. These opinions from various delegations coincide with the theoretical analysis. It is reasonable to conclude that consultations provide a venue for settling disputes and narrowing down differences for future Panel and/or AB work.

4 Korea, according to statistics in Table 3.1, has a high rate of filing cases before the Panel as a complainant. All eight disputes before the Panel/AB were trade remedy cases (AD, CVD, SCM and safeguard) and another three resolved during the consultation stage were also trade remedy cases. As a respondent, the measures covered other subjects, such as taxation and government procurement. The counterparts of Korea before the Panel/AB were the EC or the US. Korean interviewee believed that Asian counterparts are more easily able to accept amicable resolutions.

II. Conduct of Consultations

In order to know the real practice of Member states, the ideal way is to collect information from the entire process, including pre-consultations, during the consultations and after the consultations.

A. *Before Formal Consultations*

Initiating the dispute under Article 4 of the DSU means that the pre-consultation is unsuccessful or the complaining party is not satisfied, or partially satisfied but not enough with their bargaining during the pre-consultation stage.

For some countries, pre-consultations are more useful than formal consultations. This attitude could influence their behaviour during the pre-consultation and consultation stage. However, other representatives are not in agreement. The question is whether the initial contact, beginning at the pre-consultation or consultation stage, could affect the outcome of a mutually agreed-upon solution.

Table 3.3. Frequency of countries that pre-consult

Number of pre-consultations	*Countries*
Maybe none	2: ARG, BRA
Unknown or uncertain	2: CH, HUN
A few, but depends on the case	5: MEX, CAN, THA, KOR, CHN
Several or many	8: EC, NZ, NOR, CHI, JAP, IND, BAN, AUS

Two countries thought that there might not be pre-consultation before formal consultations. Argentina provided two possibilities: one is an antidumping case, which means once a determination is made, it is difficult to change the result of the investigation; another is a very complex or politically sensitive case that may lead to the counterpart not being able to negotiate, or the counterpart being unlikely to negotiate. These two situations usually appear in trade remedy cases.

Two other representatives, because of lack of experience, could not offer an answer.

Five Members expressed the view that there are a few contacts before the consultation stage. It depends on the case, but there at least one informal pre-consultation should be held.

Why some disputes require multiple pre-consultations, while others need only one or few, is another question. The answers of interviewees are almost identical. If it is a trade remedy case, the informal pre-consultation is held during one or a few rounds. If it is not a trade remedy case, most likely, the pre-consultations can be held several times. This could explain why the trade remedy cases are much more likely to go to the panel stage. Another response is that some other factors influence the number of pre-consultations, including political, economic and legal issues.

Table 3.4. Frequency of panel composition according to types of disputes

Type of disputes	*Number of disputes*	*Constitution of the Panel*
Trade remedies	137	68
Others	180	61

Eight diplomats replied that they have several or multiple rounds of pre-consultations. The reasons vary. For example, EC Members concluded that knowing each other is an extremely important factor. The EC understands its counterparts more and more through the contact of each stage: pre-consultations, consultations and litigation. After a long period of such experience, the EC can foresee the reaction of their 'old counterparts' and even the outcome of the disputes. An example is the US: the EC knows what happens in the US; and they have no language barriers, information exchange, cultural connotation, social rules and personal behaviours. Therefore, the pre-consultation to the EC is a part of understanding.

The representative of India believed that once Article 4 is initiated, the issue becomes more legal or legally-motivated, but intention of settlement is less because of formally filing a dispute to the WTO. For instance, in the *GSP* case, the parties, during the pre-consultations stage, examined all issues and solutions apart from legal issues. This solution-oriented pre-consultation lasted one year. Then, India had to trigger Article 4 to solve the dispute. For some reason, the EC preferred the ruling of a Panel through litigation. In his view, the formal consultation, because of its legal approach, is less amicable than the informal one to resolve the conflict.

New Zealand has its own attitude with regard to the pre-consultation. Because it is cautious at every stage of the proceedings, the dispute could be resolved at any time, including pre-consultation stage.

B. *Personnel during Consultations and Pre-consultations*

Which factor plays the most important role to solve the disputes? The answer is human beings, since the dispute is produced by them and has to be settled between them.

Table 3.5. The personnel

Personnel	*Number of the Member States*
Same	9: CHN, JAP, THA, ARG, CHI, HUN, NOR, CH
Depends on the case	3: NZ, AUS, MEX
Different	5: BAN, IND, KOR, BRA, EC

Nine representatives indicated that there is no change of personnel in consultations and pre-consultations. The combination of participants could be the Geneva-based delegation, the capital-based delegation, specialists in particular areas, relevant departments, relevant people, legal experts and lawyers.

Three missions stated it depends on the case. Australia mentioned that if the meeting is held in Geneva, the Geneva-based delegation participates. Otherwise, it should be the same person.

New Zealand kept with its prudent way: if it is a technical case, during the consultation stage experts should be involved.

On this point, Mexico shared the same experience and additionally mentioned that the formal consultation may require more lawyers.

Five interviewees offered their opinions that the participants differ. Bangladesh includes relevant government sectors and the Geneva-based delegation during pre-consultations. As well as the above personnel, the capital-based delegation may be exporters; the Advisory Centre on WTO Law (ACWL) participate during the consultation stage.

India provides capital-based and Geneva-based officials in pre-consultations: they are initially at counsellor level, then ambassador level. Consultations involve trade ministries, diplomats and, perhaps, lawyers.

Korean practice is that the bilateral trade bureau is involved in informal consultations; at the formal consultation stage, the international trade law team, the Geneva-based delegation and international lawyers are included.

The Brazilian appconsultation stage is to require Geneva-based and capital-based diplomats and perhaps international lawyers, and in pre-consultations participation of the private sector as well.

The EC's behaviour at the pre-consultation stage is for the Commission to participate by representatives of particular Member(s) of the EC; and when it is a formal consultation to include relevant departments, the legal service and representatives from particular EC Member states.

How many countries will involve lawyers or legal experts? Do they improve the consultation process?

Table 3.6. Number of lawyers or legal experts participating

Stages	*Participation of Lawyers or legal experts*
Pre-consultations	9 Member states
Consultations	16 countries apart from CHN

Surprisingly, there are nine Members who require the participation of lawyers or legal experts during the pre-consultation stage. These countries are Japan, Argentina, Brazil, Chile, Hungary, Norway, Switzerland, Australia and New Zealand. Many are South America countries, Australasia and small European countries. Japan is an exception.

All representatives conceded that consultation is a legal proceeding. Participation of lawyers or legal experts is valuable and desirable.

China observed that they do not involve lawyers because they have few formal filing disputes, so there are few or no legal experts in this field. The cultural impact could be another important reason (see Introduction). Since pre-consultations and consultations are amicable affairs, it is better to keep out legal issues and so maintain a clear line between law and politics/diplomacy. Two possibilities are hypothesised that either China influences the WTO game rules gradually through its solid cultural background or China is assimilated by WTO's particular rules.

C. *Strategy Adoption*

Delegations agree that there is no single approach to handling disputes, because each case is unique and must be treated on its own merits. However, the application of any strategy will be introduced in special situations by most Member states.

Table 3.7. With or without strategy

Strategy adoption	*Number of missions*
No strategy	4: BAN, JAP, KOR, ARG
Generally no, but depends	6: CAN, MEX, EC, CH, NZ, NOR
Unknown	1: HUN
Strategy	6: CHN, IND, THA, BRA, CHI, AUS

Six delegations acknowledged that strategy is necessary to achieve some objectives. Half of them are Asian countries.

Many delegations replied that it depends on the situation. Therefore, the question arises what kind of factors and concerns would influence their decisions to make concessions? The Mexican diplomat said it depends on the political environment. The Canadian diplomat said it depends on whether there are strong or sensitive issues, or whether there is any room for making concessions. The EC thought that legal strength, economic stakes and political concerns are three important elements, which have an impact on their decisions. The Norway interviewee believed it depends on their counterparts and other factors. The diplomat from New Zealand stated that it depended on the particular case.

At the same time, four missions indicated that there existed no strategies or guidelines. Nevertheless, they all recognised that it depends on the measure at issue and then they make decisions accordingly. Three of them are from Asia.

Strategy is not the same as tactics, which involves intelligence and skillful organisation and management. The differences between these two concepts were discussed in the Introduction. The strategy, whatever they understand by it and they apply, is associated with a set of plans and behaviour aiming to achieve the agreement or narrow down the subjects of disagreement. The fact is that there are different attitudes associated with different countries, cases and measures. Thus, the key point is that their negotiating behaviours are either various or stable, based on their degree of involvement.

One interviewee noted that 'tough bargaining' is itself a strategy. The attitude to differences is widely accepted because it is within the scope of the WTO rules. These are not completely the same in the real world, where there exists big and small, strong and weak, rich and poor countries.

It is observed that, when talking about strategy, many of them understood it as aspects of tactics. In general, all the Member states do have a strategy, but not every country has tactics. With respect to tactics, these missions list several possibilities, namely tit-for-tat negotiations, step-by-step with clear goals, agreement on part of issues, sacrificing one or more comparatively minor issue(s) in exchange for one or more major benefit(s), or merely presenting as a listener rather than a defendant.

The practice of tough or soft tactics depends on which position you are in. Generally the complainant is more active than the defendant. Interestingly, it is not restricted to powerful or weak states, small or big countries, oriental or western Members. Most Asian countries tend to treat every step more cautiously and foresee the possible results. It is not by chance, and demonstrates that cultural impact is a significant element during the course of pre-consultations and consultations, which will repeatedly show in this section.

D. *Some Influencing Factors during the Consultation Stage*

The consultation is not an isolated performance, but a systematic art, which is influenced by certain factors.

1. *Political Impact*

Apparently, the diplomatic cut of the consultation makes this the outstanding question. The trade bargaining power of each side could reflect its political power in reality.

Table 3.8. Impact of the political element

Attitude to political impact	*Number of states*
Yes (highly agreed)	6: CHN, IND, THA, CHI, HUN, CH
Depends (partly agreed)	8: JAP, CAN, MEX, ARG, BRA, EC, NOR, NZ
No, but… (slightly agreed)	3: BAN, KOR, AUS

Six interviewees identified political impact as definitely stronger than legal influence. The Indian diplomat said, during formal and informal consultations, they merely talk the facts and he believes a political solution is more enduring, provided it is equitable. The Chilean representative shared the same view about non-legal talk, but noted that it is a strategy, leaving the legal fighting for the Panel stage and especially to the AB stage.

Some stated it depends on the nature of the case, the country and the industry. Some of them acknowledged that these two factors cannot be separated: the decision may be political, but the fact is that economic interests, political pressure and legal basis are interlinked rather than merely political impact.

Three diplomats could not agree that political impact is stronger than legal influence during the consultation stage. However, they did not deny that the political factor could influence the consultation. Korea, the most active player in Asia, and Bangladesh, a first time participant from Asia, offered the same view that legal concerns *should* be the main consideration. The common ground is that they are both 'hurt' by trade remedy measures.[5]

Political impact cannot be avoided. It is not realistic to put aside political concerns when one government negotiates with another government.

5 All Korea filed and one of Bangladeshi sued cases were trade remedy cases.

2. *Other Factors*

During the process of consultation, a complainant must also take into account other factors for judging either to escalate or to withdraw from the dispute.

a. *Industry*

Table 3.9. Industry concerns

Taking into account	*Number of states*
Yes	11: ARG, AUS, BRA, CAN, CHI, EC, IND, KOR, NOR, CH, THA
Depends	1: MEX
No	2: BAN, CHN
Unknown or no response	3: JAP, NZ, HUN

Most countries deal with their industries' concerns. Brazil, for instance, indicated that Brazilian government and private companies keep strong contacts with each other when it comes to the international dispute resolution mechanism, because these industries pay the fee and the government has no specific budget for WTO dispute settlement.

All responses to the issue influencing the outcome of consultations from Mexico were that it depends on the case as 'in most things in life'.[6]

China and Bangladesh said they were not influenced by industries. The Bangladesh diplomat considered the government should decide independently rather than be influenced by others.

b. *Media*

Table 3.10. Media impact

Taking into account	*Number of countries*
Yes	10: ARG, BRA, CAN, CHI, CHN, KOR, NOR, CH, THA, HUN
Depends	1: MEX
No	6: BAN, IND, JAP, EC, AUS, NZ

6 The Mexico diplomat replied.

Many representatives expressed the view that media could affect the outcome of consultations.[7] Brazil, for example, explained that the media closely follow all cases in which Brazil is involved and highlight them in a headline. The public, therefore, is aware of the implication of the case.

Bangladesh, India and Australia shared the same view that the consultation generally is a government-to-government exercise. Japan believed media have little effect on the outcome, because the deliberations are done solely on the basis of evidence and submissions.

c. *Non-governmental Organisations (NGOs)*

Table 3.11. The element of NGOs

Taking into account	*Number of countries*
Yes	3: KOR, CAN, THA
Depends	3: MEX, NOR, CH
No	7: ARG, AUS, BAN, CHI, CHN, IND, JAP
Unknown or no response	4: EC, HUN, NZ, BRA

Many interviewees disagreed that NGOs could affect the outcome of consultations. In issues related to trade, they may not be visible in these countries and, again, believe that it is an issue to be addressed between governments.

Three representatives said that it depends on the case.In some important cases or a case on a public health issue, NGOs might substantially influence the outcome of consultations.

Korea and Thailand answered NGOs *could* affect, which implies a lower degree of impact. Canada also replied that, in every stage, the government has to face pressure and, therefore, NGOs *could* affect at domestic level.

7 Canada said, domestic media, not international ones, could affect the outcome of consultation. Other countries stated it could affect the outcome both at domestic and international levels.

d. *Civil Society*

Table 3.12. The importance of civil society

Taking into account	*Number of countries*
Yes	3: KOR, CAN, THA
Depends	3: MEX, NOR, CH
No	8: ARG, AUS, BAN, BRA, CHN, EC, IND, JAP
Unknown or no response	3: CHI, HUN, NZ

The situations and responses from missions were similar with regards to NGOs. It is reasonable to conclude that both NGOs and civil society have fairly limited or no impact on the outcome of consultations, although they are becoming more and more active.

III. The Panel and the Consultation

No distinct pattern can be discerned from the WTO cases that have so far been settled at the consultation stage. The approach in each case varies. Governments with decisions to pursue a case through litigation, or to settle a case outside the judicial phase, or to continue seeking bilaterally agreed solutions in parallel with the work of the Panel, are motivated by a number of considerations. Each case, in the experience of Members who have the most occasions to use the system, is different, and should be viewed as such.

A. *Deadlock*

The hypothetical scenario is: if consultation is at a deadlock, does a complainant usually require the DSB to immediately establish a Panel or create a chance to find negotiable issues?

Table 3.13. Consultations or the panel (scenario I)

Choice of proceeding	*Number of states*
Consultations	2: BAN, MEX
Depends	9: BRA, CAN, CHI, EC, HUN, JAP, NZ, NOR, CH
The Panel	5: CHN, KOR, THA, ARG, AUS
Other response	1: IND

It might be not difficult to understand why Bangladesh prefers to find an amicable solution, maybe because it is a Less Developed Country (LDC) and has limitedpersonnel and budget resources. It could be true for some developing countries, as well.

Over half of the delegations cautiously replied that it depends on other elements including political pressure, the nature of cases, the interests of defendants or complainants and how urgent the case is. This suggests that to escalate a dispute to aPanel stage is not as easy as it appears to be. Most developed countries are more careful than developing Members according to the resultsin the table.

Five missions, in which four of them are from developing countries, stated that they would opt for the establishment of a Panel. They prefer to seek a ruling from a Panel for fairness through jurisdiction or to unblock the proceedings. Most Asian developing countries stated that they would seek a legal way with no hesitation, even if the defendants they faced were advanced industrial countries (the US or EC) without exception.

India could not agree that that there is a situation called 'deadlocked'. The key is that the measures at issue may have lapsed or the trade interest in the measure may no longer exist. There is no need to revoke cases because something happened or consultations led to a belief that there is inadequate justification for a dispute.

B. *Threaten*

On the absence of chances to resolve a dispute during the consultation stage, does the request for a Panel increase the pressure to find an amicable solution?

Table 3.14. Consultations or the panel (scenario II)

Threaten	*Number of states*
Yes	7: BAN, JAP, THA, BRA, CHI, CH, NZ
Depends	9: ARG, AUS, CAN, CHN, HUN, EC, KOR, MEX, NOR
No	1: IND

Only one country, India, indicated, as a complainant that it usually tries as much as possible to resolve the matter before the Panel process is initiated, and, as a respondent, it will try to address the trade concern of the complainant, rather than focus on the legal issue. However, once the Panel process is invoked, the focus becomes much more legal. Again, the traditional antilegal belief is firmly rooted.

Many interviewees conceded that a request increased the pressure to find an amicable solution. New Zealand and Bangladesh interpreted it as a strong signal from a complainant. Chile, on the contrary, added that it is a strategy. Japan offered its views that the Panel process would inevitably incur costs, human resources as well as financial, and it makes sense if one can avoid these costs by reaching a mutually satisfactory resolution. Switzerland stated that it becomes public through newspapers, for example, and, therefore, is a pressure.

The response 'depends', is diversified. Korea mentioned that there is no pressure if it is a trade remedy case, since the Panel stage is unavoidable.Canada argued that it might increase or relieve the pressure to request a Panel. Under the former circumstance, the request to establish a Panel indicates how serious a party is in proceeding to a case. If there is indeed a willingness to negotiate, or there is an assessment on the part of the defending party that it might lose, then the Panel request increases pressure for settlement. However, in some cases there is a recognition that litigation takes years and so, by requesting a Panel, the complaining parties relieve the pressure from a partner to negotiate, or to settle, because they allow the defending party to keep the issue in dispute settlement for years.

Argentina pointed out that the motivation to go for litigation is complicated. The government has no other alternative, either as a complainant or as a respondent, since domestic industries would apply pressure.

China looked at it from another angle pointinmg out that the request for a Panel could be a signal for further bargaining.

These answers to some extent revealindividual attitudes to 'being sued'.

C. *Information Collection*

Due to the requirement of confidentiality, it is impossible to gain the transcript of any consultation stage. Nonetheless, Panel reports (maybe AB reports) are available to the public. Is there any linkage between these two stages on the issue of information usage? Do they use the information obtained during the consultations in the Panel stage?

Table 3.15. Information usage during the Panel stage

Use it in the Panel stage	*Number of missions*
Yes	11: ARG, AUS, BRA, CHN, EC, IND, KOR, NZ, NOR, CH, THA
Depends	2: JAP, MEX
No	2: CHI, CAN
No experience	2: BAN, HUN

Canada explained that because the information is either publicly available or not helpful, in most case they do not use it in the later stage. Chile, on the other hand, stated that consultations are confidential and, in principle, nothing can be used in later stage(s), unless both parties agree.

Japanese representatives stated that Member States are usually careful in dealing with information at any stage of a dispute, because that information could be used against the supplying party, and at the same time it could help the defending party's interests by demonstrating, before the Panel/AB, that measures in the dispute were indeed legitimate under the WTO Agreement.

Most interviewees explained that they use the information to clarify the facts and gauge the merit of each argument, and, in turn, narrow down the scope of the case. Meanwhile, they complained that it is not always possible to get information from a respondent, particularly if they believe that the dispute can only be resolved by litigation.

The next question asked to countries answering 'yes', was how they use the information relevant to confidentiality during the consultation stage.

Almost all missions acknowledged that they keep full records of consultations and submit the information partially or wholly to the Panel. Then, it is the Panel's responsibility to determine which information can be used. Thailand added that, with time, the nature of the case at hand may change. In some Members' perspective the strategy to deal with the information could be 'the less given, the better'.

Concerning confidentiality, some delegations considered it a separate issue, and others affirmed that any confidential information will not be released.

IV. Third Parties during Consultations

Once the request for consultations has been filed, Members who feel that they have substantial interests in the dispute could join the consultation if the situation complies with Article XXII or Article XXIII of the GATT. Are Member States concerned about third-party impact? Is it reasonable to limit third-party rights?

A. *Impact*

Table 3.16. The impact of a third-party

The impact of 3rd party	*Number of countries*
Yes	3: IND, THA, CHI
Depends	7: JPA, MEX, ARG, EC, BRA, HUN, AUS
No	7: BAN, CHN, KOR, CAN, NOR, CH, NZ

Chile believed that the more third parties you have, the more pressure your counterpart feels. India, however, suggested that, it might have negative impacts if a complainant brings too many representing their own interests and interpret the provisions based on their own position (i.e. *Generalised System of Preferences* (GSP) case); or if they put political issues, which are irrelevant to the proceedings, as did Brazil and Thailand in *EC – Sugar* case.

Some representatives noted it depends on the third-party countries: big players, like the EC and US and some Member States with strong arguments, like Norway and New Zealand, can make a good case.The EC suggestedthat there are two aspects to the argument: the political aspect and the contribution which they could make that has not been made by either party. Mexico preferred to regard all third parties as being on the complainant's side.

Other interviewees pointed out that the consultation is merely an exercise between two disputants. If third parties participate, they may intervene for the purpose of acquiring inside information, rather than influencing one side on the other – a Member looking for more impact could opt to be a co-complainant rather than a third party.

All missions agreed that third parties have a stronger impact during the Panel and AB stages.

B. Their Rights

Table 3.17. Third-party's rights

Dealing with their rights	*Number of states*
Yes	2: CHN, IND
Depends	4: JAP, MEX, HUN, NZ
No	9: ARG, AUS, BAN, BRA, CAN, CHI, EC, KOR, THA
No experience	2: NOR, CH

China mentioned that if the concerns of the party to the dispute are to be addressed appropriately, the desires of a third-party are satisfied for the sake of the MFN rule. India asserted that the WTO rules should apply to every Member.[8] The cultural factor plays a crucial role to influence its behaviour.

8 India is a religion-driven and village-based society. Everybody can participate in the 'Gospel', which should be equal to everyone. There is a hierarchy in India, as an individual he/she could be hurt by others, but the whole society functions well.

The influences on whether the violating state deals with third-party's rights are political and/or trade interests, the proximity of the factual bases and the country of that third-party.

Many representatives admitted that they cannot deal with third-party interests. If they wish to be dealt with, they should file a case not come in as a third party. A few developing countries felt that they do not have the capacity to deal with third-party rights. Sometimes third parties focus on frivolous issue rather than address issues of serious concern. Their common attitude to third parties is that they are limited to taking the floor and listening.

V. Reform and Suggestions

On the whole, no fixed formula can be followed to settle a dispute during the consultation stage. Nevertheless, this exploration never stops. Whatever those interviewees criticise or praise about the consultation stage in the DSU, their real intention is to expect that it can function efficiently.

A. *Reform*

Based on the WTO Chairman's text, which contains proposals from many Members on a substantial number of issues of importance to the DSU, four key issues could be improved in the consultation stage. Does this text reflect current views of delegations?

This belief determines the Indian constitution. The idea of third Third Third parties may not be good for India or the DSU, but good for building the WTO. Every Member should participate, and third parties make the whole WTO society better.

1. *Notification*

Table 3.18. Reform on notification

Attitudes to this issue	*Number of states*
Yes	9: CHN, IND, KOR, THA, ARG, BRA, CH, AUS, NZ
No	4: MEX, CHI, EC, HUN
No response/ unknown	4: BAN, CAN, JAP, NOR

All developing Asian countries, bigger South American countries and Australasian countries were invited to comment. At the same time, a few delegations admitted some disputes had to be pended on the list for certain unspecified reasons.

Some countries argued that transparency was not an issue in helping to resolve disputes efficiently. One delegation added that it is reasonable to believe that cases were dead or resolved after two years pending, without further notification.

2. *Enhancing Third-Party Rights*

Table 3.19. Reform on enhancing third-party rights

Attitude to this issue	*Number of countries*
Yes	2: THA, NZ
Depends	3: ARG, CHN, CHI
No	6: BAN, KOR, BRA, CH, AUS, MEX
No response/unknown	6: IND, CAN, EC, JAP, HUN, NOR

New Zealand pointed out that at the moment the respondent can refuse a request by a third party to join consultations. No explanation need be forthcoming; discrimination between third parties, who claim the substantial trade interests in the dispute, could be a reason why. Many countries would welcome some improvement of third-party rights, but simultaneously claim that it should not be overstated.

Six Members disagreed that it would be helpful to enhance third-party's rights. Brazil replied that, in any event, developing countries do not have resources to follow allimportant cases.

3. *Time Framework*

Table 3.20. Reform of time framework

Shorten the present time framework	*Number of countries*
Yes	3: BAN, CHI, THA
Depends	4: ARG, AUS, KOR, NZ
No	3: CHN, BRA, MEX
No response/unknown	7: CAN, EC, HUN, IND, JAP, NOR, CH

Three interviewees expected that the framework of consultations could be shortened from 60 days to 30 days, or even be eliminated. Chile suggested that some changes could be made to avoid delaying a final solution of the dispute when it is clear that an amicable solution is not possible.

Korea expressed pros and cons. It could expedite the dispute settlement procedures at the cost of slightly cutting down the chance of resolving disputes in the consultation stage.

Three larger developing countries have stressed that there is no need to change the current time frame.

4. *Special and Deferential Treatment (SDT)*

Table 3.21. Reform on SDT provision

Improve the SDT	*Number of countries*
Yes	2: IND, THA
Depends	2: AUS, KOR
No	6: CHN, BAN, ARG, BRA, CHI, MAX
No response/unknown	7: CAN, EC, HUN, JAP, NZ, NOR, CH

India's purpose in raising this issue in its proposal is to let all Member states understand that developing countries and LDCs do not have the capacity to fully benefit from the dispute settlement mechanism of the WTO and those steps are needed to add such capacity, such as by providing them with litigation costs. In terms of the specific needs ofcountries that become losers in disputes, if those countries have to amend their legislation, they shall be allowed to extend within reasonable period of time. LDCs can claim even longer time frames and request money back from developed countries. The DSB shall specify the requirements. Some reports of the Panel and AB gave guidance, but were not sufficient in the SDT area.

Australia supported some changes on this issue, such as their proposal to explore having consultations in the capital cities of LDCs.

Six interviewees offered controversial opinions that SDT provisions do not really solve the big problems these countries face. The Chilean representative, for example, asked why some Members should have special treatment when the measure produces adverse effects and nullification or impairment for other Members.

Some delegations were silent on these four issues, especially the last three. Regarding the status of the reforms, it seems that opponents outnumber supporters except in the area of improvement on notification. Therefore, there are two possibilities: one could be that consultation provisions are too difficult to develop, at least in practice; another could be that those provisions function so well that it is not desirable to improve them.

Sixteen missions admitted that the current procedure works well. Meanwhile, one interviewee emphasised that it works, but not well. Thus, the answer seems to point to the latter hypothesis.

B. *Suggestions*

Most representatives expressed the view that reforms of the consultation stage are not generally desirable. Some countries have filed many cases because they have to relieve trade pressures, not because the DSU has problems *per se*.

Table 3.22. Suggestions

Type of suggestions	*Number of countries*
Keep the present status	13: AUS, BRA, CAN, CHI, CHN, EC, HUN, JAP, KOR, MEX, NZ, NOR, CH
Article 5 or ADR	2: BAN, THA
Others	2: IND, ARG

Japan and Korea noted that there may be some room for improvement in a number of areas of the DSU, including the consultation proceeding. However, if reform is likely to bring some imbalance in terms of rights and obligations *vis-à-vis* the Members, one might as well settle for no change in the DSU.

Mexico believed that reform of the consultation stage is not desirable. Norway claimed that it could be improved, but whether this would make a difference is another issue, since it depends on the political willingness of the parties involved.

Thailand suggested that the DSB should encourage the parties to use Article 5 and 25. It used to invoke Article 5, but it was refused by the counterpart who preferred to refer to the principles underpinning such Article outside the context of the DSU. If the DSB does not elaborate these provisions, in practice they will be difficult to apply. Bangladesh pointed out that Article 5 should be applied before the Panel stage and every ADR should be exhausted before the Panel stage as well.

Argentina proposed that parties should provide questions properly and fully. India expected transparency and predictability.

VI. Conclusions

The perception of the role of consultations is diverse among Member States, because of differences in individual interests, experiences and unique cultures. Hence, it is difficult to provide an objective evaluation or simply a 'yes' or 'no' answer to this issue.

Some interviewees argued that it is better to distinguish every situation of the dispute as each case is unique. It is unreasonable to compare one case with another case which may appear the same. The fact is that the course of different consultations differs, even though the starting point and end point are identical.

The value of consultations is in making available a preliminary discussion of the issue between the concerned parties towards an eventual resolution of the dispute. The purpose of a transcript is not to find a shortcut to win, but to create additional opportunities for resolution.

Current opinion of interviewees is that consultations are a useful and important phase of the whole proceedings, but their efficiency needs to be improved particularly by strengthening the notification with simple information (for transparency), fully using the function of information exchange (for proper understanding) and enhancing the quality of the pre-consultation stage (which could be a valuable supplement to the formal consultation stage).

The present consultation proceedings operate well in general. The exploration of specification to Article 5 could assist the diplomatic methods and diminish some disadvantages of consultations on the whole. Third-party rights shall be restrained since the consultation procedure is strictly a bilateral operation between contestants.Understanding is one of the important requirements of this stage. Good understanding means the battle is half done.

However, developing and LDC countries believe that SDT should be reflected in any substantial reforms.[9]

9 For example, the issue of costs is one of the substantive reforms.

Chapter 2

Overview of the Consultation Stage of the DSU

The WTO builds an umbrella framework, and the consultation procedure is adapted by a new agreement, namely Understanding on Rules and Procedures Governing the Settlement of Disputes. The WTO's procedure for resolving trade quarrels, under the DSU, is vital for enforcing the rules and therefore for ensuring that trade flows smoothly.

This section will first define some concepts relevant to consultation in the DSU, then, state the provisions of the consultation under the relevant Articles (especially Article 4) and, finally, indicate some current debates within the consultation provision.

I. Two Concepts

In public international law, the concepts of 'dispute' and 'negotiation' have many definitions due to their important position and complicated situation under different circumstances. In the WTO, however, these two concepts have clear definitions. Negotiations and consultations are easy to confuse; it is difficult to distinguish them in international law, but simple within the carefully constructed DSU.

A. *Definition of a Dispute under the DSU*

A dispute arises when a Member government believes another Member government is violating an agreement or a commitment that it has made in the WTO. The authors of these agreements are the Member governments themselves – the agreements are the outcome of negotiations among Members. Ultimate responsibility for settling disputes also lies with Member governments through the Dispute Settlement Body. In other words, a dispute arises with Member states and the dispute settlement relies on Member states. "Wherever several Members have made a joint request in a single document, this is accounted as one dispute. Conversely, claims brought in distinct documents circulated under distinct 'DS' numbers are counted as distinct disputes, even if they relate to the same matter".[1] Recourse to good offices, mediation or conciliation under Article 5 of the DSU may not be notified to the DSB. In one instance, a mediation was carried out by the Director-General (DG), which was conducted in accordance with the procedure foreseen in that provision.[2] This was nevertheless not 'a dispute'. The arbitration procedure in Article 25 was resorted to in one dispute, which is WT/DS160/ARB25/1, *United States – Section 110(5) of US Copy Right Act.*[3]

All of the 330 disputes, until 30 April 2005, began with a period for consultations under Article 4 of the DSU, except for five cases.[4]

1 WTO, Special Session of the Dispute Settlement Body: Statistical Information on Recourse to WTO Dispute Settlement Procedures (1 January 1995–31 October 2003) Background Note by the Secretariat, 11 December 2003, JOB (03) 225.

2 See WT/GC/66 and Add.1, and WT/GC/71. On 10 October 2002, the DG was informed of a request for mediation by the Philippines, Thailand and the EC. The Chairman of the DG then nominated Deputy Director-General Rufus H. Yerxa as the mediator. The purpose of the requested mediation process was to examine the extent to which the legitimate interests of the Philippines and Thailand were being unduly impaired as a result of the implementation by the EC of the preferential tariff treatment for canned tuna originating in the African, Caribbean and Pacific (ACP) states. In the event that the mediator concluded that undue impairment had in fact occurred, the mediator could consider means by which this situation might be addressed. Finally, he completed his work in accordance with the timetable agreed by the requesting Members and an amicable outcome had been reached among the parties concerned based on the Advisory Opinion of the Mediator. The only mediation practice made a successful outcome.

3 See WT/DS160/ARB25/1, *United States – Section 110(5) of US Copy Right Act.* On 23 July 2001, the US and the EC mutually agreed pursuant to Article 25.2 of the DSU to enter into arbitration to determine the level of nullification or impairment of benefits to the EC as a result of Section 110(5)(B) of the US Copyright Act. On 23 June 2003, the US and the EC notified to the WTO a mutually satisfactory temporary arrangement regarding the dispute. The arrangement covered the three-year period ending December 21, 2004. However, this dispute is still pending on the implementation stage as of 8 April 2005.

4 *US – Measures Affecting Imports of Women's and Girls' Wool Coat* (WT/DS32), *US – Measures Affecting Imports of Woven Wool Shirts and Blouse* (WT/DS33),

However, there is a consultation procedure in the TMB, and these five cases initiated consultations as a first step.[5] The Panel on *US – Wool Shirts and Blouses* discussed the role of Panels under the DSU and the role of the TMB under the ATC. With respect to consultations, the Panel stated:

> We note also that, according to Article 8.10 of the ATC, when the TMB process has been completed, a Member, which remains unsatisfied with the TMB recommendations, can request the establishment of a Panel without having to request consultations under Article 4 of the DSU. This is to say that the TMB process can replace the consultation phase in the dispute settlement process under the DSU and is distinct from the formal adjudication process by Panels.[6]

Therefore, strictly speaking, these five cases are without exception concerning the existence of the consultation both in the legal text and in the factual cases although this is in the Article 8.4 of the ATC rather than Article 4 of the DSU. Moreover, DS32, DS181, and DS190 were solved respectively prior to the Panel stage.

B. *Conduct of Negotiations in the WTO*

The negotiations and consultations in public international law are hard to distinguish, as noted previously. However, when we examine these two terms in the field of WTO law, there is a clear line of distinction between consultations and negotiations.

Colombia – Safeguard Measure on Imports of Plain Polyester Filaments from Thailand (WT/DS181), *Argentina – Transitional Safeguard Measures on Certain Imports of Woven Fabrics of Cotton and Cotton Mixtures Originating in Brazil* (WT/DS 190), and *US – Transitional Safeguard Measures on Combed Cotton Yarn from Pakistan* (WT/DS192) which were considered by the Textiles Monitoring Body (TMB) before a Panel request was made.

5 According to the footnote 4 under the Article 4, it lists the covered agreements containing corresponding consultation provision. The Agreement on Textiles and Clothing (ATC), paragraph 4 of Article 8 states “Member shall afford to each other adequate opportunity for consultations with respect to any matters affecting the operation of this Agreement”.

6 See WT/DS33/R, *United States – Measure Affecting Imports of Woven Wool Shirts and Blouses from India* – Report of the Panel, para. 7.19.

One of the purposes of the WTO is to act as a forum for the reduction and elimination of trade barriers, to be undertaken through negotiations. The number of barrier reductions is performed by multilateral trade negotiations – the so-called 'rounds' (such as the Doha Round) and sectoral trade negotiations (such as negotiations on agriculture). All WTO Members have the right to participate in them.[7] These negotiations are as in Table 3.23:[8]

Table 3.23. GATT trade rounds

Year	*Place/name*	*Subjects covered*	*Countries*
1947	**Geneva**	Tariffs	23
1949	**Annecy**	Tariffs	13
1951	**Torquay**	Tariffs	38
1956	**Geneva**	Tariffs	26
1960–1961	Geneva **Dillon Round**	Tariffs	26
1964–1967	Geneva **Kennedy Round**	Tariffs and anti-dumping measures	62
1973–1979	Geneva **Tokyo Round**	Tariffs, non-tariff measures, "framework" agreements	102
1986–1994	Geneva **Uruguay Round**	Tariffs, non-tariff measures, rules, services, intellectual property, dispute settlement, textiles, agriculture, creation of WTO, etc.	123

(Source: *GATT Trade Rounds,* WTO website)

The Doha Round started in November 2001, and there is no further report when it will reach the final agenda; although the Doha Declaration sets 1 January 2005 as the date for completing all but two of the negotiations. These two exceptions are negotiations on the DSU and those on a multilateral register of geographical indications for wines and spirits.

7 Goode, W. World Trade Organisation: Dictionary of Trade Policy Terms (4th ed.), Cambridge: CUP, 2003, p. 245.

8 See http://www.wto.org/english/thewto_e/whatis_e/tif_e/fact4_e.htm last visited 5 December 2004.

The negotiations take place in the Trade Negotiations Committees and their subsidiaries.[9]

In general, 'negotiation' as a legal term in the WTO is irrelevant to the dispute settlement system. A definition of a dispute lists various kinds of dispute settlement methods. Unlike in public international law, where the negotiation is a common way to resolve international disputes, the WTO prefers to treat it as an only means to complete each round between or among Member states, which is a mode of international affairs rather than a means of international law. Therefore, it is not in the scope of the DSU.

Nevertheless, its *likely synonym*, 'consultation' in the WTO, (precisely speaking under the DSU), continuously plays an important role both in the area of dispute settlement and of dispute prevention.

II. Consultations under the DSU

In this section, research on the consultation is generally on the basis of the consultation provisions under the DSU. These relevant provisions will be explained one by one combined with case study and textual analysis in the WTO, following the definition of the consultation concerned.

> While what has been achieved is undoubtedly important, a more realistic appraisal isneeded to understand what has actually happened, and what is going to happen from here on in.[10]

After reviewing the factual provision of the consultation, we will turn to the arguments relevant to consultation, concerning its present situation so as to improve the process in the future.

9 See Chapter 1: Basics, About the WTO – Understanding the WTO, under WTO website: http://www.wto.org/english/thewto_e/whatis_e/tif_e/utw_chap1_e.pdf last visited 18 April 2005.

10 Hudec, R. E. International Economic Law: The Political Theatre Dimension, 17 U. Pa. J. Int'l Econ. L. 1996; 9:11.

A. *Definition of Consultations under the DSU*

> The consultation is the first stage in the WTO dispute settlement procedure, aimed at resolving issues cooperatively. The fact-finding nature of consultation between parties often leads to a solution. WTO Members receiving a request for such consultations must therefore treat them seriously. They cannot use them to gain extended breathing space.[11]

Thus, the first step to initiating dispute settlement procedures is the consultations stage, which serves as a dispute resolving mechanism (or an informal pre-trial discovery proceeding).

B. *Legal Framework of Consultation Provisions*

The WTO dispute settlement framework is set principally under the DSU. As in the DSM under the GATT, the WTO encourages its Member states to settle their disputes through consultations.

1. *Importance of Consultations*

The WTO dispute settlement process begins when a WTO Member state formally requests consultations with another Member state. Article 4.1 of the DSU affirms their goal to strengthen and improve the effectiveness of consultation procedures. Moreover, since the WTO is a formal international organisation, the DSU provides more specific rules and procedures to fill the gaps than during the GATT period.

In the *India – Patent Protection for Pharmaceutical and Agricultural Chemical Products* case (WT/DS50), the US argued that if India had disclosed, during consultations, the existence of certain administrative instructions, the US would have included in its request for establishment of a Panel, a claim under Article 63 of the TRIPS Agreement. With respect to disclosure of information during consultations, the AB noted:

> All parties engaged in dispute settlement under the DSU must be fully forthcoming from the very beginning both as to the claims involved in a dispute and as to the facts relating to those claims. Claims must be states clearly. Facts must be disclosed freely. This must be so in consultations as well as in the more formal setting

11 Goode 2003; 79.

> of Panel proceedings. In fact, the demands of due process that are implicit in the DSU make this especially necessary during consultations. For the claims that are made and the facts that are established during consultations do much to shape the substance and the scope of subsequent Panel proceedings. If in the aftermath of consultations, any party believes that all the pertinent facts relating to a claim are, for any reason, not before the Panel, then that party should ask the Panel in that case to engage in additional fact-finding.[12]

Therefore, the AB suggested defining the shape of the consultation to strengthen and improve the effectiveness of consultations from legal proceedings. This had the character of a partly legal procedure for the consultation under the DSU. The other provisions confirm its legal features with a deeper analysis.

Under Article 4.2, the DSU clarifies the coverage of the consultation. Each Member state undertakes to accord sympathetic consideration to and afford adequate opportunity for consultation regarding any representations made by another Member concerning measures affecting the operation of any covered agreement taken within the territory of the former.[13] That is to say, the consultation shall be applied to any Agreements under the WTO both in practice and in theory if the dispute emerges.

Furthermore, the DSB states the prevailing position of the special consultation provisions.[14] Where the provisions of any other covered agreement concerning measures taken by regional or local governments or authorities within the territory of a Member contain provisions different from the provisions of Article 4.2, the provisions of such other covered agreement shall prevail.[15]

a. *Corresponding Consultation Provisions*

The list of the corresponding consultation provisions in the covered agreements is contained in Footnote 4 of Article 4.11. These Agreements are Article 19 of the Agreement on Agriculture, Article 11.1 of the Agreement on the Application of Sanitary and Phytosanitary Measures (SPS), Article 8.4 of the ATC, Article 14.1 of the Agreement on Technical Barriers to Trade (TBT), Article 8 of the Agreement on Trade-

12 See WT/DS50/AB/R, Appellate Body Report on *India – Patents*, para. 94.

13 Article 4.2 under the DSU.

14 See DSU, Footnote 3 of Article 4.2.

15 See Footnote of Article 4.2 under the DSU.

Related Investment Measure (TRIM), Article 17.1–17.4 of the Agreement on Implementation of Article VI of GATT 1994, Article 19.1–19.3 of the Agreement on Implementation of Article VII of GATT 1994, Article 7 of the Agreement on Preshipment Inspection, Article 7 of the Agreement on Rules of Origin, Article 6 of the Agreement on Import Licensing Procedures, Article 30 of the Agreement on Subsidies and Countervailing Measures (SCM), Article 14 of the Agreement on Safeguards, Article XXII of the Agreement on Trade in Services (GATS),[16] Article 64.1 of the Agreement on Trade-Related Aspects of Intellectual Property Rights (TRIPS), and any corresponding consultation provisions in Plurilateral Trade Agreements as determined by the competent bodies of each Agreement and as notified to the DSB.

This list consists of all the agreements under the WTO relevant to the consultation. After carefully checking all these agreements, most of the corresponding consultation provisions have no difference with the consultation part under Article 4 of the DSU or Article XXII and Article XXIII of the GATT 1947. It states usually as simply as this: "Members shall afford to each other adequate opportunity for consultations with respect to any matters affecting the operation of this Agreement".[17]

From the point of view of substance, there is no change and conflict between these agreements and that of the DSU or the GATT 1947 provisions of the consultation. The only exception is in Article 19.3 of the Agreement on Implementation of Article VII of GATT 1994. It requires that the Technical Committee shall provide upon request advice and assistance to Members engaged in consultations. As a matter of fact, this provision does not change anything, but adds an obligation on the Technical Committee upon request by Member states. The whole consultation provisions integrate well without confusion. Thus, it is easy for Member states to refer to them.

b. *Implication Drawn from the DSU*

The aim of the WTO dispute settlement system is to secure a positive solution to a dispute under the Article 3.7 of the DSU. Under the same provision, the DSU sets its preferential hierarchy from top to bottom: a mutually agreed solution, the withdrawal of the measures concerned if

16 This one is not in this list, but actually it is in the text of Article 4.11.

17 Article XXII:1 under GATT 1947.

these are found to be inconsistent with the provisions of any of the covered agreements through the dispute settlement mechanism.[18]

The DSU expresses a clear preference for solutions mutually acceptable to the parties to the disputes, rather than solutions resulting from adjudication by a Panel.

Resolving disputes through consultations is obviously cheaper and more satisfactory for long-term trade relations with the other party of the dispute than adjudication by a Panel. The consultation enables the disputing parties to understand better the factual situation and the legal claims with respect of the dispute. Such understanding may allow them to resolve the matter without further proceedings. If not, it will allow the parties to learn more about the facts and legal arguments that may lead to basic understandings, eliminate some mistakes or misunderstandings and prepare future documents when the dispute goes to adjudication stage. Under the latter circumstance, the consultation serves as an informal pre-trial discovery mechanism. However, the main object is to settle disputes amicably.[19]

In the *Korea – Tax on Alcoholic Beverages* case, Korea argued before the Panel that the US violated Article 3.3, 3.7 and 4.5 of the DSU by not engaging in consultations in good faith to reach a mutually agreed solution. Korea maintained that there had been no meaningful exchange of facts, because the complainant treated the consultations as one-sided question and answer sessions. Korea, thus, asserted that such an approach frustrated any reasonable chance for a settlement and considered the non-observance of specific provisions of the DSU as a, "violation of the tenets of the WTO dispute settlement system".[20] The Panel stated, "we do not wish to imply that we consider consultations unimportant. Quite the contrary, consultations are a critical and integral part of the DSU".[21]

18 The dispute settlement mechanism here includes voluntary procedures (good offices, conciliation and mediation), the Panel, the AB, alternative means of dispute settlement (arbitration), surveillance of implementation of recommendations and rulings, compensation and the suspension of concessions.

19 Van den Bossche, P. United Nations Conference on Trade and Development: Course on Dispute Settlement World Trade Organisation – 3.2 Panels, New York and Geneva: UNCTAD, 2003; 3.

20 See WT/DS75/R and WT/DS84/R, Panel Report on *Korea – Taxes on Alcoholic Beverages*, para. 10.19.

21 *Ibid.*

The Panel in the *Turkey – Textile* case expressed that consultations are a crucial and integral part of the DSU, and are intended to facilitate a mutually satisfactory settlement of the dispute consistent with Article 3.7 of the DSU.[22]

The practices and the provisions confirm that the consultation is a significant method of dispute resolution under the DSU.

2. *Time Limits*

One of the improvements under DSU is a strict time frame. The Member shall respond within 10 days after the date of receipt of the request; the involving Members shall enter into consultations within a time limit of no more than 30 days.[23] The consultation time limit is 60 days normally after the date of receipt of the request for consultation.

Notwithstanding, it is almost impossible to conclude consultations within 60 days. For instance, in the *India – Measures Affecting Export of Certain Commodities* case, the date from the expiration of consultation period to the request for establishment of a Panel was more than 29 months.[24] There is, in fact, a period of 71 days minimum between the request for consultations and the establishment of a Panel, according to Davey's observation.[25]

a. Exceptions

There are three exceptions that allow Members to request the establishment of a Panel earlier than 60 days.

22 WT/DS34/R, Panel Report on *Turkey – Restrictions on Imports of Textile and Clothing Products*, para. 9.22.

23 Article 4.3 under the DSU.

24 See WT/DSB/W/244/Add.1, *India – Measures Affecting Export of Certain Commodities*, the date of expiration of consultation period is on 10 May 1998 (WT/DS120/1), and the date of request for establishment of a Panel is on 13 October 2000 (WT/DS120/2).

25 See Davey, W. J. The WTO Dispute Settlement System: the First Decade, in World Trade Forum 2004, Bern 2004: 4–5 June.

(1) *First Exception*

If the involved Members reach a mutual agreement that consultations cannot solve the disputes, then the Member may proceed directly to request the establishment of a Panel.[26]

A few countries invoked Article 4.3 before 30 April 2005: the *United States – Standards for Reformulated and Conventional Gasoline* case (WT/DS4/2),[27] the *European Communities – Trade Description of Scallops* case (WT/DS7/7[28] and WT/DS14/5[29]), the *Canada – Export Credits and Loan Guarantees for Regional Aircraft* case (WT/DS222/2),[30] and

26 Article 4.3 under the DSU.

27 See *ibid.* document, this is the same case as WT/DS2, in the communication under the WT/DS4/2, it states that "the parties have agreed that further consultations are not likely to be productive and, with a view towards harmonising the scheduling of this matter with that of the Panel previously established with regard to the similar complaint of Venezuela, Brazil hereby requests that a Panel be established at the next meeting of the Dispute Settlement Body". The expiration of consultation period is on 9 June 1995, but the request for establishment of a Panel is 22 May 1995, and the Panel established on 31 May 1995. It is most likely that the main reason is the Panel of WT/DS2 had established on 10 April 1995, Brazil purposed to be included in the same proceeding so as to save more time.

28 See the *ibid.* document, the expiration of consultation period is 18 July 1995, and the request for establishment of a Panel is 10 July 1995. Canada required invoking Article 4.3 of the DSU with reference to WT/DS7/7 and Corr.1.

29 See the *ibid.* document, the situation of this case is similar to WT/DS4. The expiration of consultation period is on 22 September 1995. Chile requested to establish a Panel on 15 September 1995, the same day with Peru request for establishment of a Panel, as this is the same case with WT/DS7 and WT/DS12. These three disputes including WT/DS7, WT/DS12 and WT/DS14 were solved before the final Panel report. The *Scallops* cases will be analysed in detail afterwards because of its exceptional situation.

30 See the *ibid.* document and WT/DSB/M/106, Canada did not provide any significant information on its programmes. Brazil regretted that the consultations had not been meaningful, especially in light of Article 4.3 of the DSU, which provided that Members should enter into consultations 'in good faith [...] with a view to reaching a mutually satisfactory solution'. Since no such a solution had been found, Brazil requested the establishment of a Panel. The Panel established as early as on 12 March 2001, when was before the expiration of consultation period. The DSB on 18 March 2003 authorised Brazil against Canada by suspending concessions in order to push Canada to implement its obligations.

the *United States – Definitive Safeguard Measures on Imports of Certain Steel Products* case (WT/DS258/9).[31]

The above five disputes can be categorised into two types: mutually agreed pursuant to Article 6.2, according to Article 4.3 of the DSU;[32] and with regard to the similar complaint of previously established Panel, under the situation of unfruitful consultations and in order to save time, therefore, establishment of a single Panel for multiple complainants, agreed pursuant to Article 9.1 of the DSU.[33] This can also be applied to Article 4.7, which explains that the complaining party may request a Panel during the 60-day period if the consulting parties jointly consider that consultations have failed to settle the disputes.

(2) *Second Exception*

Under the second circumstance, in case of urgency (particularly concerning perishable goods), Members shall enter into consultations within 10 days, and settle the disputes within 20 days. Otherwise, the complaining party may request the establishment of a Panel.[34] In practice, a few cases were referred under this circumstance, namely the *Peru – Tax Treatment on Certain Imported Products* case (WT/DS255/3)[35] and *Romania – Import Prohibition on Wheat and Wheat Flour* (WT/DS240/1/Add.1),[36] although some cases are relevant to perishable goods. To put the true situation of these together, 30 day consultations seem absurd in the sense that these goods are perishable and would not last the time.

31 See the *ibid.* document and WT/DSB/M/129, the situation of this is also the same as WT/DS4. The consultation period expired 13 July 2002. New Zealand requested to establish a Panel on 28 June 2002 since the DSB agreed that the Panel established on 3 June 2002 to examine the complaint by the EC would also examine the complaint by New Zealand pertaining to the same matter.

32 See WT/DS7 and WT/DS222.

33 See WT/DS4, WT/DS14 and WT/DS258.

34 Article 4.8 under the DSU.

35 See WT/DS255/3, in the request for consultations and during the consultations, Chile invoked the provisions relating to cases of urgency in Article 4.8 of the DSU, as the measure affects natural, and hence perishable products. This case was finally resolved prior to Panel establishment by Chile's withdrawal. See below case study on DS255.

36 See below case study on DS240.

Another provision is relevant to perishable goods under Article 4. In cases of urgency parties to the dispute, Panels and the AB shall make every effort to accelerate the proceedings to the greatest extent possible.[37]

In the *Canada – Patent Protection of Pharmaceutical Products* case (WT/DS114), the US submitted a request for expedited consideration of the dispute under Article 4.9 of the DSU on the grounds that the premature expiration of patents, during the dispute settlement procedure, caused irreparable harm to the patent owners. It referred to the alleged simplicity of the issues in dispute, the absence of third parties and other circumstances. The Panel indicated that owing to other demands on its Members' time, it could not accelerate the timetable prior to the first substantive meeting. However, the Panel stated that it undertook to make every effort to issue its report as soon as possible after the second substantive meeting.[38] This provision appears to be the supplement of Article 4.8. Considering that few Member states invoke Article 4.8, it is possible that few countries apply this provision as well. The above dispute is quite special indeed, since it raised a question of whether a patent is a *perishable good* under the TRIPS Agreement.

(3) *Third Exception*

Another circumstance under Article 4.3 does not seem to have been applied (so far) by Member states:

> If the Member does not respond within 10 days after the date of receipt of the request, or does not enter into consultations within a period of no more than 30 days, or a period otherwise mutually agreed, after the date of receipt of the request, then the Member that requested the holding of consultations may proceed directly to request the establishment of a Panel.[39]

It can be assumed that the disputants need the procedure of consultations, since no Member state has invoked this circumstance.

37 Article 4.9 under the DSU.

38 See WT/DS114/R, Panel Report on *Canada – Patent Term*, para. 1.5.

39 DSU, Article 4.3.

(4) *Combination of Flexibility and Strictness*

Strict time limits make consultation procedure more efficient. Furthermore, in practice, it shows flexibility as well as strictness. The complaining party may request to establish a Panel if consultation fails to settle disputes, or the complaining party can go on consultations after 60 days limit. In fact, most disputes through consultation were settled within five to fifteen month periods, according to the WTO survey.

Some cases may last even longer. For example, the inspection requirement of consultations between the US and Korea about agricultural products entry into Korea was raised 6 April 1995. Surprisingly, it is still pending at the consultation stage.[40]

It is impossible that the complaining parties can request to establish a Panel immediately in practice, because they need a period of time to prepare material on the basis of information and divergent points that have emerged during the period of consultations, in order to state their requirement precisely and comprehensively.[41]

Some Member states submitted a proposal to reduce the time framework on the consultation such as the EC. Meanwhile, other Member states requested to extend the time limits such as some developing countries. The reform of the time framework and proposals from Member states will be discussed later in the Conclusions section.

3. *Notification*

In Article 4.4, the DSU states that all consultation requests *shall* be notified to the DSB and the relevant Councils and Committees by the Member who requests consultations. For instance, on 7 March 2002, the European Union (EU) ambassador sent a letter to the American ambassador to request consultations on steel imports limitation measures in

40 WT/DS3, *Korea – Measures Concerning the Testing and Inspection of Agricultural Products*. Presumably this case was solved as no further report has been submitted to the WTO Secretariat. The Korean representative acknowledged it was over (see below).

41 Yang, G. H. Analysis consultations in the WTO Dispute Settlement Mechanism, at http://chinalawinfo.com/research/academy/details.asp?lid=3525 last visited 5 December 2004.

America on 5 March.[42] Since the EU requested consultation involving the question of steel imports safeguard measures, the EU shall notify the Council for Trade in Goods Committee on Safeguards and the DSB. In practice, this provision is operated successfully without any exception. At the DSB meeting on 19 July 1995, it agreed that delegations would send one single text of their notifications to the Secretariat (Council Division), simply specifying in that text, the other relevant Councils or Committees to which they wished the notification to be addressed. The Secretariat would then distribute it to the specified relevant bodies.[43]

According to Article 3.6, a mutually agreed solution to matters formally raised under the consultation and dispute settlement provisions of the covered agreements *shall* be notified to the DSB and the relevant Councils and committees, where any Member may raise any point relating thereto.

Since the process of consultation is confidential, the obligation of notification, therefore, is very important. Unfortunately, in practice, some Member states have not implemented this obligation to give a notification. If we check WT/DS/OV documents, as of 31 January 2006, there are 120 disputes pending on the consultation. In fact, the accurate numbers of resolved cases are much lower than 106. For example, on 23 December 2003, the US requested consultations with Egypt regarding the tariffs applied to textile and apparel products and the Decree of the President of the Arab Republic of Egypt No 469 of the year 2001 Decree No 469 and any amendments, related regulations or other implementing measures.[44] According to the Office of the United State Trade Representative (USTR) website, in January 2004, Egypt informed the US that it had issued a decree applying ad valorem rates to these imports and setting the duty rates within Egypt's tariff bindings.[45] That is to say, this

42 See http://www.wto.org/wto/disputes/bulletin/ (April, 2002) last visited 5 December 2004.

43 See WT/DSB/M/6, Dispute Settlement Body – Minutes of Meeting – Held in the Centre William Rappard 19 July 1995.

44 See WT/DS305/1, *Egypt – Measures Affecting Imports of Textile and Apparel Products*. During the Uruguay Round, Egypt agreed to bind its duties on these imports (clarified under HS Parts 61, 62 and 63) at rates of less than 50% (ad valorem) in 2003 and thereafter. The US believed the duties that Egypt actually applied, on a 'per article' basis, greatly exceeded Egypt's bound rates of duty.

45 See http://www.ustr.gov/enforcement/update.pdf (March 9, 2004), last visited 10 December 2004.

dispute was solved during the consultation, but the DSB was not notified by either the US or Egypt.

The significance of the notification is disclosed under Article 3.5 of the DSU in an indirect way. All solutions to matters formally raised under the consultation and dispute settlement provisions of the covered agreements, shall be consistent with those agreements and shall not nullify or impair benefits accruing to any Member under those agreements, nor impede the attainment of any objective of those agreements.[46] Thc notification to the DSB can supervise whether the violating states are in compliance with the rules under the covered agreement.

The DSU notes that any requests for consultations shall be submitted in writing.[47] Due to the confidential consultations, there are no formal records. There is no Panel-style record of consultations, which might figure in later proceedings.[48] As an authoritative source has indicated, consultations last no longer than two or three hours, generally conducted in English with no interpreters, no transcript and taping, and closed to the public and other WTO Members.[49] On the other hand, we should note that it is vital for complaining parties to keep the records of consulting items after formal consultations, which is actually affirmed by many missions. If requiring entry into the next stage of the Panel and perhaps the further AB, complaining parties need to collect more information.

The records of consulting items can also be the starting points to prepare the litigation materials. The measures are taken by the responding parties, and are considered by the complaining parties whose benefits are impaired according to direct or indirect measures taken by responding Members.[50] Compared with the Panel stage and the further AB stage, there are no formal records in the course of consultations. It is therefore related to the subject of the notification. If there is no written record during the consultation, it is hard to imagine whether the involving countries are able to notify the DSB and how they prepare the requisite documents, on the basis of original records, if they have to go to further judicial proceedings.

46 Article 3.5, under the DSU.

47 Article 4.4, under the DSU.

48 See Davey, W. J. & Porges, A. Performance of the System I: Consultations & Deterrence, 32 INT'L LAW 1998; 696: 705, from WESTLAW.

49 *Ibid.*

50 Article 3.3 under the DSU.

4. *Legal Basis*

The DSU requires that Members "*shall* give the reasons for the request including identification of the measures at issue and an indication of the *legal basis* for the complaint".[51]

'Legal basis' means the detailed Article(s) in the WTO Agreements which complaining parties consider the responding parties violate. For instance, in the *Steel Safeguard* case the EU ambassador required consultations with the US under Article 4 of the DSU, Article XXII(2) of the GATT 1947 and Article 14 of the Agreement on Safeguards.[52] The consulting item is the decision made by the Bush Administration at 5 March 2002 to impose steep protective tariffs of 8–30% on steel imports. The EU considered that the US violated the obligations of the GATT 1947 and the Agreement on Safeguards.[53]

We cannot say if, at the stage of consultations, complaining parties do not bring up some items and the Panel cannot hear the case. Nevertheless, it is unfair to responding parties to some extent in that consultation is a prerequisite for establishing a Panel.[54] If complaining parties do not raise all the necessary questions at consultation stage, but raise them to the Panel or the AB, it is likely that they contravene the necessary procedure. The responding parties are deprived of the rights of equal procedure, and it is obvious not in line with the rule of 'in good faith' in Article 3.10 of the DSU. In view of the importance of consultation to later procedures, such as the Panel or arbitration, the consulting contents are always broad so as to cover every possible issue.[55]

51 Article 4.4, under the DSU.

52 Article 4 of the DSU and Article XXII are provisions of consultations, meanwhile, Article 14 of the Agreement on Safeguards is dispute settlement provision.

53 See http://www.metalcenternews.com/2002/April/, www.ustr.gov/releases/2002/04/02–47.htm, www.europa.eu.int/comm/trade/goods/steel/pr_270302.htm , www.asil.org/insights/insigh84.htm, www.whitehouse.gov/news/release/2002/03/20020305–8.html, www.globalpolicy.org/socecon/bwi–wto/wto/2002/0307.htm and www.bbc.co.uk/hi/english/business/newsid_1881000/1881821.stm last visited 15 December 2004.

54 Yang 2003 http://chinalawinfo.com/research/academy/details.asp?lid=3525 last visited 5 December 2004.

55 *Ibid.*

5. *Confidentiality*

While the request for consultations is notified to the DSB, the consultation itself is confidential in accordance with Article 4.6. In general, it is held in Geneva and involves Geneva-based diplomats, as well as capital-based trade officials of the parties to the dispute. The WTO Secretariat is not present at, and is in no other way involved with, the consultation.[56] No one knows the result of 'the bargaining' behind that secret door except for the disputants.

The confidentiality requirement exists under Article 4.6 which provides that consultations shall be confidential, and without prejudice to the rights of any Members in any further proceedings.

In the *Korea – Alcoholic Beverages* case, Korea argued before the Panel the confidentiality requirement of Article 4.6 by referring in their submissions to information supplied by Korea during consultations. The Panel, in a finding not reviewed by the AB, held that, while confidentiality in consultations between parties to a dispute was *essential*, it also found that, "parties do not thereby breach any confidentiality by disclosing in those proceedings information acquired during the consultations".[57] Additionally, the Panel noted in detail:

> This is essential if the parties are to be free to engage in meaningful consultations. However, it is our view that this confidentiality extends only as far as requiring the parties to the consultations not to disclose any information obtained in the consultations to any parties that were not involved in those consultations. We are mindful of the fact that the Panel proceedings between the parties remain confidentiality by disclosing in those proceedings information acquired during the consultations. Indeed, in our view, the very essence of consultations is to enable the parties gather correct and relevant information, for purposes of assisting them in arriving at a mutually agreed solution, or failing which, to as assist them in presenting accurate information to the Panel. It would seriously hamper the dispute settlement process if the information acquired during consultations could not subsequently be used by any party in the ensuing proceedings. We find therefore, that there has been no breach of confidentiality by the complainants in this case in respect of information that they became aware of during the consultations with Korea on this matter.[58]

56 Van den Bossche 2003; 4.

57 See WT/DS75/R, Panel Report on *Korea – Taxes on Alcoholic Beverages*, para. 10.22.

58 *Ibid.*, para. 10.23.

The Panel on *Australia – Automotive Leather II* repeated the findings of the Panel in *Korea – Alcoholic Beverages* as above. Australia, as the defending party, demanded the information, which the US, as the complaining party, had obtained during consultations preceding a previous Panel.[59] The US requested that it was declared inadmissible in the second proceeding. The Panel rejected this request by Australia:

> As Australia rightly notes, Article 4.6 of the DSU provides that 'consultations shall be confidential, and without prejudice to the rights of any Member in any further proceedings'. However, in our view, this does not mean that facts and information developed in the course of consultations held pursuant to one request cannot be used in a Panel proceeding concerning, as it does in this case, the same dispute, between the same parties, conducted pursuant to another, different request.
>
> We recall that Article 11 of the DSU obliges a Panel to conduct 'an objective assessment of the matter before it'. As discussed earlier, any evidentiary rulings we make must be consistent with this obligation. The Panel in *Korea – Taxes on Alcoholic Beverages* confirmed the right of a Panel to a WTO disputes to use information learned in consultations in Panel proceedings.
>
> Given that, in this case, the parties and the dispute are the same, no Panel was actually composed or considered the dispute in the first-requested proceeding, and there are no third parties involved in either proceeding who might have learned information in the course of consultations, we cannot see any reason to exclude the United Sates from our consideration, merely because it was developed in the course of the consultations held pursuant to the first request[60]. Australia has failed to specify what other, if any, facts might have been derived by the United States from the earlier consultations, and so there is no basis for us to exclude any such facts.[61]

These two cases illustrate the importance of confidentiality, as well as the significance of consultations, and introduce the relationship between the Panel and the consultation. The course of consultations is not always

59 A Panel, which had been established, but never composed and as a result, never became active.

60 (original footnote) There is nothing to indicate that there would have been any different answers had the same questions been asked by the United Sates during consultations held pursuant to the second request. We note Australia's view that there were no consultations held pursuant to the second request, although there was a meeting between the parties. Presumably, this view is based on Australia's position that the second request for consultations, and the second request for establishment, like this Panel that flowed from those requests, were inconsistent with the DSU.

61 See WT/DS126/R, Panel Report on *Australia – Subsidies Provided to Producers and Exports of Automotive Leather*, paras. 6.32–6.35.

an independent procedure. It may directly influence any further proceeding(s).

In my view, confidentiality is an extremely important principle during the course of consultations, even the most effective weapon in the consultation, although it seems antagonistic to the requirement of transparency in the DSU proceedings. The consultation has a mysterious content of diplomacy.

6. *Types of Consultation*

The consultation forms are classified as sole consultation and joint consultation. The former means one Member consults with another Member. The latter means several Member states consult with one Member, a procedure which is used more today than in previous years. The *Steel* case is a good example. In addition to the EC, Japan, Korea, Norway, Switzerland, Brazil, New Zealand and China requested a joint consultation.

Consultations can be requested, either pursuant to Article XXII of the GATT 1994, or corresponding provisions in other covered agreements. The Member requesting consultations is free to choose either type of consultation.

There is only one, albeit significant, difference between the two types of consultation. Merely in the context of consultations pursuant to Article XXII, or corresponding provisions, can a Member other than the consulting Members be allowed to participate. A Member that considers it has a substantial trade interest may notify the consulting Members and the DSB of such interest (within 10 days after the date of the circulation of the request for consultations). Provided that the responding party to the dispute agrees that the claim of substantial interest is well founded, this Member shall be allowed to join in the consultations.

If consultations are conducted pursuant to Article XXIII, or corresponding provisions, it is not possible for other Members to join in the consultations. This distinction allows the requesting party to make the tactical decision of whether it wants the presence, and presumably the support, of third parties or not. In some cases, requesting parties have used Article XXIII, presumably to keep outsiders out of the consultation.[62] For example, in the *European Communities – Aid for Commercial*

62 Van den Bossche 2003; 4.

Vessels case, Korea requested consultations with the EC and with the EC Member States pursuant to Article 4 of the DSU, Article XXIII: 1 of the GATT 1994 and Articles 4, 7 and 30 of the SCM Agreement with regard to measures affecting trade in commercial vessels.[63] No other Member joined in this dispute. It is likely that Korea expects other Members to be excluded during the course of consultations.

7. *Third Parties*

Interestingly, under Article 4, there is such a concept as, 'third parties', within any of the provisions.[64]

According to the definition in the *Dictionary of Trade Policy Terms*, third parties are:

> Members who are not directly involved in the launch of a dispute, but who participate in the proceedings because they have a substantial interest in the matter. A mere interest in the proceedings is not enough. Members wishing to become third parties must show that they have a trade interest at stake.[65]

The key requirement for third parties is they should have a substantial trade interest.

The DSU explains that whenever a Member other than the consulting Members considers that it has a substantial trade interest in consultations being held pursuant to provisions in covered agreement,[66] such a Member shall be joined in the consultations.[67] Semantically speaking then, joint Members have a similar meaning to third parties.

However, in practice, there exist two possibilities when disputing Members decide to go to further proceedings: one is to be a third party, the other a co-complaining party. In the *Steel Safeguard* case, Japan, Korea, Norway, Switzerland, Brazil, New Zealand, China, Venezuela, Mexico, and Canada during the consultation stage were joined with the EC. Afterwards, the EC, Japan, Korea, Norway, Switzerland, Brazil,

63 See WT/DS307/1, *European Communities – Aid for commercial vessels* – Request for Consultations by Korea.

64 Article 10 of the DSU states third parties during the Panel process.

65 Goode 2003; 342.

66 The covered agreements are listed above, under the subtitle of the Importance of the Consultation.

67 Article 4.11 of the DSU.

New Zealand, and China sued the US as co-complainants. Canada, Mexico and Venezuela requested that they be regarded as the third parties in this case.

A request to join the consultation may be accepted or refused. The DSU interprets that Members of a substantial trade interest in consultations may notify the consulting Members and the DSB within 10 days to join in consultations, under Article 4.11. A well-founded, substantial interest is addressed by the consulting Members. Otherwise, the joint request may be refused. If the joint request is not accepted, the applicant Member shall be free to request consultations.[68] That is to say, third-party Members participate in consultations only with the acceptance of the defending Member under the DSU. Otherwise, the Members who are refused by the right to participate in such consultations, may request their own consultations with the defendant, who may then decide to coordinate the consultations in both disputes.

Practically there is no obligation to notify the DSB of any refusal to have a third-party join into consultations.[69] In *US – Trade Act 1974* case, Japan argued that the US could not refuse its request to join in the consultation. Japan requested the US should provide the reasons with regard to its acceptance or refusal, and should supply them with copies of all the US responses made to each request in view of transparency.[70]

Under the WT/DS200/13, the Chairman of the DSB suggested that, in light of the Secretariat's overload of translation work and the important number of requests to be joined in consultations, the circulation of just the names of Members accepted to join in consultations would be a considerable practical improvement.[71] Hence, the notification of names of Members accepted by the defending party is of concern to the DSB,

68 Article 4.11 of the DSU.

69 When one checks the whole proceedings of one case, it is impossible to find 'Rejection by the Defendant Party of the Requests to Join Consultations'. Normally, it may or may not have an acceptance report. For instance, in the Steel Safeguard case, under the WT/DS248/11, the Permanent Mission of the US informed the DSB that it had accepted the requests of Canada, China, Japan, Korea, Mexico, New Zealand, Norway, Switzerland and Venezuela to join consultations titled 'Acceptance by the United States of the Requests to Join Consultations'.

70 WT/DS200/12, *United States – Section 306 of the Trade Act of 1974 and Amendments Thereto* – Communication from Japan.

71 WT/DS200/13, *United States – Section 306 of the Trade Act of 1974 and Amendments Thereto* – Communication from the Chairman of the DSB.

since it has an interest in finding out: which Members have been invited for such consultations with regard to the increasing requirement of transparency.

One observes that a third party who has joined another Member's consultations is not able immediately to take the role as a claimant and request a Panel without separately requesting its own consultations.[72]

In my view, if too many parties become involved in a consultation, it could lead to complications that get in the way of the efficient settlement of disputes. To enhance third-party rights during the consultation stage could impede rather than improve this diplomatic method. Replies from some interviewees of delegations support this hypothesis.

In fact, the position of a third party is attractive to more and more Members, who raise many proposals about their status throughout whole procedures of the DSM.

There exist slight differences between joint consultations and third parties. The comparison of a third party during the consultation stage and during the Panel stage is provided below.

8. *Special and Deferential Treatment (SDT)*

Special and deferential (S&D) is the concept that exports of developing countries should be given preferential access to markets of developed countries, and that developing countries participating in trade negotiations need not reciprocate fully concessions they receive. Developing countries can enjoy longer timeframes for phasing in new rules and lower levels of obligations for adherence to the rules.[73]

The DSU states that Members should give special attention to the particular problems and interest of developing Members and Least Developed Countries (LDCs).[74] Asglobalisation is progressing, developing countries need to participate in some international organisations in order to improve their international positions and enhance their peoples' living standard. Additionally, developing countries need access to foreign markets if they are to reap the benefits of globalisation. Thereby, the SDT

72 Waincymer, J. WTO Litigation: Procedural Aspects of Formal Dispute Settlement, London: Cameron May, 2002; 212.

73 Goode 2003; 323.

74 See Article 3.12, 4.10, 8.10, 12.10, 12.11, 21.2, 21.7, 21.8, 24, and 27.2 in the DSU.

can encourage developing countries to embark on open trade growth policy.

Simultaneously, goal of the WTO is to improve the welfare of the peoples of the Member states. Yet, throughout the global economy, pressures for protectionism abound, threatening the improvement of market access. In order to approach this aim, the WTO shall pay much attention to developing states, which account for above three fourths of WTO Members.

The WTO dispute settlement system can help insure against trade protectionism by maintaining market access. This is particularly crucial because most of developing countries have fewer alternative export markets and fewer export goods, it therefore will undermine trade reform in developing countries. The SDT is a benchmark to evaluate whether the DSU is the most critical and successful dispute settlement mechanism in the trade regime.

There are many special rules for developing Members under some WTO Agreements and Articles. With regard to consultation phase, Article 4.10 defines the special treatment permitted.[75]

Although more and more developing Members and LDCs[76] have been involved as complainants, they only accounted for 28.2%. The number

75 It states that during consultations Members should give special attention to the particular problems and interests of developing country Members.

76 According to United Nations statistics, as of December 2003 there are 50 LDCs on its list. Social Council of the United Nations used the following three criteria for determining the new list of the LDCs, as proposed by the Committee for Development Policy:
a low-income criterion, based on a three-year average estimate of the gross domestic product per capita (under $900 for inclusion, above $1,035 for graduation);
a human resource weakness criterion, involving a composite Augmented Physical Quality of Life Index (APQLI) based on indicators of: (a) nutrition; (b) health; (c) education; (d) adult literacy;
an economic vulnerability criterion, involving a composite Economic Vulnerability Index (EVI) based on indicators of:(a) the instability of agricultural production; (b) the instability of exports of goods and services; (c) the economic importance of non–traditional activities (share of manufacturing and modern services in GDP); (d) merchandise export concentration; (e) the handicap of economic smallness (as measured through the population in logarithm).
In the 2000 review of the list, a country qualified to be added to the list if it met the above three criteria and did not have a population larger than 75 million. See

of participants has increased, compared with the GATT period, but 23 out of 65 traditional countries have not been involved. One view is that it is not a good idea to encourage developing counties and LDCs to use some of the WTO Agreement, since these rule-based solutions would not provide security and predictability to these Member states, rather, it would leave them once again "at the mercy of the major powers" (i.e. Ecuador in *EC – Banana* case).[77]

Some developing Members have used the WTO dispute settlement system to great effect, proving the system's worth from a development perspective. For example, Brazil has made most extensive use of the WTO dispute settlement system. As of 30 April 2005, Brazil has brought 19 cases and been respondent in 8 cases.[78] Nonetheless, the technical and legal complexity of this regime makes it difficult for other developing

---

http://www.un.org/special–rep/ohrlls/ldc/ldc%20criteria.htm last visited 21 December 2004.

There is no list of developing countries in the UN. However, the World Bank (WB) gave identifications to countries with developing economies status, there are 149 countries under this category, see http://www.reading.org/Membership/devel_countries.html last visited 21 December 2004). Meanwhile, the UN publishes a list of 48 Small Island Developing States (SIDS) (See http://www.un.org/special-rep/ohrlls/sid/list.htm last visited 21 December 2004) and a list of 31 Landlocked Developing Countries (LLDCs) (See http://www.un.org/special-rep/ohrlls/lldc/list.htm last visited 21 December 2004). Deducting overlapped number, we have an extra 17 countries not on the list of the WB. Therefore, the total number of developing countries is 166. The Member States of the UN is 191 countries, roughly developing countries including LDCs account for 87% of total countries (LDCs are 26%, developing countries are 61%).

In reference to present WB statistics, there are 162 developing countries. The classification of the WB is a bit different from the UN. For operational and analytical purposes, the World Bank's main criterion for classifying economies is gross national income (GNI) per capita. In previous editions of its publications, this term was referred to as gross national product, or GNP. Based on its GNI per capita, every economy is classified as low income, middle income (subdivided into lower middle and upper middle), or high income.

See http://www.worldbank.org/data/countryclass/countryclass.html last visited 21 December 2004. The WB has 184 Member States, in which developing countries account 88%.

77 Steger, D. P. Afterward: the 'Trade And...' Conundrum – A Commentary', 96 A.M.J.I.L 2002; 135: from WESTLAW. In the *EC – Banana* case, although Ecuador won the case, it had no ability to retaliate againstthe EC'sinconsistent regime.

78 See http://www.wto.org/english/tratop_e/dispu_e/distabase_wto_members1_e.htm for detailed disputes of Brazil.

countries to use the system effectively, of which LDCs have filed only one dispute.[79]

The biggest barriers during the dispute settlement proceedings are the high costs and necessity of professional legal experts. Developing countries usually lack the resources. Therefore, the consultation procedure for them seems more realistic, since it is a low-cost option.[80] Especially, LDCs are always in a disadvantaged position when they try to achieve a bargaining symmetry with some powerful Members, since they have few in-house experts and are 'less sophisticated buyers of legal advice'.[81] Many LDCs cannot maintain a permanent Geneva-based WTO delegation and have rarely participated in prior WTO disputes due to their lesser role in world trade, relatively undiversified export portfolios and smaller market capacity. LDCs participate in WTO disputes less frequently than they should because of these reasons. This suggests that WTO should put more emphasis on helping LDCs in general and at consultation stage in particular.[82]

As developing countries and LDCs recognise their disadvantages, if possible, they will try their best to solve divergence at consultation stage. Jamaica, for example, put forward its proposal to strengthen the significance of the consultation stage. It pointed out that a strengthened consultative process would allow developing countries to use more frequently the DSM if a dispute could be resolved without resort to the Panel process which can be very costly and time consuming.[83]

79 See WT/DS306 *India – Anti-dumping measure on batteries from Bangladesh.* This case was settled bilaterally according to the answer from the Indian representative in Geneva.

80 Horlick, G. N. & Butterton, G. R. A Problem of Process in WTO Jurisprudence: Identifying Disputed Issues in Panels and Consultations, L.P.I.B.2000; 31(3–4): 573 from WESTLAW.

81 Advisory Centre on WTO Law, Trade and Development Centre, Agreement Establishing the Advisory Centre on WTO Law at www.itd.org/links/char1611.doc last visited 20 December 2004.

82 Busch, M. L. & Reinhardt, E. Bargaining in the Shadow of the Law: Early Settlement in GATT/WTO Disputes, FDM.I.L.J.; 24:158 from WESTLAW.

83 TN/DS/W/21, Contribution by Jamaica to the Doha Mandated Review of the DSU, 10 October 2002.

It is said that the WTO will not change its character as a rich man's club if it does not completely transfer to adjudication from diplomacy.[84] However, 'law is the tool of the ruling class to perpetuate injustices' according to Marxist theory.[85] Once the class exists, domination will not die out. Therefore, leading countries and developed countries will always dominate developing countries and main international organisations. The WTO is no exception. For example, legal methods under the DSU have never been initiated by any LDCs to date. Mere legalisation cannot change anything fundamentally for developing Members.

Article 3.7 states that the aim of the dispute settlement mechanism is to secure a *positive* solution to a dispute. A solution *mutually* acceptable to the parties to a dispute and consistent with the covered agreements is to be preferred. At the same time, Article 3.2 requires that the dispute settlement system of the WTO be a central element in providing *security* and *predictability* to the multilateral trading system.

Moreover, there is always an argument that favours the judicial mechanism, whether or not the DSU is more responsive to the interests of the strong than of the weak. Some scholars have thought that consultations could be useful particularly for smaller countries whose requirements for dialogue might be ignored by the larger players in the system.[86] It is more likely that consultations can be useful for weaker states that have a need for dialogue with the stronger counterparts, provided the effects of power bargaining asymmetry of members are achieved.

We have already discussed the consultation provisions under the DSU. In Part III we concluded that the consultation is a legal procedure in public international law. Consultations under the DSU affirm this because it is a procedure designed to initiate further procedure(s) without exception and the DSU indicates that there is a duty to consult in respect of Article 3.3, Article 3.7, Article 4.1 and Article 4.2. Moreover, the regulations of time limit, notification, legal basis and third parties during the consultation support its character as a legal procedure.

84 See Jackson, J. H. The Jurisprudence of GATT& the WTO, Cambridge: CUP, 2000; 402.

85 See Collins, H. Marxist and Law, Oxford: OUP, 1984.

86 See Davey, W. J. & Porges, A. Performance of the System I: Consultations & Deterrence, Int'l Law 1998; 32: 696 from WESTLAW.

C. *Duty to Consult*

There is no doubt that consultations are a prerequisite to Panel proceedings.[87] There is no exception under the DSU to the fact that the consultation is the first step of the whole proceedings.

In Part I, we concluded that there is a duty to consult for both parties in practice and theory. Likewise, there is a duty to consult when disputes arise in the WTO. There are two exceptional provisions in Article 4, but these two have never been invoked to date.

In the *Brazil – Measures Affecting Desiccated Coconut* case, the Panel states that "Members' duty to consult is absolute, and is not susceptible to the prior imposition of any terms and conditions by a Member".[88]

It is noteworthy that Members are not entitled to impose any terms and conditions as a precondition, different from the consultation stage which is a precondition of a Panel request. Also in the *Brazil – Measure Affecting Desiccated Coconut* case, the Philippines argued that Brazil had refused to consult. The Panel considered that Brazil's submission in document WT/DS22/3 did not make a claim on behalf of the Philippines, and that there is nothing in the record of the discussions in the DSB meeting of 21 February 1996 that would lead to the conclusion that the requested Panel would be asked to make any finding regarding Brazil's failure to consult. Examining terms and conditions of the consultation are not within a Panel's terms of reference. Thus, the Panel excluded the Philippines' claim regarding Brazil's failure to consult.[89]

In the *US – Certain EC Products* case, AB stated that a complaining party *must* request consultations and consultations *must* be held before the establishment of a Panel.[90] EC acknowledged that there was no formal statement of the subject of the consultations held on 19 April 1999. Therefore, the AB considered the 19 April action was not a measure at issue in this dispute and did not fall within the Panel's terms of reference.

87 See WT/DS132/AB/RW, Appellate Body Report of *Mexico – Corn Syrup* (Article 21.5–US), para. 58 and WT/DS267/AB/R, Appellate Body Report of *United States – Subsidies on Upland Cotton*, para. 284.

88 See WT/DS22/R, Panel report of *Brazil – Measures Affecting Desiccated Coconut*, para 287.

89 *Ibid.*, paras. 287–288.

90 See WT/DS165/AB/R, Appellate Report on *United States – Import Measures on Certain Products* from the European Communities, para. 70.

In the *US – Upland Cotton*, AB disagreed with the US argument that measures whose legislative basis had expired were incapable of affecting the operation of a covered agreement and expired measures could not be the subject of consultations under the DSU. AB supported the view that measures whose legislative basis had expired affected the operation of a covered agreement was an issue that must be resolved on the facts of each case.[91] However, at the same time, AB emphasised that consultations are the first step in the WTO dispute settlement process, and were intended to "provide the parties an opportunity to define and delimit the scope of the dispute between them".[92] AB hesitated to impose too rigid a standard for the 'precise and exact identity' between the scope of consultations and the request for the establishment of a Panel, as it would substitute the request for consultation for the panel request.[93]

That is to say, although there is a duty to consult, this does not mean that there is a duty to check the adequacy of consultations. To put it more precisely, it is impossible to set the terms and conditions, since the consultation is a diplomatic method, which is a freely bilateral negotiation. It is not essential to give any terms and conditions, since the secrets of successful consultations have no strictly legal terms of reference nor any compromise of confidentiality. Moreover, practically it is difficult to make a rule for such a private activity as a consultation, although there exists the customary conduct of the consultation during its course.

D. *Evidence and Positions*

If consultations are not successful and a Panel is established in due procedure, questions may arise whether the evidence of the consultation can be used or not.

From a policy perspective, it is difficult to resolve this question properly, since the DSU and other covered agreements do not expressly an-

91 See WT/DS267/AB/R, Appellate Report on *United States – Subsidies on Upland Cotton*, para. 262.

92 *Ibid.*, para. 293 and WT/DS132/AB/RW, Appellate Body Report on *Mexico – Corn Syrup* (Article 21.5–US), para. 54.

93 *Ibid.*, para. 293 and WT/DS46/AB/R, Appellate Body Report on *Brazil – Financing Programme for Aircraft*, para. 132.

swer the evidentiary questions.[94] However, a number of propositions are clear: the consultation occurs between the parties themselves; the content is confidential; there is no obligation to disclose the results to the Secretariat or other Member states.

Then the next question is whether the parties can unilaterally disclose some information during the consultation to the Panel. On the one hand, the consultation is confidential, but on the other, it should not prejudice the rights of Members in further proceedings, particularly considering that any question to the Panel is put in a controversial situation.

In practice, the Panel or the AB more or less gave an explanation to this evidentiary argument in the *Korea – Alcohol* case, when the Panel stated that, "it would seriously hamper the dispute settlement process if the information acquired during consultations could not subsequently be used by any party in the ensuing proceeding".[95]

The AB in the *India – Patent* case indicated that parties must be fully forthcoming from the very beginning both as to claims and the facts relating to those claims. Fact-finding is a major function of the consultation process.[96]

The Panel in *Argentina – Textiles and Apparel* believed that the evidence received by the US from the consultation stage with Argentina should be relied upon. Therefore, it was considered valid evidence of the trade issues in that case.[97]

Nevertheless, Member States still seem to be confused by the extent of confidentiality in the consultation. In the *Mexico – HFCS* case, Mexico argued that the US's first written submission contained improper references to confidential aspects of the consultation. It put forward that one reason for the need for confidentiality over such information arose because of the power to limit the involvement of third parties at the consultation period. The Panel did not accept this argument.[98] It made the

94 Waincymer 2002; 220.

95 See WT/DS75/R, WT/DS84/R, Panel Report on *Korea – Taxes on Alcoholic Beverages*, para. 10.23.

96 See WT/DS50/AB/R, AB Report on *India – Patent Protection for Pharmaceutical and Agricultural Chemical Products*, para. 94.

97 See WT/DS56/R, Panel Report on *Argentina – Measures Affecting Imports of Footwear, Textiles, Apparel and other Items*, para. 3.211.

98 See WT/DS132, Panel Report on *Mexico – Anti-Dumping Investigation of High-Fructose Corn Syrup* (HFCS) from the United States, para. 7.42.

same analysis as in the *Korea – Alcoholic* case that it would seriously hamper the dispute settlement process if a party could not use information obtained in the consultation in subsequent Panel proceedings merely because third parties did not participate in the consultation, but chose to participate in the Panel proceedings. Thus, there was no violation of the requirement of confidentiality of consultations in these circumstances.[99]

It can be concluded, given the Panel and the AB's reasoning, that in most cases, the evidences submitted during the consultation proceedings can be used in the subsequent Panel stage. Then, the following question is whether the Panel is under no limitation to use such information during the consultation phase.

An offer of compromise on a particular issue will not be used against that particular Member.[100] If one party discloses information unilaterally to the Panel, the Panel should not use it in its decision-making process.

In the *US – Underwear* case, Costa Rica submitted to the Panel information concerning the bilateral negotiations that took place between Costa Rica and the US before and after the imposition of the restriction. More specifically, Costa Rica submitted information relating to settlement offers made by the United States concerning the level of the restriction to be imposed. In this respect, the Panel noted that the wording of Article 4.6 of the DSU makes it clear that offers made in the context of consultations are, in case that a mutually agreed solution is not reached, of no legal consequence to the later stages of dispute settlement, as far as the rights of the parties to the dispute are concerned.[101] Consequently, the Panel would not base its findings on such information.

By means of the Panel and the AB's reports, it seems that they intend to use information obtained in the consultation in general but excluding a particular issue against a particular party in one dispute, in which an offer is made but without settlement. It can be understood that either the

99 *Ibid.*, para. 7.42.

100 Waincymer 2002; 207.

101 See WT/DS24/R, Panel Report on *United States – Restrictions on Imports of Cotton and Man-Made Fibre Underwear*, para. 7.27 The notion that details of settlement negotiations are inadmissible is consistent with the practice of the ICJ. In The Factory at Chorzow case the Court said that it "cannot take into account declarations, admissions or proposals which the parties may have made during negotiations between themselves, when such negotiations have not led to a complete agreement". *Factory at Chorzow* (Merits), 13 September 1928, PCIJ Series A No 17 at 51.

Panel or the AB remains reluctant to judge the adequacy of the consultation, as the consultation stage is bilateral and private. The parties may simply put forward information they believe to be in their tactical best interests.

E. *Good Faith and Consultation under the DSU*

In international law, good faith is an important and basic principle derived historically from *pacta sunt servanda*. Similarly, good faith in the DSU is a fundamental and vital principle. Article 3.10 is clear that, "if a dispute arises, all Members will engage in these procedures in good faith in an effort to resolve the dispute".[102]

The Consultation provision requires that the Member shall enter into consultations in good faith.[103] If one party cannot fulfil 'good faith', another party can challenge through an invocation of this paragraph.

In the *Philippines – Motor Vehicle* case, after the US requested the establishment of a Panel, the Philippines claimed that this would violate WTO decision-making processes and, therefore, must be rejected. One of the arguments against the establishment of a Panel was that the Philippines engaged in negotiations with the US in good faith. The reasons were stated as follows:

> The Philippines demonstrated considerable flexibility since its original extension request. In a letter from the Philippines to the US dated 14 July 2000, the Philippines manifested: (i) its willingness to accept a shorter time frame, from five years to three and half years; and (ii) a phase-out plan.[104]

The Philippines was committed to establishing a liberal trade and investment regime for the automotive industry and had demonstrated its flexibility. A multilateral solution, however, required more than flexibility of the Philippines.

The Philippines believed that US demands were targeted at preferential tariffs arising out of the Philippine Motor Vehicle Development Pro-

102 Article 3.10 of the DSU.
103 Article 4.3 of the DSU.
104 See WT/DS195/4, *Philippines – Measures Affecting Trade and Investment in the Motor Vehicle Sector* – Communication from the Philippines, para. 2.

gramme. The US request for a Panel made a specific reference to preferential tariffs. Their request was inappropriate leverage on tariffs by means of a dispute ostensibly on trade-related investment measures.

According to the United States Trade Representative (USTR) website, this case was resolved to the satisfaction of the US without litigation.[105] One might assume that the US did not negotiate in good faith during the consultation stage, although the Philippines finally made concessions.

Contrary to Article 3.10, which envisages both the Members involved in conciliation and/or dispute settlement procedures, as indeed all Members of the WTO should resolve disputes in good faith, Article 4.3 has a more limited scope and addresses only the, "Member to which the request [for consultation] is made".[106] It is somehow the disharmony with Article 3.7, which requires both Members to try to resolve their dispute in good faith.[107]

As of 31 July 2004, six Panel reports contained a reference to Article 4.3, namely, *Brazil – Coconut* (WT/DS22/R), *EC – Bananas* (WT/DS27/R, four disputes, i.e. EC against Ecuador, Guatemala/Honduras, Mexico, and the US), and *US – FSC* (WT/DS108/R), as well as one AB report which is the *Mexico – HFCS* (WT/DS132/AB/RW).

In *Mexico – HFCS,* the AB elaborated firstly on the issue of confirming that consultations are a prerequisite for initiating a Panel procedure.[108]

Then, the AB emphasised the importance of consultations: through consultations, parties exchange information, assess the strengths and weaknesses of their respective cases, narrow the scope of the differences between them, and, in many cases, reach a mutually agreed solution, provide the parties an opportunity to define and delimit the scope of the

See Snapshot of WTO Cases Involving the United States (Updated: March 21, 2005), on website: http: //www.ustr.gov/assets/Trade_Agreements/Monitoring_Enforcement/Dispute_Settlement/WTO/asset_upload_file555_5696.pdf last visited 18 April 2005.

106 Article 4.3 of the DSU.

107 See Panizzon, M. Good Faith and Legitimate Expectations in WTO Adjudication: Integrating a General Principle of Law into the WTO Acquis (PhD Dissertation), Bern, 2003; 306.

108 See WT/DS132/AB/RW, *Mexico – Anti–Dumping Investigation of High Fructose Corn Syrup* (HFCS) from the US – Recourse to Article 21.5 of the DSU by the United States – Report of the AB, para. 52.

disputes between them even where no agreed solution is reached.[109] Furthermore, the AB evaluated that practice of consultations is testimony to the important role of consultations in dispute settlement through Article 4.1.[110]

The AB further explained:

> Article 4.3 of the DSU relates the responding party's conduct towards consultations to the complaining party's right to request the establishment of a Panel. When the responding party does not respond to a request for consultations, or declines to enter into consultations, the complaining party may dispense with consultations and proceed to request the establishment of a Panel. In such a case, the responding party, by its own conduct, relinquishes the potential benefits that could be derived from those consultations.[111]

Article 4.3 imposes a good faith obligation on the right of the complaining party to request the establishment of a Panel. Good faith thus limits the scope of the complaining party's right to request a Panel. Good faith balances the right of the responding party to request consultations with the right of the complaining party to move ahead and request a Panel.[112]

Moreover, good faith imposes a limitation on the right of the defending party to enter into consultation, prohibiting abuse of this right "as a litigation technique either to gain time or deter from the substantive issues".[113]

Nevertheless, Article 4.3 in combination with Article 4.6 establishes that a Panel has no obligation to withhold the adjudication of a dispute for the absence of consultations. Good faith, on the one hand, limits a party's claim that a Panel has breached its authority by adjudicating a dispute without prior consultation, and, on the other hand, limits the Panel's obligations *vis-à-vis* Member's conduct of consultations.[114]

The AB interpreted Article 4.7 relating to the conduct of consultations that, "this provision states the responding party may agree with the

109 *Ibid.*, para. 54.
110 *Ibid.*, para. 55.
111 *Ibid.*, para. 59.
112 Panizzon 2003; 307.
113 *Ibid.*, p. 307.
114 WT/DS132/AB/RW, paras. 62–65.

complaining party to forgo the potential benefits that continued pursuit of consultations might bring".[115]

In the *US – FSC* case, the Panel spent eleven pages on interpreting the evidence function of the consultation. Good faith depends on the adequacy of the consultation. Good faith covers the proper conduct of evidence submission so as to render consultations meaningful and perhaps avoid further Panel procedures.[116]

In the *EC – Bananas* case, the EC tried to demonstrate the bad faith of the complainants during consultations. The EC was of the view that consultations in the present case had not been able to fulfil their function because the complaining parties were not prepared to wait for a further exchange of questions and answers as agreed during the oral consultations.[117]

The complaining parties considered that they had provided the EC with ample notice and explanation of their concerns during the consultation phase, going beyond any DSU requirement by providing a detailed, seven-page, joint statement and a hundred questions detailing the many aspects of the EC banana regime about which they had concerns.[118]

Good faith can arbitrate whether the consultation is a null and void procedure in a particular dispute. In this case, the Panel rejected the EC's claim.

In the *Brazil – Coconut* case, the Philippines argued its request for establishment of a Panel and accused Brazil of refusing a request for consultations. "The obligation to consult would be meaningless if WTO Members could refuse to consult when they did not consider the legal claims of the WTO Member requesting consultations to be justified".[119] Therefore, the Philippines submitted that a finding on this issue was necessary to strengthen the consultative process in general and, in particular, to reduce

115 *Ibid.*, para. 61.

116 See WT/DS108/R, *United States – Tax Treatment for "Foreign Sales Corporations"* – Report of the Panel, paras. 4.18–4.88.

117 See WT/DS27/R/USA, *European Communities – Regime for the Importation, Sale and Distribution of Bananas* – Complaint by the US – Report of the Panel, para. II.4.

118 *Ibid.*, para. II. 12.

119 See WT/DS22/R, *Brazil – Measures Affecting Desiccated Coconut* – Report of the Panel, para. 100.

the likelihood of Brazil's resort to similar arguments to avoid consultations in the future.[120]

However, Brazil disputed the Philippines' contention that it 'refused' to consult. Brazil noted that it had offered to consult under the Tokyo Round SCM Code three times. In addition, Brazil submitted a list of the informal consultations that were held, noting that these consultations were considered 'informal' at the request of the Philippines.[121]

The Panel finally concluded that the Philippines' claim regarding Brazil's failure to consult was not within its terms of reference. In this case, good faith is the fact of consultations being held regardless of formal or informal consultations which depend on each Member's understanding as it goes beyond the Panel's term of reference.

The principle of good faith and the duty to resolve disputes in good faith are the most far-reaching expressions in the WTO dispute settlement system. Good faith balances the principle of fundamental fairness and due process that underlie and inform the provisions of the DSU against the right of other Members in a correct exercise of due process right.[122]

Good faith is indeed a broad and abstract expression, but it permeates every procedure of the DSU including the consultation. The ultimate function of good faith is fair, prompt and effective settlement of disputes summed up by *US – FSC* case.[123]

The understanding of good faith during the consultation phase differs from delegation according to the outcomes of research interviews from many Geneva-based missions.

120 *Ibid.*, para. 101.

121 *Ibid.*, para. 102.

122 See WT/DS132/AB/RW, *Mexico – Anti-Dumping Investigation of High Fructose Corn Syrup (HFCS)* from the US – Recourse to Article 21.5 of the DSU by the United States – Report of the AB, para. 107.

123 WT/DS108/R, *US – FSC*, para. 166.

III. Debate about Consultations

Although the consultation is contained in DSU, the debate about its usefulness remains.

During Ministerial Seattle, America requested that the time allotted for consultations should be reduced from 60 days to 30 days.[124] As the diplomatic/negotiating side of the WTO becomes increasingly unable to perform its obligations, there is a strong temptation within the system to take problems to the dispute settlement system and this may incur excessive burdens on the DSM, (by causing the DSM to address issues and legal problems that are not particularly addressed in a rule-applying or judicial-type institution).[125]

The consultation stage is 'waning in its efficacy' to settle disputes before they reach the Panel stage, since very few cases, since 1998, have been settled during this stage.[126] For example, in 1998, only five disputes under the DSU were resolved during consultation stage; in 1999, only one case was settled before a Panel issued any reports.[127] Even in that case, New Zealand and the EC resolved the matter by agreement after a Panel had been formed.[128] Under the domain of legal-orientation of WTO dispute settlement system, the importance of consultations has faded considerably. The current Consultation is merely a *pro forma* stage.

Nevertheless, many scholars and practitioners give a positive evaluation to consultations. In keeping with the goal for the mutual resolution of disputes, the WTO dispute settlement system was designed to ensure

124 See for example Lichtenbaum, P. Dispute Settlement and Institutional Issues, 3(1) J.I.E.L. 2000; 173: 173.

125 See Jackson, J. H. Perceptions About the WTO Trade Institutions' Inauguration Ceremony for the Advisory Centre for WTO Law Keynote Address, 5 October 2001, at http://www.acwl.ch/e/tools/news_detailsphoto_e.aspx?id=7192a684-8dac-4d91-974d–4f4f9ed3a682 last visited 6 December 2004.

126 See Wethington, O. J. Commentary on consultation Mechanism under the WTO Dispute Settlement Understanding During Its First Five Years, L.P.I.B. 2000; 31(3–4):583; Feeney, S. P. The Dispute Settlement Understanding of the WTO Agreement: An Inadequate Mechanism for the Resolution of International Trade Disputes, PEPD.R.L.J. 2002; 2:99 from WESTLAW.

127 *Ibid.*

128 WT/DS72/7, *European Communities – Measure Affecting Butter Products* (Nov. 18, 1999).

that states attempt a mutually agreed upon solution before resorting to a Panel.[129] In fact, according to the statistics over the years, in a great number of cases consultations took place without leading to requests for establishment of a Panel. Up to the end of April 2005, above half of the disputes ended before a Panel had to be set up. The above opinions are partly from practitioners who find that what they are concerned with most depends on the final results and statistical evidence.

Both the GATT's and the WTO's statistics provide evidence that consultations have been playing and will continue to play an important role in the WTO dispute settlement system. During the time of the GATT, Hudec and Busch's empirical study showed that two thirds of the disputes were solved before going to the Panel. Under WTO, between 1 January 1995 and 30 April 2005, a total of 330 disputes were initiated under the DSU. Since, in a number of cases, no notification had been circulated to the DSB, only incomplete information about dispute settlement before invoking a Panel is available. The exact status of each dispute is in Annex (II).

Nonetheless, it may be useful to check the other side of the coin. According to the statistics of Davey, with reference to the WTO, USTR and EU's websites on the dispute settlement, there are 106 out of 309 disputes pending at the stage of request for consultations as at 31 April 2004. In 75 cases, Panels have issued reports, 15 are at the Panel adjudication stage and six Panels are being established. There are at least 107 disputes (52.7%) solved before going to the Panel. Even among the 106 pending consultation disputes, 78 have actually been resolved.[130] That is to say there are about 185 out of 309 disputes (60%) resolved without resorting to Panel.

Although it is difficult to say that these disputes were solved through consultations, theoretically this hypothesis can be maintained. The rea-

129 Stewart, T. P. & Karpel, A. A. Review of the Dispute Settlement Understanding: Operation of Panels, 31(3–4) L.P.I.B.2000; 593:595 under the WEST LAW.

130 In the absence of empirical statistics onthe WTO website, the USTR and the EU websites provide latest reports on WTO dispute settlement resolution relevant to them. In addition, Professor Davey indicated from a practical point of view that after 18 months pending on consultations and no further report, disputes were most likely to have been solved already if the US and the EC were disputants. Some of the data were from his course on Dispute Settlement in Bern, MILE IV, 29 March to 1 April 2004. Others were from interviewed delegations.

sons are as follows: the disputes seem to have ended during the stage of request for consultations or before the issuance of final Panel reports. Since disputes were resolved without recourse to Panel reports, they used the non-litigant method to solve conflicts. Under the DSU, dispute settlement means the incorporation of consultations, good offices, conciliation and mediation, (which are diplomatic methods), with arbitration, Panels and the AB (which are judicial methods). Since there is no notification to the DSB for recourse to its good offices, conciliation or mediation under Article 5, the only non-litigant resort is to consultation under Article 4. Due to the clear definition of the concept of the negotiation in the GATT/WTO, the DSU does not contain the provision of negotiations, although it is customary for Member states to resolve disputes through negotiations rather than consultations.[131] Therefore, the logical inference is that consultation solved these disputes. To be more precise, the disputes solved by consultations can be categorised as falling into one of three different situations, namely, (1) at the stage of requiring for consultations, (2) after the stage of requiring for consultations but before the stage of composing the Panel, (3) after the stage of composing the Panel but before the stage of issuing final Panel reports.

Some have gone so far as to criticise the judicial role, although they did not praise consultations. For instance, from Bourgeois's perspective, issues raised *ex officio* by Panels or the AB raise significant practical problems,[132] and not all Members want a juridical system in the WTO.[133]

Meanwhile, others who give their views of consultations, ignoring how the consultation is conducted could significantly undermine its role.[134] Although the consultation does not impose a major obligation, this right is useful.[135] Busch observed that, in the position of the 'shadow of the law', defendants would like to plead stronger cases and complainants would presumably withdraw weaker ones, and found particularly

131 The distinction between the negotiation and consultation in the WTO was explained before.

132 Bourgeois, J. H. J. Reflections on the WTO Dispute Settlement System from a Practitioner's Perspective, J.I.E.L. 2001; 4(1): 145–151.

133 Palmeter, D. The WTO Appellate Body Needs Remand Authority, J.W.T. 41 1998; 32(1): 44.

134 See Davey, W. J. & Porges, A. Performance of the System I: Consultations & Deterrence, 32 Int'l Law 1998; 32:696 from WESTLAW.

135 See Jackson, J. H. The World Trading System: Law and Policy of International Economic Relations, MIT: Cambridge, 1992; 134.

that cases filed for consultations were no more likely to go to a Panel after the improvements than before. Thus, he pointed out that the experience of the GATT should remind us of the fact that the real action is still likely to be found in pre-trial negotiations.[136] There is no reason to depart fundamentally from the system-based legitimate dispute settlement to a traditional diplomatic means.[137] Moreover, the well-known *Banana* and *Hormones* cases have uncovered a potential weakness in the litigation mechanism.[138] Butler, an economist, established the 'pay-off structure' to express his views that the result of bilateral settlements should be similar to the expected ruling of the DSB and that the losing party can avoid reputation losses by agreeing upon a mutually accepted solution.[139] Scholars usually put forward their opinions on the position of theory in order to understand the true nature of events or objects or, they say, to expose the problems.

In general, this debate is still going on in academia and in the field. The debate itself is good for the improvement of consultations and the WTO dispute settlement system. At the same time, it raises a question how we identify the consultation phase.

136 Busch, M. L. & Reinhardt, E. Bargaining in the Shadow of the Law: Early Settlement in GATT/WTO Disputes, 24 FDM.I.L.J.158: from WESTLAW.

137 Cottier, T. The WTO Dispute Settlement System: New Horizons, 92 A.S.I.L.PROC 1998; 86: from WESTLAW.

138 Bulter, M. & Hauser, H. The WTO Dispute Settlement: A First Assessment from An Economic Perspective, J.L.Econ.Org 2000;16:503: from WESTLAW.

139 *Ibid.*, Bulter established three payoffs to express his four views in this article by economic perspective.

Chapter 3

Assessment of Consultations in the GATT/WTO

The WTO era seemingly treats the DSU methods as a fact without any divergences. However, the fact is that WTO has already established a legal framework for the dispute settlement system. It is likely that there is no incentive to discuss it against a judicial background.

Nonetheless, as has been noted, the argument about the consultation remains within the academic and practical circles.

The purpose of this section is to overview the current research situation into attitudes towards the consultation. The contribution of scholars to this field may impact on future practice and procedure. It is also essential, in my view, to analyse the effectiveness of the consultation in the WTO. In particular, the conclusion of this thesis, which addresses the balance between the consultation and the Panel rather than overstating either of them, may result in compromise (and the best choice).

As the assessment of the GATT dispute settlement system was explained in Part II, this section will focus on the debate between adjudicatory and diplomatic orientation. Most researchers support more legalised dispute settlement procedures. Other scholars, however, have criticised the adjudicatory orientation.

Jackson advocates that the dispute settlement system should continue to be legal-oriented, as it still has to face judicial issues (many of which have often conflicted with a domestic legal system). He concludes with the observation that, "all politics is local, and all economics is international".[1] Some of his articles are developed by refinement of this observation. Meanwhile, this leaves plenty room for researching the orientation of the dispute settlement mechanism, since economic and political factors intertwine. Other authors offer their opinions from various angles for or against his adjudicatory orientation.

1 Jackson, J. H. Afterword: The Linkage Problem-Comments on Five Texts, 96(1) A.J.I.L. 2002; 118:120 (footnote 14).

I. Literature on Rule-orientation: a Review

The supporters of rule-orientation generally criticise the GATT history of dispute settlement practices.[2] As the GATT has increasingly found itself in a position of deciding matters that entailed a balance of competing or diverse policy values, for example, in the trade and environment area, such an approach has threatened its legitimacy.[3]

However, there are two key issues. First, the reason, why the GATT was treated freely, is to help in solving disputes at that time and it was fairly successful, in general. Second, the GATT/WTO would improve accordingly when it could not meet the requirements of social development, such as the environmental problem.

In Howse's articles and books, there are two things that are of special note, namely the Trade Stakeholders Model and the Social Legitimacy Theory.

The Trade Stakeholders Model views trade dispute resolution as part of a wide-ranging deliberative process by which an emerging global social system can set its priorities.[4] Since dispute rulings directly impinge on the constituencies that affect the legitimacy of states themselves,[5] the commitment to a co-operative balance by those states will depend, not only on the appropriate sanction of 'cheating', but also on how dispute settlement is perceived by constituencies to affect their own bargain with the state or the domestic welfare calculus. Thus, Howse deduces that the implication of the Model, is that WTO dispute resolution process should be open to all groups, with a stake in the outcomes of trade decisions. What this does imply is transparency and publicity in the process through written or oral submissions by affected non-

2 They believe the Panel treated the GATT law rather freely in order to obtain outcomes that were thought to be diplomatically viable and to be helpful in sustaining the overall trade liberalisation bargain.

3 Trebilcock, R. J. & Howse, R. The Regulation of International Trade (2nd ed.), London: Routledge, 1999; 395.

4 Shell, G. R. The Trade Stakeholders Model and Participation by Nonstate Parties in the World Trade Organisation, 17 University of Pennsylvania Journal of International Economic Law 1996; 359: from Westlaw.

5 Howse admits at the same time that dispute rulings always indirectly affect domestic distributive outcomes, but do not entail constraint of domestic policy instruments.

governmental and transnational organisations. In fact, Howse strongly advocates the participation of non-governmental organisations (NGOs) to make the dispute settlement more legitimate.[6] The stakeholder model is more like a kind of metaphorical method, which is frequently used by Howse besides case study and textual analysis.

The social legitimacy of dispute settlement outcomes is relevant to the Trade Stakeholder Model.[7] Howse finds, with respect to dispute settlement under the GATT, the trade liberalisation elite was aware of the limits of formal legitimacy. The effectiveness of the system, either during the time of the GATT or during the time of the WTO depends on the willingness of the states to adopt rulings as binding and to implement them.[8] The gap between formal and social legitimacy relied heavily on validating dispute settlement results as the product of technical, institutional expertise about the trading system. The Social Legitimacy Theory, like the Trade Stakeholder Model, is in order to lower the threshold to let more into the system. As a critical legal researcher, Howse finds his own ways to combine the liberty with the legitimacy. But, in operation, it may be hard to carry out because the WTO is an international organisation which has to deal with the disputes of 148 Member states. Additionally, the WTO as an international trade organisation arguably may not go much further since trade liberalisation is its final goal.

An article written by Lennard is one of the typical pieces from the rule-oriented approach. He applies the method of treaty interpretation, which allows more confident predictions about how future issues would be solved in WTO jurisprudence. He criticises the teleological method, which is more likely to develop 'a life of its own'.[9]

6 He mentions the rejection of participation by interested stakeholders represented, for instance, by environmental NGOs served to rob the outcome of social legitimacy. He also observes that in Doha the way in which NGOs are intervening in the ongoing services negotiations indicated the WTO is involving towards great openness.

7 Social legitimacy means "a basis sensitive to the concern of critics or sceptics concerning the project of global economic liberalism that the whole undertaking of international trade law is titled towards the privileging of free trade against other competing, relevant values of equal or greater legitimacy in themselves".

8 It can be related to the 'all politics is local' of Jackson's view.

9 See Lennard, M. Navigation by the Stars: Interpreting the WTO Agreements, 5(1) J.I.E.L. 2002; 17:17–24,

While explaining the 'supplementary means' of Article 32 of the Vienna Convention, Lennard argues that they need to be treated with caution, since they are extremely difficult to justify under the interpretative rules of the Convention.[10] He discusses several interpretative maxims or principles in interpreting WTO obligation for existence of the gap. Although in theory these maxims assist in the development of a legally coherent text-based WTO jurisprudence; in practice, they will lead the Panel and AB away from a textual approach to create great uncertainty as to the applicable rules, and to risk altering the balance of WTO institutions.

He likens the textual approach to the North Star, and various disputes dealt by the Panel or AB as a navigation tool. You can use any way to identify the direction, but the only authoritative criterion is the North Star. In this article, Lennard uses most of the methods to justify his argument. These typical methods are comparative methods, such as the teleological and the textual approach, the metaphor (such as North Star and navigation), treaty interpretation (such as the Vienna Convention), textual analysis (such as the DSU) and case studies (such as the Panel and AB reports). He explains positive and negative aspects, by and large keeping a balance between them. There is always a gap between practice and theory. The aim of the DSU is to achieve a satisfactory settlement of the matter. From this perspective we cannot ask too much from the system.

Trachtman in his assessment examines two related analytical techniques of law and economics in an attempt to suggest the reasons for the assignment of competence to WTO dispute resolution as opposed to WTO legislation.[11] He intends to outline a more realistic picture. The two techniques he referred to are 'incomplete contracts' and 'rules versus standards'. The incomplete contract theory argues that all treaties (like all contracts) are necessarily incomplete in their capacity to specify the norms that will be applied to particular conduct. In the rules versus standards theory, a law is a rule that is specified in advance of the conduct to which it is applied. Each law is a compromise in that it is a combination

10 *Ibid.*, p. 22.

11 Trachtman, J. P. The Domain of WTO Dispute Resolution, 40 Harvard International Law Journal 1999; 333: from WESTLAW.

of rules and standards. He argues there could be gaps in the dispute resolution structure that leave the international law enforceable.

The rules of interpretation of customary international law have been adopted into WTO law. International treaties are often subject to the problem of incompleteness.

Law is worked out by human beings, who are not perfect. Thus, one cannot expect international law to be perfect. Trachtman believes a domestic legal system can be relied upon through 'complete contract'.[12] It can be argued that the domestic legal system is also formulated by persons who have the same mode of thoughts as the persons who work out the international legal framework. The difference is that knowing the domestic situation well, does not mean knowing the international situation well, with its complications and varieties. At this point, it is better to say that the dispute resolution process in a domestic legal system is considerably more complete than the international one. We should bear in mind that nothing can be perfect, including law – either domestic or international.[13]

Trachtman's article addresses the rule-oriented approach, which is demonstrated by another technique – rules and standards. He indicates that both of these are in the law-oriented approach. The choice between rules and standards is not a decision between more or less international law. While rules may be developed by tribunals, the decision is often an institutional choice between adjudicators and legislators. This observation depends on the perception that tribunals applying standards legislate. Furthermore, he refers to theories of jurisprudence to support his observations such as Hart's concept of law, which is also applauded by other researchers.

There is plenty of literature being produced in this area, especially on the rule-oriented approach. Jackson is the leading advocator of this orientation, while other authors develop this trend with reference to his views. Nevertheless, contemporaneously, some scholars put forward different ideas that challenge the rule-orientation approach.

12 *Ibid.*
13 See Part I.

II. Diplomatic Orientation (a Balance Preferential): Literature Review

Jackson and Hudec share the opinion that, in general, a strong feature of the GATT dispute settlement is diplomatic, and the biggest flaw is its political colouration. The argument is whether we should supersede the diplomatic means.

Much literature criticises the roles of the judicial means, rather than supporting the diplomatic orientation. Researchers treat the GATT experience as a mirror, which reflects the effective results at that time, and remind us that diplomatic means are still ways to solve divergences. Legal means cannot solve all disputes. Additionally the WTO has a huge package of tasks to fulfil.[14]

A. *The Legal Aspect*

Cottier explains the relationship between law and diplomacy: the legal and judicial nature of WTO dispute settlement is often built on the impression that law and diplomacy (politics) are too closely intertwined with its carefully 'crafted' balance of law and policy components.[15] The 'balance theory' penetrates his work, and his remarks basically rely on his experiences as a panellist. He reviews two stages among the dispute settlement procedures through his observational analysis.

The first one is the consultation. He argues that the initial step of consultation and possible conciliation leave the system within the realm of overall negotiated settlements, even upon the establishment of a Panel.[16]

The consultation stage is obviously a diplomatic means to solve disputes, but how to understand the phrase 'even upon the establishment of

14 The WTO Agreements consist of goods, services, intellectual property, and investment. They involve cultural, educational, environmental, healthy, labour and human rights aspects. In addition, the WTO is truly a universal organisation, which needs to harmonise among 148 Member states.

15 Cottier, T. Dispute Settlement in the World Trade Organisation: Characteristics and Structural Implications for the European Union, C.M.L.Rev 1998; 35(2); 335.

16 *Ibid.*, p. 337.

a Panel'?[17] Panels should "make findings as will assist the DSB in making the recommendations or in the rulings provided for in the covered agreements. Panel should consult regularly with the parties to the dispute and give them adequate opportunity to develop a mutually satisfactory solution".[18] This provision reflects the traditional conciliatory functions of the Panel. Again in his experience, legal dispute settlement may only be introduced to 'tip' the balance of power with a view to bringing about a negotiated settlement, and this strategy does not impair the legal quality of the Panel process.

The second stage is the Panel stage. During this, parties can continue to negotiate; in some disputes a settlement has been reached. Nevertheless, if a Panel report has to be issued, the reasoning of the Panel is always and has to be legal. Cottier's evaluation of the balance of law and diplomacy is realistic. His attitude to dispute settlement procedures is modest. From his perspective, the 'balance theory' helps to avoid abusing the litigation aspect of the system in any sense.

Horlick's comments express the opinion that consultation once was, now is and, in the future will remain an important way to solve disputes, as a diplomatic means, to be used by Member states.

The argument about the consultation as a mid-way station on the road to a Panel rather than as a means of final settlement has been debated for a long time.[19] Horlick claims there are alternative functions of consultation other than settlement.

17 *Ibid.*, pp. 337–338.

18 Article 11 of the DSU.

19 In July 2000 there was a special issue of the Law and Policy in International Business about the proceedings of a symposium on the first five years of the operation of the WTO. The purpose of the symposium was to convene a group of experienced and knowledgeable individuals to review the performance of the WTO to date. One of the sections during the symposium was a review of the operation of the DSU. In regard to consultation, the key issue raised was whether the system helps to solve disputes before their going to a Panel. Some sentiment was expressed that the system in this area was working adequately. However, the strongest opinion by far was that more and more cases were going to a Panel and the parties were coming to view the consultation process as a pro forma step, rather than as an opportunity to resolve disputes as provided under the Article 4 of the DSU. There were three articles about consultation in that symposium, which were presented by Horlick, Parlin and Wethington respectively. See Wethington, O. L. Commentary on the Consultation Mechanism under the WTO Dispute Settlement Understanding During its First Five Years, 31LPIB 2000; 583: from WESTLAW.

Horlick proposes that consultations can serve as 'action forcing events' for the two governments to rethink the merits of their cases and their desirability of moving forward. In some cases, settlement can occur at any time, not just in pre-Panel consultation.[20]

The consultation can be treated as a forum for exchanging data in private. Member states can seek to gather useful information, explaining their factual arguments or political needs, making their legal and factual arguments to try and avoid a Panel, resolving uncertainties about the scope and nature of the measures at issue and eliminating fruitless or invalid claims.[21] As a matter of fact, WTO dispute settlement procedures have to include the option for governments to consult in private as in the consultation procedure. They need to make all possible efforts privately before the adjudicatory procedure(s) start.

The consultation as a prerequisite is a significant means of focusing the dispute, and setting up the case to facilitate the Panel's work (similar to the role of pre-trial conferences between parties in domestic litigation).[22] Although Davey advocates a rule-oriented dispute resolution system, he acknowledges that to some extent consultation cannot be ignored. He structures his paper by the methodology of a skilful presenter of case studies who has rich statistical resources.

He concedes that consultation can be useful, particularly for smaller countries whose needs for dialogue might be ignored by the larger players in the system. The larger players Davey referred to are developed countries, particularly Australia, Canada, Japan, the US and EU. The smaller countries he referred to are developing countries or LDCs that have certain GDP levels not limited to the size of national territory.

The dispute settlement system as a whole reflects an ecological balance between settlement values and enforcement values. Settlement values support the complainant or respondent who wants to have a private discussion without non-relevant parties such as arbitrators. Enforcement values support the quasi-working party approach of plurilateral Article

20 The *EC – Trade Description of Scallops* case was settled at the course of the Panel (WT/DS7). See Part III.

21 The US in the *Shrimp/ Turtle* case is a good example to demonstrate these points (WT/DS58/R).

22 Davey, W. J. & Porges, A. Performance of the System I: Consultations & Deterrence, International Law 1998; 32:695 from WESTLAW.

XXII consultation. 'Balance theory' is applied again to explain one of the functions within consultation.

B. *Views of Economists*

Most economists share the view that the best way to settle trade disputes is through an out-of-court agreement; the consultation period is in large part intended for that purpose.[23] One article written by Butler and Hauser constructs the theoretical model of WTO dispute settlement procedures.

At the beginning, they introduce the participating players: the defendant (D) is a country which has taken an action (trade restriction) and is subsequently accused of violating WTO law by a complainant (C), who files the suit.[24]

Then, the game begins. In the background is D who introduces a trade-related measure, C requires to consult D afterwards, then goes to Panel, or furthermore sues AB, and the final step is the implementation stage.

Next, they build up their payoff model structure including directly trade-related gains and losses, reputation gains and losses and litigation costs. They analyse four stages, which are consultation, a Panel, the AB and implementation in the line of this payoff model, and quote 38 cases to prove the scientificity of this model.

Finally, they conclude by the methods of model-prediction and empirical evidence as follows:[25]

1) The preventive power of WTO dispute settlement system is too limited to discourage new trade restrictions. A complaint is only filed if

23 Most of them use the game theory, particularly the prison dilemma case to explain why the early settlement/out-of-court agreement is the best choice. There are four possibilities to get the final result, which includes win/win, lose/win, win/lose and lost/lose. It is clear that the outcome of the settlement resolved after litigation could be win/lose, lose/win, or lose/lose (no implementation). That is to say, the win/win situation only takes place in mutually agreed solution stage because two parties more or less get something. However, it is impossible to reach win/win situation after rulings by courts.

24 Buetler, M. & Hauser, H. The WTO Dispute Settlement System: A First Assessment from an Economic Perspective, Journal of Law, Economics, and Organisation 2000; 16(2): 503–510.

25 *Ibid*., pp. 527–528.

the probability of winning is sufficiently high. By the end of 2000 there had been 219 cases on files, in which settled by a Panel or AB reports were 55, accounting for 25.1%.[26] By the end of 2001 the number of cases had been 242, out of which 62 were resolved by Panel or AB reports accounting for 25.6%.[27] By the end of 2002, there had been 276 disputes, 72 of which had been settled by adopted Panel or AB reports, accounting for 26.1%.[28] By the end of 2003, there had been 305 complaints, of which 81 had been resolved by Panel or AB reports, accounting for 26.5%.[29]

2) There is a strong tendency for the losing government to appeal Panel decisions, even if the chances of a revision are slim. An appeal delays the implementation of negative findings, and suits the interests of domestic groups.[30] Moreover, according to the statistics, as of 1 January 2001, 49 Panel reports had been issued, among which 10 were not appealed; AB reports were invoked 78%.[31] As of 1 January 2002, 57 Panel reports had been issued, among which 14 were not appealed; AB reviews were invoked 75%.[32] As of 1 January 2003, the percentage of Panel reports that had been appealed is 72%.[33] As of 1 January 2004, the percentage of Panel reports is 71.6%.[34]

3) In clear-cut cases, the results of bilateral settlements should be similar to the expected rulings of the DSB. Bilateral settlement is the most economical way to solve a dispute. Direct trade gains and losses are reduced in relation to the litigation time saved, the losing party can avoid reputation losses by agreeing upon a mutually accepted solution

26 Park, Y. D. & Umbricht, G. C. WTO Dispute Settlement 1995–2000: A Statistical Analysis, J.I.E.L. 2001; 4(1): 217.

27 Park, Y. D. & Panizzon, M. WTO Dispute Settlement 1995–2001: A Statistical Analysis, J.I.E.L. 2002; 5(1): 227.

28 Leitner, S. & Lester, K. WTO Dispute Settlement 1995–2002: A Statistical Analysis, J.I.E.L. 2003; 6(1): 252.

29 Leitner, S. & Lester, K. WTO Dispute Settlement 1995–2003: A Statistical Analysis, J.I.E.L. 2004; 7(1): 170.

30 The FSC case between the US and EC with an affected trade volume of several billion dollars gains due to the delay in the procedure before the end of reasonable period of implementation time.

31 Park & Umbricht 2001; 219.

32 Park & Panizzon 2002; 230.

33 Leitner & Lester 2003; 255.

34 Leitner & Lester 2004; 175.

> and litigation costs will be the lowest. The statistics strongly support this model. Among 103 settled complaints by the end of 2000, 48 were resolved in other ways apart from litigation procedure(s), of which 32 were solved by bilateral settlement, sharing 31% of the whole settlement.[35] Among 128 settled complaints by the end of 2001, 58 were solved in other ways of which 39 were settled bilaterally, sharing 30%.[36]

The 'cost accounting' leads to the conclusion that settlement by litigation is neither the only method nor the one that provides satisfactory results. What we should be concerned with is, how to solve disputes effectively and efficiently – either by diplomatic or legal means. Although the model construction is not a legal analytical method, it gives a direct and clear perception of the pros and cons of settlement through adjudication. As developing countries are mostly concerned about their unfavourable position economically, this model provides theoretical evidence for these Member states to understand whether litigation is truly necessary in specific cases, especially from an economic point of view.

C. *Views from Political Science (Systematic Assessment)*

In Busch and Reinhardt's article their observations are different from Davey's. They found, during the GATT period, that highly democratic countries (e.g. the US, Canada) were up to 21% more likely to settle their disputes co-operatively in consultation compared to states that are not fully domestic countries (e.g. Mexico, Guatemala).[37]

Through their statistics and a WTO survey, by the end of April 2002, there had been 35 disputes settled by mutually agreed solutions out of 153 active complaints, accounting for 23%, of which 32 cases involved 'big players', accounting for 91%. The results seem to lead in the opposite direction to Davey's observation.

Bush and Reinhardt's general opinion is that defendants tend to offer the greatest concessions in the consultation stage, or at the Panel stage

35 Park & Umbricht 2001; 218.

36 Park & Panizzon 2002; 229.

37 Busch, M. & Reinhardt, E. Bargaining in the Shadow of the Law: Early Settlement in GATT/WTO Dispute, 24 FDM.I.L.J. 2000; 158: from WESTLAW.

before a ruling. Interestingly, their analysis is combined with economic (e.g. statistical, model), legal (e.g. case study, textual interpretation) and political perspectives, although it is categorised as 'political views' concerning their background. They use a compelling combination to attain their empirical research objective. Moreover, their research is ecologically balanced, given developed Members and developing parties.

1. *Dispute between the US and the EC*

The outcomes of US-EC cases have not demonstrated any improvement of legal reforms *per se*. According to statistics until 2001, a large majority, 58%, of US-EC disputes had been solved during consultations or Panel deliberations.[38] In their view, this percentage speaks to the significance of early settlement under the WTO, and is entirely in keeping with figures drawn from empirical work looking at all GATT-era disputes.[39] So, their first observation to the US-EC is to compare WTO with GATT and dispute results.

The second finding is that the frequency of early settlement in WTO disputes is probably driven not by any improved threat of enforcement, but by diplomacy and the normative weight of the institution.

Their empirical quantitative findings include:

Defendants are 22% less likely to concede in multilateral as opposed to purely bilateral disputes; 43% less likely to concede in SPS or cultural cases; 33% more likely to concede in cases involving purely discriminatory measures; 24% more likely to concede in agricultural cases.[40]

A ruling for the defendant reduces the probability of full concessions by about 63%; a mixed ruling by 43%; even a ruling for the complainant reduces the chances of concessions by roughly 25%.[41]

More to their point, the majority of US-EC disputes under TRIPS have centered on the phase-in of commitments that were already in progress. The DSU boasts a poor track record in resolving high stakes US-EC disputes, and has hardly proved effective when given a second 'kick

38 *Ibid.*

39 Busch, M. L. & Reinhardt, E. Transatlantic Trade Conflicts and GATT/WTO Dispute Settlement in Petersmann, E. (ed.), Dispute Prevention and Dispute Settlement in the Transatlantic Partnership, Florence: EUI, 2002; 6.

40 *Ibid.*, p. 12.

41 *Ibid.*, pp. 12–13.

at the can' in those disputes, but the true measure of the success of a dispute settlement mechanism is how it handles the toughest cases. These high-stakes disputes include *Hormones, Banana, FSC,* and *Anti-Dumping Act of 1916*.[42]

They also found that those GATT cases recurred under the WTO, but the record is no better than that of the GATT. For example, the GATT *DISC*[43] ruling was criticised for its legal incoherence, and the parties were blocked from adoption for many years. The WTO ruling on the FSC allowed the EC to force the issue to retaliate against the US. Both of the cases were brought by the EC against US tax practices that subsidised exports, along with the accompanying counter-complaints by the US against alleged similar EC Member state subsidies. Thus, the WTO legalism has not induced any more change from the *status quo* US policy than the GATT complaint did.[44]

They then concluded that the real action in US-EC disputes is in early settlement. Furthermore, they implied that it is easier to achieve a compromise which may be relatively less transparent, is consultations. Since after rulings, pressure from legislators and industries at home will invariably be greater, if for no other reason than any post-ruling will leave a clear paper trail, and policy changes at that point are more likely to require implementing legislation.[45]

2. *Disputes involving Developing Members*

Contrary to the data of the developed Members, developing parties have not benefited as much under the WTO as their counterparts. They note that parties can no longer significantly delay or block the establishment of Panels, which means that legal preparation carries more weight in the pre-Panel bargaining process.

42 What they mean by the high stake or toughest case is annual affected trade levels or authorised retaliation levels above 150 million USD and/or intense perceived significance for the future of WTO dispute settlement or the US-EC trading relationship.

43 See Part II.

44 Busch & Reinhardt 2002; 12–15.

45 Busch, M. L. & Reinhardt, E. Testing International Trade Law: Empirical Studies of GATT/WTO Dispute Settlement, in Kennedy, D. L. M. & Southwick, J. D. (ed.), The Political Economy of International Trade Law: Essays in Honour of Robert E. Hudec, Cambridge: CUP, 2002; 477.

The new premium on legal capacity under the DSU is less burdensome for most of the advanced industrial states, since they generally maintain large, dedicated, permanent legal and economic staff tasked with WTO and trade law matters. However, most developing countries lack market size and, thus, retaliatory power, also legal capacity. Busch discloses that, even for some developed Members, the costs of legal work related to trade disputes have mushroomed in recent years. For instance, expenditures by the Canadian Department of Foreign Affairs and International Trade on just the private component of legal representation for trade disputes tripled from 2000 to 2002 alone.

They argue that legal capacity as evidenced by the level of development, ironically matters less once the parties resolve to use litigation rather than a settlement option because its effects on litigation performance are largely realised during consultations. Therefore, the problem is that developing-country complainants are losing out in pre-litigation negotiations rather than losing verdicts after litigation.

Developing countries have, in fact, been more active in WTO dispute settlement and more likely to have Panel disputes against developed countries. However, a poor plaintiff – i.e. a plaintiff possessing less legal capacity or facing higher transaction costs, relative to the potential winnings of the case – might file weaker cases on average in the first place, or might lose 'winnable' cases more often if it went to trial. While complainants, for whom litigation is costly or difficult, would be less likely to induce early settlement by defendants, they may not be any less likely to win the verdicts ultimately issued.

Hence, Busch and Reinhardt draw two conclusions: first, under the WTO poorer complainants are likely to have become significantly less able to induce early settlement by defendants than wealthy complainants; second, developing countries are disadvantaged in achieving early settlement because of their limited legal capacity and not their inability to threaten retaliation. This is because the main obstacle to retaliation is the mustering of the political will to follow through an authorisation, rather than securing it. The DSU has merely improved the latter.[46]

According to statistical data until the end of 2000, 50% of disputes ended with substantial concessions, 20% with partial concessions, 31%

46 Busch, M. L. & Reinhardt, E. Developing Countries and General Agreement on Tariffs and Trade/WTO Dispute Settlement, 37(4) J.W.T 2003; 719:722–723.

with no concessions.[47] Notwithstanding, they did not clearly define what 'substantial concessions', 'partial concessions' and 'no concessions' mean. Since most of their data is in line with Hudec's empirical research, these categories are assumed to be similar to his work. Hence, according to Hudec:

> Full satisfaction describes cases where the legal claim has been fully (or most fully) vindicated, usually by removing a measure found to be in violation of GATT.
>
> The partial satisfaction category consists of those cases in which some significant remedial action was taken by the defendant, short of complete removal but sufficient to justify treating the legal claim as having been successful.
>
> Negative outcome describes cases in which the legal system has failed to enforce a valid claim.[48]

Developed Members shifted from an initially comparable success rate of 40% (under the GATT) to a remarkable 74% (under the WTO) through their prior experience. However, the developing countries changed from 36% under the GATT to 50% under the WTO. To this point, they believe that the relatively small gains for developing country complainants moving from the GATT to the WTO thus overstate the likely effects of the reforms for more typical developing states.[49]

Factors for getting full concessions or to make the dispute easier/harder to resolve include the complainant's income, its GDP, characteristics of the defendant, WTO Panel formation and rulings and observable aspects of the disputed policy.[50]

Another imbalanced behaviour is seen with wealthier complainants who have dramatically increased the proportion of their complaints filed against developing countries from 8% to 37% in the GATT versus the WTO eras. Poor defendants are significantly more likely to concede, thus suggesting that many gains from richer complainants have been made in inducing concessions from poor defendants under the WTO.[51]

However, a developing Member may not able to compel the defendant to liberalise even with a legal victory in hand since its threat to re-

47 *Ibid.*, p. 725.

48 Hudec, R. E. Enforcing International Trade Law: the Evolution of the Modern GATT Legal System, Salem, NH. Butterworth Legal Publishers, 1993; 276.

49 Busch & Reinhardt 2003; 725–726.

50 *Ibid.*, pp. 726–730.

51 *Ibid.*, p. 730.

taliate lacks credibility.[52] In the *Banana* case, for example, although Ecuador was authorised to retaliate against the EC, it actually did not impose tariffs on the EC's exports. This is not surprising because Ecuador lacks a big enough market size to exert much influence on the defendant.

The primary difficulty from the poor complainant's standpoint, 'lies early in a dispute's origins, not in litigation once embarked upon, nor in the retaliatory endgame, despite the oft-noted (and valid) point that weak market power severely curtails a complainant's leverage, even if it wins a ruling'.[53] This may deter developing Members from filing complaints. A developing country might also be reluctant to initiate a dispute because of fears of reprisals such as the suspension of foreign aid or unilateral trade preferences.[54]

Afterwards, they suggest that the complainant's level of development speaks directly to its capacity for recognising, and aggressively pursuing, legal opportunities as a complainant.[55]

The methodologies used by the US and EC analysis, are similatr in that they raise an hypothesis, then create models and tables through economic formulae and theory, and finally deduce their opinions by legal and political implication.

All in all, they try to demonstrate that past successes of the dispute settlement system measured in terms of the level of liberalisation on the part of the defendant, make all Members less likely to file new complaints. The intuition about complaints being the result of 'growing confidence' in the dispute settlement system is misleading. Instead, the ballooning caseload is mostly a function of the expansion of the organisation and of world trade more generally; disputes are just as likely to be responses to the failure rather than success of the adjudication system.

52 Busch, M. L. & Reinhardt, E. The WTO Dispute Settlement Mechanism and Developing Countries, from http://userwww.service.emory.edu/~erein/research/SIDA.pdf, p. 3, last visited 30 December 2004.

53 Busch & Reinhardt 2003; 732.

54 Busch & Reinhardt 2000; 165.

55 This capacity they referred to can be widely understood as legal capacity, because they further explain that having this capacity, a complainant is in a much better position to hit the right legal buttons in the request for consultations, to pressure the defendant on its weakest legal points during consultations, and to give the impression that the issue might well be pushed to a successful conclusion. See Busch & Reinhardt 2003; 732.

In addition, as three-quarters of disputes ending at pre-ruling stage yield at least partial concessions from the defendant, the consultation meets the purpose of international dispute settlement.[56]

They intend to agree that the stages of legal activity per dispute, such as appeals, compliance reviews and compensation arbitration merely find an excuse for defendants to add a potential two years or more to legally permissible delay in complying with adverse rulings. Furthermore, they believe that the involvement of third parties or additional disputants reduced the prospects for concessions by a defendant.

However, what they point out is one side of the law rather than whole picture. It is useful to be more rounded. Law as a defensive system in disputes is not perfect. Diplomacy or politics is also logically incomplete. In a perfect world, they would be interactive rather than overstating the case for either one.

The major debate about orientation of dispute settlement helps to integrate WTO law, lays invaluable practical and theoretical foundations through conscientiously dedicated research. The various research methods enrich this field as well, with methods that include observation, comparison, case study, model-construction, treaty interpretation, textual analysis, metaphor and critical legal study.

Alternative functions of consultation have been summarised by many practitioners especially by lawyers in their literature, which possesses an important reference value. At the same time, the diplomatic method has its own dispute settlement system, different from adjudicatory systems and not limited to solving disputes in ways that are similar to theirs.

III. GATT/WTO Dispute Settlement in China: A Literature Review

The concept 'rule of law' has only recently begun to resonate in China mainly through the country's agreement to settle disputes using the WTO dispute settlement mechanism.

56 *Ibid.*, p. 725.

'Globalisation' in Chinese and most Asian people's view can be regarded as the dominance of Western economic and cultural interests over the rest of the world.

In the name of globalisation, economic development has reconstructed traditional social norms. Although 'Western' legal systems and thoughts have greatly influenced China, fundamental differences remain. The dispute settlement system in the WTO based on 'the rule of law' or 'rule orientation', challenges the traditional Chinese belief of 'rule by law'. The dispute settlement mechanism, under the old GATT regime, aiming at lowering tensions, defusing conflicts and promising diplomatic orientation, was consistent with the spirit of Chinese culture.

A. *Overview*

Systematic research on GATT/WTO dispute settlement in China is from the mid-1980s.[57] Nevertheless, Chinese academia and practitioners made their contributions in order to catch up with the 'world level'. What they expect is to master the 'rules of the game' of dispute resolution and the WTO law, especially how to adapt the WTO legal system to their domestic legal system so as to keep on the right track according to the interpretation of current Chinese law, (and on how to adapt to a 'new trade' and legal environment). In general, their research direction is primarily to enhance international competitive abilities and to make profits from international trade.

Although China was not the CP of the GATT and not a Member of the WTO until 11 December 2001, it is a major participant, particularly a defendant, in international trade cases.[58] The Chinese government expects to protect its legitimate rights and interests through WTO entry.Differing from Western experts in their attitude to dispute settlement orientation, Chinese scholars tend to adopt eclecticism, which means they welcome the rule-orientation and do not reject diplomatic orientation, toaccord with Chinese situations and the cultural influences of

57 Later, China applied to entry into the WTO.

58 Plenty of complaints from the US and EC are on the field of dumping investigation. Many articles from other WTO Member states criticise the dumping conduct of Chinese government ignoring Chinese national conditions at the moment. Due to the cheaper labour resource, China is always a victim in international trade area.

deep-rooted Confucism.[59] The Golden Means is different from most western theories that rigorously stick to either rule orientation or diplomatic orientation. It looks like the 'balance theory' to some extent.

Chinese legal scholars working in the WTO field, usually begin with trade freedom[60] and comparative superiority theories[61] from the economists Adam Smith and David Ricardo[62] at the end of 18th century. Marxist theories on or related to legal issues also play a leading role, in such as the theory of economic base. The aim of the WTO is to promote the free flow of international trade, which cannot be divorced from economic considerations. From this perspective, authors argue that the jurisdictional interpretation of the WTO agreements must follow economic and political theories if they are to be more persuasive and effective.

Similar to their colleagues in the West, Chinese scholars put their efforts on research of dispute settlement procedures into theory and practice.

B. *Dispute Settlement Mechanism through Case Study: China's Behaviour*

Many scholars note that trade conflicts are expected to arise with China, since it is difficult for that country to meet all of its obligations in the short term.

It is a newly emerging research field for Chinese scholars because China only recently joined the WTO. Therefore, it is early days for Chinese researchers, especially in the dispute resolution field, since there are only two complete cases involving China (although China has surprisingly participated in 31 other disputes as a third party, as of 30 April

59 See Kong, Q. J. Will China Behave well in the WTO Dispute Settlement Mechanism: the Law and Practice of the Chinese Approach to Trade Disputes?; Yang, G. H., What will it mean to China after entry into the WTO; Zhao, W. T. WTO and China; Zou, R. The WTO and Regional Integration, on website:http://chinalawinfo.com/research/public/article_search.asp last visited 31 December 2004.

60 See Smith, A. The Wealth of Nations, London: Penguin Book, 1999.

61 See Ricardo, D. Principles of Political Economy and Taxation, Amherst (NY): Prometheus Books, 1996.

62 Both of them were against mercantilism which was popular throughout the world at that time.

2005).[63] Generally speaking, the aims of their research are to master the rules of dispute settlement procedures, and to guide the national government in understanding these new legal rules so they can fully participate in the international economic system without violating international regulations. Will China be the next major litigious target, after Korea and India? In laborious negotiations with the other 142 Member states, particularly with the US and the EC, China made many promises in its entry protocol.[64]

However, like other Members, a problem for China in formulating its policies is that it must do so in consideration of international, national and local interests. A genuine consideration in adopting trade policies is the requirement to understand the effect of institutional change in policy, socio-economic and legal institutions and the impact of China's ontological base in tradition or Confucianism. In terms of Western universalism and litigation consciousness, China obviously cannot be an exception. Trade disputes are certain to occur between China and other Member states, and China has begun referring to the WTO rules to protect its perceived interests.

Nevertheless, a powerful Chinese legal tradition is to pursue a voluntary and consultative dispute resolution mechanism, which is based on harmony, ambiguity and flexibility. These features reflect Chinese traditional values, and are unlikely to be completely changed in the short term.

It is true that WTO rules help China establish an integrated legal framework in order to meet some universally recognised regulations and to remedy domestic legitimate inadequacies. However, it is not necessary to overstate the 'Western litigious approach' and weaken the 'Chinese/ Asian non-litigious approach' to resolve disputes in the WTO.

Not surprisingly, China has scuffled with its major trade partners due to its trade surges. The US, EC, Korea and Japan have been encountering disputes with China for a long time.

63 WT/DS252, *United States – Definitive Safeguard Measures on Imports of Certain Steel Products*. However, at the same time, China was involved in one case as a respondent, WT/DS309, *China – Value Added Tax on Integrated Circuits*, and is involved in another as a joint complainant, WT/DS301/2, *European Communities – Measures Affecting Trade in Commercial Vessels* – Request to Join Consultations.

64 Protocol on the Accession of the People's Republic of China, WT/L/432, Decision of 10 November 2001.

1. *China – US Dispute over Textile Transhipment*[65]

This is a case where the dispute was settled with concessions by China.

China is the third largest supplier of imported textile and apparel products in the US, after Mexico and Canada. Textile exports account for about 10% of the overall Chinese exports to the US. In February 1997, China and the US concluded an agreement on textile trade. Under this four-year agreement, the US promised to raise quotas for Chinese textile imports in exchange for Chinese promises to reduce tariffs and non-tariff barriers to US textile imports and to crack down on transhipments.

However, on 5 May 1998, the US announced it would impose punitive charges of US$5 million because of actions that resulted in the export of textiles to the US via third countries to escape quotas. China claimed that the US was in violation of the bilateral agreement by unilaterally deducting the quotas. After several negotiations for solving the dispute, China finally did not resort to retaliation. Instead, it tightened its enforcement of the rule against transhipments.

2. *China – EU Dispute over the Interpretation of Trade Agreement*[66]

This case ended in an agreed solution based on China's concession.

The Agreement on Trade and Economic Co-operation between the EU and China is the guiding agreement on trade relationships. However, this agreement does not contain a provision for the resolution of disputes and, therefore, no reference can be made to this agreement to solve trade disputes between the two parties.

In 1994, China and the EU reached agreement on administrative production for pharmaceutical and agrochemical product inventions. At the conclusion of the agreement, the EU consisted of 12 Member States.

65 Under the November 1999 US-China WTO agreement, the US agreed to end its textile and apparel quotas on Chinese products in 2005, while China agreed to allow the United States to utilise a special safeguard provision once China entered the WTO until 2008 that would allow it to impose restraints on textile and apparel imports from China if such imports caused market disruptions to US domestic producers.The detailed information about textile transhipment and market access issues between the US and China is in Morrison, WM. China-US Trade Agreements: Compliance Issues, http://www.usc.cuhk.edu.hk/wk_wzdetails.asp?id=3142 last visited 20 December 2004.

66 See http://www.businessnewsguide.com/feb28ec.htm for detail, last visited 20 December 2004.

When, later, three other States, i.e. Austria, Finland and Sweden, acceded to the EU, the Chinese authorities followed previous performances (given a restrictive interpretation) and, thus, denied administrative protection to applicants from these new Members.

Since then, the EC raised the issue of equal treatment to these particular three on several occasions. In June 2000, EU Commissioner Pascal Lamy requested urgent action for equal treatment of all Member States from China's trade Minister Shi Guangsheng. At the subsequent EU-China Joint Committee in October 2000, Minister Shi agreed in principle to an extension. In February 2001, the two sides reached final agreement to end this long-running dispute on China's extension of three new EU Member States through a seven-year-negotiation.

3. *China – Korea Dispute over Garlic Export*[67]

This is a case where China and its counterpart agreed on a mutual solution, with Korea making more concessions.

China was the third largest trade partner of Korea, and Korea the fourth trade partner of China. The total volume of the trade between the two countries has exceeded US$300 billion in 2000.

In 1999, there was a 30% drop in garlic prices in Korea, and the Korean farmerblamed cheap foreign imports. The Korean Finance and Economy Ministry issued its No. 141 order on May 31, 2000, which declared that, starting from 1 June 2000, Korea would adopt limitation measures on garlic imports and a tariff rate as high as 315% would be levied on imported garlic.

China is the major garlic exporter to Korea. Therefore, China thought Korea's limitation on garlic import was targeted at China. China argued that the assertion that the increase of garlic imports caused a reduction in garlic prices and damaged the garlic industry in Korea was unjustified. China claimed that any damage to Korea's garlic industry was caused entirely by the sharp increase of its garlic production at home rather than the minor increase of its imports.

The Chinese government further asserted that the unilateral measures not only seriously obstructed China's garlic export and affected the nor-

67 See Synder, S. The Insatiable Sino-Korean Economic Relationship: Too Much for Seoul to Swallow? http://www.csis.org/pacfor/cc/003Qchina_skorea.html last visited 22 December 2004.

mal development of bilateral trade, from which China had sustained huge amount of deficits for a long time, but also did not accord with the regulations of the WTO.[68]

China thus announced its suspension of the import of Korean mobile telephones and polyethylene on 7 June 2000. A dispute arose between the two Asian countries.

After six weeks, China announced the lifting of its ban on import of mobile phones and polyethylene from Korea after the two countries reached an agreement on garlic trade. The decision was made as the two parties reached an agreement after several diplomatic consultations.

Under this agreement, Korea would import 32,000 tons of Chinese garlic at low tariffs in 2000, and the amount would grow by 5.25% annually within a term of three years. For the purpose of implementing this agreement, the Chinese Ministry of Foreign Trade and Economic Cooperation (MOFTEC)[69] promulgated the 'Provisional Rules on Management of Export of Garlic to South Korea' to regulate and rectify garlic exports to Korea.

4. *China – Japan Dispute over Agricultural Products*[70]

This is another dispute to be settled with the other disputant making concessions.

Japan is China's largest trade partner and China is Japan's second, without much of an imbalance, importing US$41.7 billion goods from China and exporting US$41.5 billion in 2000.

On 11 April 2001, Japan decided to impose temporary restrictions on the imports of Chinese leeks, mushrooms and straw for a period of 200 days starting from 23 April 2001. China protested that Japan used double standards, which were against the principle of fairness. From the Chinese perspective, the Japanese decision was politically motivated.

The MOFTEC further argued that the Japanese decision ran against the WTO rules in several respects, namely the selection of products to

68 China at that time was not a Member State of the WTO, but Korea is.

69 MOFTEC was changed under the name of "Ministry of Commerce of the People's Republic of China".

70 See http://www.japantoday.com/gidx/news36341.html for further information, last visited 22 December 2004.

investigate, the basic conditions to impose the protective measures, the objectivity of the decisions and some others.

While strongly urging Japan tosuspend the restrictions, China threatened that a possible retaliation would be imminent if Japan did not. Japan responded that imposed safeguard measures are in the WTO rules, which precluded retaliation. Furthermore, Japan decided from 7 June to temporarily stop the importation of Chinese poultry on alleged 'bird flu' fears, while China denied any local outbreak of the virus.

On 19 June, China announced it would impose prohibitively high tariffs on imports of Japanese cars, mobile phones and air conditioners, with a value of about US$500 million. China required the Japanese to immediately correct its wrong decision and discriminatory actions against China's export goods.

However, the extra tariffs were not expected to have much influence on Japanese manufacturers, since the majority of brands are produced in China through joint ventures. The Chinese move was believed to be more symbolic than anything else.

Japanese Prime Minister Junichiro Koizumi, in markedly milder language, urged calm. He thought it appropriate to listen to the Chinese arguments carefully and hold talks to improve the situation in a calm and constructive manner.

The two parties afterwards engaged in talks. The signals from Japan made one speculate whether the trade dispute could be resolved without resorting to a war of retaliation.

5. *US – Steel Safeguards*

On 26 March 2002, China requested consultations with the US, with regard to the definitive safeguard measures imposed by the US on imports of certain steel products. The US measures were in the form of increased duties and a tariff rate quota ranging from 8 to 30%, which became effective on 20 March 2003 for a period of three years.[71]

This case is a special one, since the US restricted steel imports from the rest of the world including the EC, Brazil, Japan, Korea, New Zealand, Norway and Switzerland. There is no such thing as a US steel industry crisis, but only a crisis of an integrated and politically powerful

71 See WT/DS252/1, *United States – Definitive Safeguard Measures on Imports of Certain Steel Products* – Request for Consultations by China.

sector of the industry. The US frequently attributed its industry's difficulties to competition from subsidised imports and opposed the financing of new plants by international lending organisations such as the World Bank. The expansion of the mini mill sector in the US had been encouraged by subsidies from governments and local communities. In fact, these mills had always significantly lagged behind their competitors. Consequently, there is no American company amongst the world's ten largest steel firms. However, the US announced safeguard measures for mostly political reasons.[72]

In this case, because of US political alignments, the consultation became an extra proceeding for these co-complainants, so givingthe US time to delay removing the inconsistent measures.

6. *China – VAT on Integrated Circuits*

On 18 March 2004, the US filed the first case against China at the WTO regarding China's value-added tax (VAT) on integrated circuits (ICs). Before that date, the USTR warned that America would take its case against China to the WTO because the administration had been pressed to file the case by the US$70 billion semiconductor industry in the US.

China had a 17% VAT on ICs, but enterprises in China were entitled to a partial refund of this. The US further claimed that China allowed a partial refund of VAT for domestically designed ICs that, because of technical limitations, were manufactured outside China.[73]

According to US media, China and its trade policies dominated much of the economic debate during 2004, presidential election year, and the move was seen as a way for the administration to counter accusations from Democrats that it was not doing enough to protect American workers. The Commerce Secretary and the USTR representative travelled to China to convey the message that the US was losing its patience with China's refusal to adapt more quickly to WTO rules. Chinese officials told a senior administration official that they would not lift the tax on

72 See WTO Dispute Settlement, Case Involving the EU, WT/DS248, Other Information, in http://trade–info.cec.eu.int/wtodispute/show.cfm?id=166&code=1 last visited 10 December 2004.

73 See WT/DS309/1, *China – Value-Added Tax on Integrated Circuits* – Request for Consultations by the US.

foreign semiconductors. This paved the way for the case filed by the US.[74]

Foreign imports account for 80% of China's IC market, which is valued at US$19 billion – the third largest in the world. China's semiconductor industry is growing. Meanwhile, the chip industry in the US employs 255,000 Americans, according to the Semiconductor Industry Association, and US companies have a 50% share of the world market. The USTR noted that, while US exports to China support more jobs for American workers, and they faced a number of persistent problems that must be resolved. Some critics argued that the case filed was politically motivated because of a rising trade deficit with China.[75]

In China's view, this filing was sudden and non-understandable, since there had been several rounds of negotiations between the two countries on the right track over this issue, which had gained some improvement.[76]

On 26 March, 31 March and 1 April, the EC, Japan, Taiwan and Mexico requested joint consultations.

The consultations were held on 27 April 2004 between China and the US in Geneva to exchange information without substantial improvement. However, China disclosed it might adjust some refunding policies of VAT on ICs. Afterwards, they culminated several rounds of discussions between negotiators and legal experts from the two countries meeting in Washington and Beijing where they approached the final agreement.[77]

On 14 July 2004, China and the US notified the DSB that they reached an agreement:[78]

By 1 November 2004, China would amend the measures to eliminate the availability of VAT refunds to firms producing ICs in China on their

74 See Becker, E. US Files A Complaint Against China At the WTO, 19 March 2004, http://query.nytimes.com/gst/abstract.html?res=F20D10F738550C7A8DDDAA0894DC404482 last visited 8 December 2004.

75 *Ibid.*

76 See Wen, Y. Trade Conflict between China and the US Upgrades and China Feels Surprised, 20 March 2004, in http://tech.sina.com.cn/other/2004-03-20/0928336599. shtml last visited 9 December 2004.

77 See Mills, R. & Moorjani, N. US, China Settle Dispute Over Semiconductor Tax Refunds: China to Stop Refunds Favouring China-Designed Circuits, 08 July 2004, http://hongkong.usconsulate.gov/uscn/trade/general/ustr/2004/070801.htm last visited9 December 2004.

78 See WT/DS309/7, *China – Value-Added Tax on Integrated Circuits* – Joint Communication from China and the US.

domestic sales. The effective date of these amendments will be no later than 1 April 2005. Until the effective date of these amendments, VAT refunds will be available only to IC enterprises certified under the measures as of 14 July 2004.

By 1 September 2004, China would issue a notice to revoke the measure that provides for VAT refunds on ICs designed in China but manufactured abroad. The effective date of revocation will be no later than 1 October 2004.

According to Chinese media, China will work out other policies, which encourage building up domestic IC production so as to compete with foreign products conforming to WTO rules.[79]

This did not merely apply to *the Art of War* going back 2500 years.[80] Instead, it worked within today's field of international dispute settlement.

Through the above case studies against big players within or outside the WTO dispute settlement framework, one has reason to believe that the Chinese response has brought a pause rather than an escalation to disputes. The impact of the traditional legal culture in China is undoubtedly maintained.

As a matter of fact, DSU should not be too legalistic for China, because DSU ratified and legitimised some of the practices under the GATT. On the contrary, the Chinese non-litigious approach may influence future reforms of DSU (although on the domestic level China is reconstructing the rule of law). A good example is the dispute settlement mechanism in Asian-Pacific Economic Co-operation (APEC).

In international arenas, such as the WTO, Asian countries have no choice but to adjust to the so-called 'Western legal culture'. The numerical dominance and growing significance of Asian countries, however, alters the international dynamics within APEC. APEC's dispute settlement mechanism is a voluntary and consultative dispute resolution mechanism.

There is no win or lose confrontation in such a dispute mediation system, and there is no threatening atmosphere for solving disputes, yet it is

79 See China Will Formulate New Policies for Supporting the Production of IC Industry, 10 July 2004, in http://tech.sina.com.cn/it/2004-07-10/0743385876.shtml last visited 9 December 2004.

80 The Art of War (Original Title of Chinese: Sun Zi Bing Fa, ca. 490 BC) by Sun Tzu is Classic work of Chinese History contributing to the tactics of war.

an argument for efficiency in the international dispute settlement field. The Asian approach to legal culture reflectstraditional values, and is unlikely to completely change in the near future, particularly in China. Contrasting Confucian and non-Confucian societies reveals an Oriental/Western legal culture dichotomy between litigious and non-litigious approaches.[81]

IV. Conclusion

Researchers examine the GATT/WTO cases widely either in practice, in theory or both. Their goals are to improve dispute settlement procedures and to shorten the distance between theory and operation.

They obtain their perspective from different academic disciplines including law, economics and politics. At the same time, they adopt various methods consisting of observation, treaty interpretation, case study, comparison, metaphor, model-construction and critical legal analysis. These methods and perspectives enrich the research area of GATT/WTO dispute settlement mechanisms through their empirical studies.

Researchers from developed countries (Canada, the EC and the US) are more likely concentrating on their own national interests. Their rich experiences and knowledge can contribute further to the rest of the world and are not limited to their own nations or regions (i.e. the EC or the NAFTA). Therefore, this can establish channels of communication between developed and developing countries in order to reach the goal of universal prosperity rather than labelled merely a 'rich man's club'.

Busch and Reinhardt distinguish between two types of participant: developed players (the EC and US) and developing Members, combining political science with law and economics.

Inregard to China, this country should, for traditional reasons, push the improvement of rule of law; on the other hand, China should contribute its unique legal culture to WTO's dispute settlement mechanism, which is non-litigation in character.

81 See Green, C. J. APEC and Trans-Pacific Dispute Management, 26 LPIB 1995; 719: from WESTLAW.

The Chinese 'Golden Mean' implies that, while there is a need to strengthen the judicial elements of the DSU, there is also a need to preserve the diplomatic elements in dispute settlement scope. From this perspective, the dispute settlement procedures should be understood, not only as an adjudication mechanism, but also as a persuasive mechanism.

The purpose of the literature assessment on consultations or early settlement is to understand the present research situation, the various arguments, the key research directions and interdisciplinary similarities and conflicts. This is a responsible decision to keep research on the track of objectivity, fairness and persuasiveness and to avoid either exaggeratingits merits or diminishingits defects.

Chapter 4

Linkage between the Panel and Consultation Stages

Article 4 of the DSU makes it clear that consultations are a prerequisite for the establishment of a Panel. If disputes can be resolved before a request for establishment of a Panel, the consultation is a completely independent proceeding, which is rarely related to the Panel.[1] If the disputes cannot be settled during the consultation phase, but be solved during the period of request for establishment of a Panel and issuing final Panel report, the consultation closely co-operates with the Panel.

I. Adequacy of the Request for Consultations

A Panel should not be able to deal with provisions not raised in consultations. Otherwise it would render meaningless the mandatory nature of the consultation phase.[2] A number of the AB's comments suggest that this is an important consideration.

Therefore, the argument comes up whether the Panel and the AB should rule on the so-called adequacy of the consultation request in order to improve the efficiency of the consultation.

In the *US – FSC* case, the AB was asked to rule on the adequacy of the consultation request. The AB disposed of the claim by noting that the US had held three separate sets of consultations and had not raised any objection until the Panel had been established. It concluded that the US acted as if it had accepted the establishment of the Panel as well as the

1 One might argue that some mutually agreed solutions are resolved under the 'shadow of the law'. This will be discussed afterwards.

2 See WT/DS8/R, WT/DS10/R, WT/DS11/R, Panel Report of Tax on *Japan – Alcoholic Beverages*, para. 6.5.

consultations preceding it. In those circumstances, the US could not subsequently make the specific claim.[3]

The Panel thought the adequacy of the consultation request was basically an unclear legal concept. For example, the Panel in the *Korea – Alcoholic Beverages* case noted that the WTO jurisprudence so far had not recognised any concept of 'adequacy'.

It is practically impossible for a Panel to check adequate or inadequate behaviour by the disputants because of confidentiality requirements during the consultation. In other words, the adequate reaction is to conditionally release the adequacy of the consultation requirement rather than being restricted by it. If no adequate requirement is given, the consultation is arguably not in good faith.

As it happens, Panels have a habit of finding the bottom-line and identifying the 'adequacy'. Again, in the *Korea – Alcoholic Beverages* case, the Panel believed that the only requirement under the DSU was that, "consultations were in fact held, or were at least requested, and that a period of sixty days has elapsed from the time consultations were requested to the time a request for a Panel was made".[4] According to the reasoning in *EC – Banana III*:

> Consultations are a matter reserved for the parties. The DSB is not involved, no Panel is involved, and the consultations are held in the absence of the Secretariat. While a mutually agreed solution is to be preferred, in some cases it is not possible for parties to agree upon one. In those cases, the function of a Panel is only to ascertain that the consultations, if required, were in fact held.[5]

Similarly, in the *Turkey – Textiles* case the Panel confirmed this approach to explain the adequacy of the consultation. The Panel concluded with reference to *EC – Bananas III* and the *Korea – Alcoholic Beverages* cases that the private nature of the bilateral consultations means Panels are normally not in a position to evaluate how the consultations process

3 See WT/DS108/AB/R, AB Report on the *US – Tax Treatment for "Foreign Sales Corporations"*, para. 165.

4 See WT/DS75/R and WT/DS84/R, Panel Report on *Korea – Taxes on Alcoholic Beverages*, para. 10.19.

5 See WT/DS27/R/ECU, *European Communities – Regime for the Importation, Sale and Distribution of Bananas* – Complaint by Ecuador – Report of the Panel, para. 7.19. This issue was not appealed.

functions, but could only determine whether consultations, if required, did in fact take place.[6]

As the terms of reference for aPanel are different from the request for consultations, the Panel cannot overstep its authority. Hence, the Panel offered its perspective:

> We note also that our terms of reference (our mandate) are determined, not with reference to the request for consultations, or the content of the consultations, but only with reference to the request for the establishment of a Panel. Consultations are a crucial and integral part of the DSU and are intended to facilitate a mutually satisfactory settlement of the dispute, consistent with Article 3.7 of the DSU. However, the only function we have as a Panel in relation to Turkey's procedural concerns is to ascertain whether consultations were properly requested, in terms of the DSU, that the complainant was ready to consult with the defendant and that the 60-day period has lapsed before the establishment of a Panel was requested by the complainant.[7]

Although the above Panels hesitate to define the adequacy of the consultation, they apparently found a definition for an adequate justification. The 'duty to consult' also discloses the adequacy of consultations.

II. From Consultations to the Panel

Once the request for consultations has been made, parties may reach the Panel process in three ways:

First, if a Member does not respond within ten days of receiving the request, or does not enter into consultations within thirty days, then the Member requesting consultations may proceed directly to request the establishment of a Panel. Second, if consultations fail to settle a dispute within 60 days after the original request for consultations is received, the complaining party may request the establishment of a Panel. Third, if the

6 See WT/DS34/R, Panel Report on *Turkey – Restrictions on Imports of Textile and Clothing Products*, para. 9.22.

7 See, for instance, the AB Report on *EC – Bananas III*, paras. 139–144; the AB Report on Brazil – Measures Affecting Desiccated Coconut, adopted on 20 March 1997, WT/DS22/AB/R (*Brazil – Desiccated Coconut*), page 22; and the AB Report on *India – Patent*, paras. 86–96.

parties jointly conclude that the consultations have failed to settle the dispute, the complaining party may request establishment of a Panel even within the sixty-day period.

It has already been mentioned that the first situation never takes place, and the third situation hardly happens.[8]

III. Relationship between Consultations and the Panel

The AB has shown its sophisticated understanding of the divergences between the consultation and the Panel.

In the *India – Patent* case the AB clarified the relationship as follows:

> All parties engaged in dispute settlement under the DSU must be fully forthcoming from the very beginning both as to the claims involved in a dispute and as to the facts relating to those claims. Claims must be stated clearly.Facts must be disclosed freely. This must be so in consultations as well as in the more formal setting of Panel proceedings. In fact, the demands of due process that are implicit in the DSU make this especially necessary during consultations. For the claims that are made and the facts that are established during consultations do much to shape the substance and the scope of subsequent Panel proceedings. If, in the aftermath of consultations, any party believes that all the pertinent facts relating to a claim are, for any reason, not before the Panel, then that party should ask the Panel in that case to engage in additional fact-finding. But this additional fact-finding cannot alter the claims that are before the Panel – because it cannot alter the Panel's terms of reference. And, in the absence of the inclusion of a claim in the terms of reference, a Panel must neither be expected nor permitted to modify rules in the DSU.[9]

8 See 'An Overview of the Consultation Stage under the DSU' in this book.

9 See WT/DS50/AB/R, *India – Patent Protection for Pharmaceutical and Agricultural Chemical Products*, para. 94. In other disputes, the AB also stressed the relationship between the consultation and the Panel, such as WT/DS27/AB/R, *EC – Regime for the Importation, Sale and Distribution of Bananas*; WT/DS22/AB/R, *Brazil – Measuring Affecting Desiccated Coconut*; WT/DS26/AB/R, WT/DS48/AB/R, *EC – Measures Concerning Meat and Meat Products* (Hormones); WT/DS46/AB/R, *Brazil – Export Financing Programme for Aircraft*; WT/DS62/AB/R, WT/DS67/AB/R, WT/DS68/AB/R, *EC – Customs Classification of Certain Computer Equipment*; WT/DS98/AB/R, *Korea – Definitive Safeguard Measure on Imports of Certain Dairy* Products, but not limited to these above cases.

Article 4 of the DSU confirmed that consultations are a precondition to establishment of a Panel. There is then a question of whether there ought to be minimum standards of conduct within this process before an establishment of a Panel. The answer is unfortunately controversial. On the one hand, it would be desirable that parties consult fully, frankly and in good faith. On the other it would be virtually impossible to define and monitor any such standards for the consultation that is essentially private and confidential.

According to the analysis of consultations in international law and current practice in WTO law, the nature of private and confidential consultations cannot be undermined as their ability to solve disputes has a close connection with the terms of reference of international law or WTO law. Furthermore, the consultation is a diplomatic type of procedure. If it is entitled to have some standards of conduct or rules, the consultation will take off its diplomatic coat. In practice, the consultation is the only diplomatic means of solving disputes and even avoiding them altogether.

WTO jurisprudence has supported the view that it would be impractical for a Panel or the AB to review the adequacy of conduct during consultations. As with the AB, the decisions of the Panels do not review the adequacy of consultation.

In the *EC – Banana* case, the Panel wrote two pages to clarity the relationships between the Panel and the consultation, and to explain the application of the adequacy of consultations. The EC argued that the consultations held in this matter between the complainants and the EC did not fulfill their minimum function of affording a possibility for arriving at a mutually satisfactory solution and a clear setting out of the different claims of which a dispute consists.[10]

Consultations are, however, a matter reserved for the parties.The DSB is not involved, no Panel is involved and the consultations are held in the absence of the Secretariat.In these circumstances, the Panel is not in a position to evaluate the consultation process in order to determine if it functioned in a particular way.The function of a Panel is only to ascer-

10 WT/DS27/R/ECU, *European Communities – Regime for the Importation, Sale and Distribution of Bananas* – Complaint by Ecuador – Report of the Panel, para 7.19.

tain that consultations, if required, were in fact held or, at least, requested.[11]

The EC argued that consultations must lead to an adequate explanation of the complainants' case. While one function of the consultations may be to clarify what the case is about, there is nothing in the DSU that provides that a complainant cannot request a Panel unless its case is adequately explained in the consultations.The fulfilment of such a requirement would be difficult, for a complainant to demonstrate if a respondent chose to claim a lack of understanding of the case, a result which would undermine the automatic nature of Panel establishment under the DSU. The only prerequisite for requesting a Panel is that the consultations have failed to settle a dispute within 60 days of receipt of the request for consultations. Ultimately, the function of providing notice to a respondent of a complainant's claims and arguments is served by the request for establishment of a Panel and by the complainant's submissions to that Panel.[12]

Therefore, the Panel rejected the EC's claim that the complainants' case should be dismissed because the consultations held did not perform their minimum function of affording a possibility for arriving at a mutually satisfactory solution and a clear setting out of the different claims of which a dispute consists.

To summarise, it is desirable for parties to have meaningful obligations to consult in good faith, but it is undesirable for them to have a so-called 'qualitative consultation' as a precondition to a complainant's right to establish a Panel.

A. *Formal Requirements of Panel Requests*

The formal requirements of Panel requests are sufficiently integrated with the necessary minimum content of requests for consultations and with the terms of reference of the Panel.[13]

The content requirements for consultation requests are less precise than those for the Panel requirement. Because the consultation is a necessary precondition to establish a Panel, the matters covered in the Panel

11 *Ibid.*, paras. 7.19–7.20

12 *Ibid.*, para 7.20.

13 Waincymer, J. WTO Litigation: Procedural Aspects of Formal Dispute Settlement, London: Cameron May, 2002; 241.

request should relate to the matters dealt with during consultation (although it is not necessary for them to be identical).

To attain this objective, Article 6.2 states that the request for the establishment of a Panel shall provide *a brief summary* of the legal basis of the complaint *sufficient* to present the problem *clearly* and the written request shall include *the proposed text of special terms of reference.* Meanwhile, Article 4.4 merely notes that all requests for consultation shall include *identification* of the measures at issue and an *indication* of the legal basis for the complaint. It is easy to tell the differences from the aspect of their degree. So, the Panel request is often more elaborated than the consultation request, and the requirements are stricter for requests for the establishment of a Panel than for requests for consultations. Of course, the similarity is that both provisions require an indication of the factual and the legal basis for the request.

However, the more they differ, the more it is arguable that consultations were not held on the issues raised in the Panel requests. In the *Brazil – Aircraft* case, the respondent claimed that the consultations held could not justify a Panel request covering regulatory instruments that came into effect after the consultations were concluded. Both the Panel and the AB held that these later instruments did not change the essence of the original subsidies. The consultations were sufficient to justify a Panel request, which included the later instruments. Moreover, the AB ruled that it does not need to "require a *precise and exact identity* between the specific measures that were the subject of consultations and the specific measures identified in the request for the establishment of a Panel".[14]

Concerning the cases that request the establishing of a Panel, it is a relatively strict interpretation to apply. For instance, the AB explained in the *EC – Banana* case that:

> A Panel request is normally not subjected to detailed scrutiny by the DSB, it is incumbent upon a Panel to examine the request for the establishment of the Panel very carefully to ensure its compliance with both the letter and the spirit of Article 6.2 of the DSU. It is important that a Panel request be sufficiently precise for two reasons:first, it often forms the basis for the terms of reference of the Panel pursu-

14 WT/DS46/AB/R, *Brazil – Export Financing Programme for Aircraft* – AB-1999–1 – Report of the Appellate Body, paras. 130–132.

> ant to Article 7 of the DSU; and, second, it informs the defending party and the third parties of the legal basis of the complaint.[15]

Apparently, as a legal interpretive method, the Panel was satisfied with the standard at a high level. Nonetheless, it may fail to apply to a case when it generously accepted the method chosen by the complainants as being sufficient to comply with such a high standard.[16]

The ideal way is to keep the detailed parts, but to carefully deal with differences to the greatest extent, particularly to avoid substantive differences. There is a need to distinguish between the pedantic and substantive challenges. Practically, in view of quantitative analysis, there is a trend to put these two into the same category.[17] This is an improvement among Member states to prevent amplifying controversy in a particular argument. It is also significant for the Panel and the AB who are reluctant to question the nature of consultations, unless there is a clear evidence that parties are not held (or do not cover a particular issue).

It is not always easy to resolve the difficulties between procedural requirements and the factual progress of the disputes. Therefore, some kind of balance should be fairly established between them. Otherwise, the chance may be lost to settle disputes without litigation.

B. *The 'Shadow of the Law'*

Reviewing all the disputes, quite a number of them have been solved after a request for a Panel but before the final Panel report. Moreover, "concessions by defendants appear significantly more likely to occur after a Panel has been established, but before it has ruled regardless of

15 WT/DS27/AB/R, *European Communities – Regime for the Importation, Sale and Distribution of Bananas* – Report of the Appellate Body, para. 142.

16 Jansen, M. Scope of Jurisdiction in GATT/WTO Dispute Settlement: Consultation and Panel Requests, in Weiss, F. (ed.), Improving WTO Dispute Settlement Procedures: Issues and Lessons from the Practice of Other International Courts and Tribunals, London: Cameron May, 2000; 47.

17 From 2001, most of the context of the requests for the establishment of a Panel is almost similar to that of the consultation in the author's observation.

which way the verdict goes".[18] So the question arises whether these disputes actually were solved under the so-called 'shadow of the law'.

The consultation serves two functions within international dispute settlement, namely dispute settlement and dispute prevention.

The stage of the request for consultations can be treated as a matter of dispute prevention if the disputes can be solved during this period of time, because the request for the consultation is a notice to raise the divergences. The 60-day-consultation is a chance to put off or cool down the conflicts rather than upgrade it to a formal dispute of litigation. That is to say, the consultation exists to prevent parties from enlarging disputes, or even completely to avoid disputes. To be more precise, the function of dispute prevention is much stronger than dispute settlement. As a matter of fact, the goal of dispute settlement exists in the whole proceedings of the DSU.

The stage between the request for a Panel and the final Panel report underlines that the function of dispute settlement is tougher than that of dispute prevention. The reason is the complainant intends to seek law to resolve disputes: there is an implication, during this stage, that the claimant will apply legal enforcement since divergences havenot disappeared and the dispute grows to a higher level.

If disputants solved the conflict during this stage, they would not need to have recourse to legal methods; there are no legal enforcement power and legal rulings afterwards, so they use the skills in 'shadow of the law' instead.

A Panel ruling carries weight to the extent that it delivers a timely and coherent normative statement. Even without a credible threat by a complainant to seek authorisation to retaliate, a definitive legal opinion from the institution may empowerdefendant groups who oppose the disputed measure. Alternatively, a ruling may enable the defendant to implement, making concessions more politically palatable by citing the need to be a good citizen of WTO.[19]

Because of these factors, and about an 87% winning rate for complainants (WTO statistics), it is possible to solve disputes during this preruling stage. Thus, "the basic force of the procedure comes from the

18 Busch, M. L. & Reinhardt, E. Bargaining in the Shadow of the Law: Early settlement in GATT/WTO Disputes', 24FDM.I.L.J. 2000; 158: 163.

19 Busch & Reinhardt 2000; 165.

normative force of the decisions themselves and from community [ie, complainants] pressure to observe them".[20]

Under the 'shadow of the law', defendants would like to plead stronger cases and complainants would like to withdraw weaker ones, and *vice versa*. This is not surprising, since after rulings of a Panel or an AB, pressure from legislators and industries at home will invariably be greater, if for no other reason than that post-ruling proceedings leave a clear paper trail and policy changes at that point are more likely to require implementing legislation or administration. The pre-trail stage, the consultation, by way of contrast, does not have to be reported to the DSB until it has been concluded. This gives the disputants more latitude to reach a deal.[21]

Additionally, under the 'shadow of the law' defendants worry about the normative condemnation that goes along with a legal defeat rather than threats of direct retaliation per se. In other words, defendants prefer to avoid being found non-compliant because such a label may damage their prospects of gaining compliance when they file as complainants.[22]

This phenomenon of non-compliance by defendants and then revenge from complainants has arisen, was not only just a tragedy in the GATT time, but also a barrier to the process of improving the dispute settlement system because both disputants end in defeat.

The *Brazil – aircraft*[23] and *Canada – aircraft*[24] cases are two examples. Canada, on 21 June 1996, argued that Brazil violated Agreement of SCM regarding certain export subsidies granted under the Brazilian Programa de Financiamento às Exportações (PROEX) to foreign purchasers of Brazil's Embraer aircraft. This claim was supported by the Panel and AB, but Brazil decided not to comply with the rulings. Afterwards, on 14 March 1997 Brazil filed a case that Canada was inconsistent with the SCM agreement regarding certain subsidies granted by the Government of Canada or its provinces that support the export of civilian aircraft. Similarly, Brazil won the case, but Canada made no compliance. Therefore, finally these two disputes were listed in the 'failed case' category.

20 Hudec, R. E. Transcending the Ostensible: Some Reflections on the Nature of Litigation Between Governments, 72 Minn. L. Rev. 1987; 211: 219.
21 Busch & Reinhardt 2000; 171.
22 *Ibid.*, p. 164.
23 WT/DS46, *Brazil – Export Financing Progamme for Aircraft.*
24 WT/DS70, *Canada – Measures Affecting the Export of Civilian Aircraft.*

C. *Two Possibilities of Reaching a Mutually Agreed Resolution in Pre-ruling Negotiation*

There are three time periods for solving disputes before the final Panel ruling.Theseare at the stage of requiring consultations, after the stage of requiring a Panel, but before the stage of composing the Panel and after the stage of composing the Panel, but before theissuing offinal Panel reports. The latter two are closely related to the Panel.

1. *Between the Request to Establish a Panel and the Constitution of a Panel*

Three examples will be discussed here out of 324 disputes by the end of 2004: (1) after request for establishment a Panel the disputants reached a mutually agreed solution or the complainants withdrew; (2) after request for establishment of a Panel no Panellist was selected; (3) after request for establishment of a Panel the Panel lapses.

The latest statistics of WTO Legal Affairs Division indicate that the number of disputes covered by Panels are 157; the number of disputes covered by Panels in composition are 129.[25] At least 18 disputes fall into the category at the head of this section.

a. *No Panelist Selected*

In June 1995, Canada requested a consultation with the EC concerning its regulations implementing some of the EC's Uruguay Round concessions on agriculture, specifically, the regulations which impose a duty on wheat imports based on reference prices rather than transaction values, with the result that duty-paid import price for Canadian wheat will be greater than the effective intervention price by 55% whenever the transaction value is greater than the representative price.[26]

On 15 September 1995, Canada requested the establishment of a Panel owing to failed consultations. A Panel was established at the DSB meeting on 11 October 1995, but no Panellists were selected.

25 See Legal Affairs Division, WTO Secretariat, WTO Dispute Settlement Statistics (as of 11 June 2004), in the 7th Annual Conference on Dispute Settlement in the World Trade Organization, Geneva, 18th June 2004.

26 See WT/DS9/1, *European Communities – Duties on Imports of Cereals* – Request for Consultations by Canada.

According to Article 8 of the DSU, if there is no agreement on Panellists within 20 days after the date of the establishment of a Panel, *at the request of either party*, Director-General (DG), in consultation with the Chairman of the DSB and the Chairman of relevant Council or Committee, shall determine the composition of the Panel by appointing the Panellists whom the DG considers most appropriate in accordance with any relevant special or additional rules or procedures of the covered agreement or coveredagreements after consulting thc parties to the dispute.[27]

In other words, if a claimant in the dispute pursues further proceedings, the no-agreement-on-Panellists situation can be resolved as there are relevant Articles covered this issue even (if they had controversy). Members shall undertake, as a general rule, to permit their officials to serve as Panellist.[28] The only possible answer is that this dispute was settled between the establishment of a Panel and the composition of the Panel, but the disputants did not notify the DSB. Meanwhile, the DG did not get a request from either party, therefore, the DG could not determine the composition of the Panel as he did not in 54 other disputes.[29]

This case involved the tariffication commitment under the Agreement of Agriculture, which is well known for controversy with the EC. How did they finally reach an agreement?

The bargaining results were ended with a so-called 'win-win' situation.[30]

The EC adjusted its import rules for common and durum wheat from 1 January to 30 June 1996, the abatement for high quality wheat would be increased from ECU 8/tonne to ECU 14/tonne; for the same period, the requirement for durum wheat of 73% of vitreous kernels would be reduced to the standard level of 60%.

Subject to implementation of these changes, Canada would terminate its present request for a WTO Panel on EC cereals regulations.

27 Article 8.7 of the DSU.

28 Article 8.8 of the DSU.

29 As of 11 June 2004, there have been 54 disputes pursuant to Article 8:7 of the DSU, which was invoked by Members annually except 1995.

30 See Canada-EU Agreements and Joint Statements: Exchange of Letters Between the EC and Canada on the Conclusion of Negotiations under GATT Article, http://www.dfait-maeci.gc.ca/canadaeuropa/caneu/eu23-en.pdf last visited 7 July 2004.

It was agreed that the two parties would enter into discussions in the first quarter of 1996 with a view to examining what measures might be necessary for subsequent marketing years.

To settle the current WTO Article XXIV, six negotiations on agriculture and Canada's claims on barley arising from past enlargements of the EU, the EC agreed a reduction in the duty rate for canary seed to zero, the MFN tariff rate quota of 50,000 tonnes for durum wheat (minimum vitreous kernel content of 73%) at zero duty and MFN tariff rate quota of 10,000 tonnes for worked oats at zero duty.

Canada accepted this as a basket of agreements.[31] Therefore, the confusion of 'no Panellist selected' was removed. They solved this dispute solely through bilateral negotiations.

b. *Panel Lapsed*

Under Article 12.12 of the DSU, if the work of the Panel has been suspended for more than 12 months, the authority for establishment of the Panel shall lapse.

Interestingly, the following three cases (four disputes) were filed by the same complainant, the EC.

(1) *US – Cuban Liberty and Democratic Solidarity Act*

In March 1996, the Cuban Liberty and Democratic Solidarity Act (Libertad or Helms-Burton) was signed into law. This law provides for legal action against any companies which made use of American property expropriated after the Cuban revolution in 1959, and bars foreign executives of these countries and their families from entering the US.[32]

The extraterritorial character of the Helms-Burton Act ran counter to basic principles of public international law. In addition, it risked harming not only the friendly relationships between the US and many other countries, but also the efforts of the international community as a whole to

31 Within this agreement, EC also promised to increase the quota of Canadian aged Cheddar and limited export subsidies on fresh, chilled or frozen beef and veal destined for Canada. As another end of the negotiations, Canada undertook the certificates of authenticity for aged Cheddar on the basis of in-quota quantities and agreed to bind at free its duty on pasta products.

32 See Libertad Act of 1996, http://www.ustreas.gov/offices/eotffc/ofac/legal/statutes/libertad.pdf for detailed context, last visited 7 July 2004.

ensure continued progress towards democracy, human rights, the rule of law, economic reform and prosperity in Cuba.[33]

On 3 May 1996, the EC required the DSB to consult with the US. The EC challenged that this Act restricts the freedom to export to Cuba or to trade in Cuban origin goods, as well as restricts the freedom of EC registered vessels and their cargo to transit through US ports. Additionally, there are provisions, which require certificates in respect trade in Cuban sugar. If such certificates are not provided, access to the US sugar quota is denied. Furthermore, there are measures which may lead to the refusal of visas and the exclusion of non-US nationals from US territory in a way that contravene US commitments under the GATS.[34]

During the following five months, the negotiations did not make satisfactory progress. On 3 October 1996, the EC requested the establishment of a Panel. The EC seemed to follow a procedural double strategy, not relying exclusively on the diplomatic mode, but rather having recourse as well to the legal ruling. This in turn raised interesting questions about the feasibility of such a claim in the multilateral trade organisation's realm.[35] On 12 February 1997, the Panel was composed.

However, on 25 April 1997, the EC requested the Panel to suspend its work. After several tough negotiations between the two big players, the Understanding on Cuba was reached and announced on 11 April 1997. The two sides in this Understanding noted that they would work cooperatively to develop binding disciplines on acquisitions and dealing in property confiscated by Cuba on Cuba and other governments in contravention of international law. The US agreed that it would help to promote a transition to democracy and the protection of property rights in Cuba. The US further avoided bringing a foreign policy dispute before the WTO. In return, the EC was required by the US to immediately sus-

33 See Resolution 1135 on the implications for Europe and the world of Helms-Burton Act of the US Congress, http://assembly.coe.int/Documents/AdoptedText/TA97/eres1135.htm last visited 7 July 2004.

34 WT/DS38/1, *United States – The Cuban Liberty and Democratic Solidarity Act –* Request for Consultations by the European Communities, 13 May 1996.

35 See Reinisch, A. Widening the US Embargo Against Cuba Extraterritorially: A Few Comments on the Cuba Liberty and Democratic Solidarity (LIBERTAD) Act of 1996, 7 EJIL 4 1996; 545:551. He argued that it was unclear whether the WTO is the appropriate forum for an international jurisdictional dispute of this kind because it is difficult to see how the extraterritoriality dispute concerning potential property claims could fall under the WTO regime in a technical sense.

pend its challenge against the Libertad Act and other components of its Cuba legislation.[36]

The US and the EC would complete their efforts to develop this agreement by October 15. They would also open a dialogue with a view to obtaining an amendment providing the President with waiver authority for Title IV of the Libertad Act once these bilateral consultations were completed and the EC adhered to these agreed disciplines. During the interim period, the EC agreed to continue enforcing Title IV of the Libertad Act.[37]

The Understanding created the opportunity to develop multilateral disciplines deterring and inhibiting investment in confiscated property and the first time the EC agreed to develop such an international norm. This Understanding required enormous efforts by both the US and EC negotiators, as well as continual consultations with the US Congress to shape and define US negotiating objectives.[38] The most important improvement is that this Understanding prevented a dispute rather than de-escalating it.

This dispute was settled. However, some interesting arguments remained for quite a long time. The EU ambassador to the US, Hugo Paemen, expressed the view that if it reached the Panel stage, the Panel might have ruled against the US because of the 'reasonable expectations' of another contracting party under Article XXIII of the GATT.[39]

The Liberto Act caused a 'nullification' or an 'impairment' of a 'benefit' in the EC's eyes. As far as the required causality was concerned, the EC would rely on the trade diminishing effect, either as between the US and the EC, or between Cuba and the EC as a result of the deterrent effect of potential lawsuits against European traders investing in Cuba. However, the dilemma is the burden of proof, namely the di-

36 See Eizenstat Announces US/EU Understanding on Cuba (EU suspends challenge to Helms-Burton in WTO) on April 11 1997, http://usinfo.state.gov/regional/ar/us–cuba/eizen.htm last visited 8 July 2004.

37 *Ibid.*

38 *Ibid.*

39 See "International Trade, EU Still Undecided on WTO Action Against U.S. over Cuba Bill, Envoy Says", the Bureau of National Affairs, Daily Report for Executives, 28 March 1996 in Reinisch, A., Widening the US Embargo Against Cuba Extraterritorially: A Few Comments on the Cuba Liberty and Democratic Solidarity (LIBERTAD) Act of 1996, 7 EJIL 4 1996; 545:547.

minishing effect on the total trade flow between the EC and the US and Cuba respectively.[40]

From the perspective of the US, although there might be a list of possible inconsistencies with various parts of the WTO legal texts, the US had valid defence, which is 'national security exceptions'.[41] These two Articles could provide a defence for the US to many, if not all, of the US Helms-Burton measures. These exceptions, nevertheless, if given a broad interpretation, could undermine the whole WTO treaty and impair the security and stability of the world trading system for which the WTO has been created.[42]

A key question for the national security exception is whether this exception permits a WTO Member to decide for itself, to 'auto-determine', whether the criteria for invoking the exception exist. There is no WTO ruling addressing the meaning of Article XXI. There was some GATT practice supporting the 'auto-determination', but the only time the GATT Panel favoured this approach, its view was constrained by particular 'terms of reference' to the Panel, which are not present in the case today. In fact, the US is notinterested in developing a complete auto-determination interpretation of the national security exception as other Members could also be tempted to invoke the exception to justify discriminatory trade actions to favour a particular country.[43]

In any case, it would be a tough decision for the Panel. At the same time, it raises the problem of contradiction in the WTO legal texts. Therefore, it is hard for the Panel or the AB to interpret these Articles persuasively. The reputation of the WTO law could be undermined if there are too many divergences.

The consultation enables more understanding of the parameters of the way forward. In this case, on the EC side, the difficulty is to prove the diminishing effect on the total trade flow, while on the US side, the pressure is to justify the national security exception. If two parties could not reach bilateral agreement, the double-dilemma would transfer to the Panel and/or the AB. As a result of resolving this dispute through consultation, the US and the EC embarked on an exercise in co-operation and

40 Reinisch 1996; 553.

41 See Article XXI of the GATT and Article XIV of the GATS.

42 Jackson, J. H. & Lowenfeld, A. F. Helms-Burton, the US, and the WTO, in http://www.asil.org/insights/insight7.htm last visited 8 July 2004.

43 *Ibid.*

worked with their allies on concrete steps toward the same goal. Nonetheless, the regret over this case is the outcome on the DSB record is a 'lapse of authority for establishing the Panel' rather than mutually agreed resolution.

(2) *Argentina – Textiles and Clothing*

On 23 April 1997, the EC requested consultations with Argentina concerning the textile, clothing and footwear sectors. Under the provisions of different governmental measures and, in particular, Decree 998/95 Argentina introduced a range of specific duties on these products. The change resulted in increasing duties and, in certain circumstances, led to applied tariffs over the 35% binding that Argentina made following the conclusion of the Uruguay Round. Therefore, the EC considered that these measures were in breach of Argentina's concessions under Article II and Article XXVIII of the GATT 1994.[44]

Concerning labelling requirements for these products, particularly Resolutions 622/95 and 26/96, the EC noted that the obligation to include the name of the importer and the number of the affidavit submitted by the importer to the Argentine authorities on labels would be obstacles to trade since this additional information would not bring any extra benefit for consumers. Thus, these measures were in violation of Article 2 of the TBT. Besides, in this case, the above labelling requirements and tariff barrier were inconsistent with Article 7 of the ATC.

Consultations were held on 12 June 1997 in Geneva. These consultations allowed a better understanding of the respective positions. The EC agreed that the measures prevented improvement of market access in the textiles and clothing sectors, excluding footwear. They also reached a mutually agreed solution regarding Argentina's labelling requirements.[45]

However, the parties failed to reach a mutual agreement on other issues during the consultation. On 10 September 1997, the EC requested the establishment of a Panel with regard to violation of Article II of GATT 1994 and Article 7 of the ATC by Argentina. The Panel was composed on 18 December 1997, but dated 29 July 1998, and the EC

44 See WT/DS77/1, *Argentina – Measures Affecting Textiles, Clothing and Footwear – Request for Consultations by the European Communities.*

45 See WT/DS77/3, *Argentina – Measures Affecting Textiles, Clothing and Footwear – Request for Establishment of a Panel by the European Communities.*

requested the Panel to suspend its work. On 24 May 2002, the Secretariat announced as of 30 July 1999, the authority for the establishment of the Panel had lapsed. The puzzle is whether the parties actually solved the dispute.

On 4 October 1996, the US filed a consultation request challenging Argentina's failure to comply with the bound rate of 35% *ad valorem* provided in its Schedule on footwear, textile, apparel and other items under the GATT Article II and ATC Article 7. In addition, America challenged the 'statistical services' tax under the GATT Article VIII. The EC requested to join consultations afterwards.[46] According to the US requirement, the DSB composed the Panel on 4 April 1997. The EC reserved its rights to participate in the Panel proceedings as a third party, as well as Hungary and India.

The Panel issued its report on 25 November 1997. It concluded that Argentina was in violation of the GATT Article II and Article VIII; for reasons of judicial economy the Panel declined to address the US claim under ATC Article 7.[47]

Argentina appealed the Panel's findings on 21 January 1998 under GATT Article II and VIII, and it also claimed that the Panel violated DSU Article 11 in its consideration and treatment of evidence. The AB concluded that the Panel did not violate DSU Article 11, and also upheld the Panel's finding that the statistical services tax was inconsistent with GATT Article VIII and specific import duty was inconsistent with GATT Article II, although under modified reasoning.[48] The EC was the only third party.

Thereafter, this case entered into implementation stage. Argentina guaranteed fulfillment in all import transactions of the commitment assumed by Argentina in its WTO Schedule to apply import duties whose *ad valorem* equivalents do not exceed 35%. At the meeting on 26 May 1999, Argentina announced that Decree 108/00, pursuant to which no import transactions covered by the statistical services tax shall be taxed

46 See WT/DS56/3, *Argentina – Measures Affecting Imports of Footwear, Textiles, Apparel and other Items* – Request to Join Consultations – Communication from the European Communities.

47 See WT/DS56/R, *Argentina – Measures Affecting Imports of Footwear, Textiles, Apparel and other Items* – Report of the Panel.

48 See WT/DS56/AB/R, *Argentina – Measures Affecting Imports of Footwear, Textiles, Apparel and other Items* – AB-1998-1 – Report of the Appellate Body.

in excess of the amounts agreed between it and the US, would enter into force on 30 May 1999. Finally, Argentina implemented in full, the recommendations of the DSB.[49]

The dispute ended, with the US winning on the core issue. As a matter of fact, the case between the EC and Argentina was over, after Argentina implemented this.

These two cases shared the same respondent, legal basis and almost similar goods. The EC participated in the whole procedure with the US filing as a third party. When Argentina fully implemented the rulings of DS56 announced on 4 June 1999, the EC let the authority for the establishment of DS77 Panel lapse on 30 July 1999. Although, strictly speaking, the EC settled the dispute through a 'legal method' as a free rider, it was a case that was resolved before the composition of the Panel. The EC won without litigation. The interesting question to ask is: if the US had lost or partly lost its case, would the EC continue suing its dispute?

(3) *US – Government Procurement*

On 20 June 1997, the EC requested consultations with the US regarding the Act Regulating State contracts with Companies doing Business with or in Burma (Myanmar) enacted by the Commonwealth of Massachusetts on 25 June 1996 (Part 130 of the Acts of 1996). This Act prohibited Massachusetts public authorities from procuring goods or services from any persons, whether the US or foreign citizens, who do business with Burma.[50]

The EC felt that Massachusetts, a state covered by the Government Procurement Agreement (GPA), violated the obligations of the US under the Agreement by contravening Article VIII, X and XIII. The EC also claimed that the Massachusetts legislation limited the access of EC suppliers to procurement by a sub-federal authority covered by the GPA. The EC additionally considered that the measure had the effect of impeding the attainment of the objectives of the GPA, including that of maintaining a balance of rights and obligations.[51]

49 See WT/DS56/14, 15, and 15/Add.1–5, *Argentina – Measures Affecting Imports of Footwear, Textiles, Apparel and other Items* – Status Report by Argentina.

50 See WT/DS88/1, *United States – Measure Affecting Government Procurement* – Request for Consultations by the European Communities.

51 *Ibid.*

The consultations were held on 22 July, 2 October and 17 December 1997 in Geneva. They exchanged views and obtained a better understanding of the respective positions, and included discussions about a possible amendment of the Act. It did not lead to a satisfactory resolution of the matter. Therefore, on 8 September 1998, the EC required establishment of the Panel with regard to the measure in breach of US obligations under Article III, VIII, XIII, and XXII of the GPA.[52]

Japan filed on the same issue against the US. On 21 January 1998 a Panel was established for both requests. However, a federal district court found the Massachusetts law to be unconstitutional in 1998 and barred its implementation. The case against Massachusetts was brought to court by the National Foreign Trade Council (NTFC), which asked cities in California, Colorado, Maryland, Massachusetts, Michigan, Minnesota, New Jersey, New York, North Carolina, Oregon and Wisconsin with similar purchasing laws, to revoke them.

In the context of the US court ruling barring implementation of the measure at issue, the EC and Japan requested the Panel to suspend its work.[53]

The NFTC's challenge to the law rested on three main constitutional arguments, all involving the relative powers of the federal government *vis-à-vis* local jurisdictions in conducting foreign affairs and commerce. Under the constitution, according to the business group, federal law and policy are supreme and automatically pre-empt and invalidate inconsistent local laws. Massachusetts, which was supported by two dozen Members of Congress from both major parties, a plethora of human-rights, environment, and labour groups, 11 states and more than a dozen cities, argued that local jurisdictions had the right to decide how they wished to spend their money and to use moral considerations in making those decisions.[54]

The NFTC won the first round on 4 November1998 when a trial court ruled that the law "impermissibly infringes on the federal government's

52 See WT/DS88/3, *United States – Measure Affecting Government Procurement* – Request for Establishment of a Panel by the European Communities.

53 See WT/DS88/5, *United States – Measure Affecting Government Procurement* – Communication from the Chairman of the Panel.

54 See Multinationals win US Court Victory over Activists, http://www.globalpolicy.org/socecon/tncs/court99.htm last visited 11 July 2004.

power to regulate foreign affairs".[55] The appeals court ruling on 22 June 1999 was even more sweeping in that it upheld each of the NFTC's three main arguments in favour of federal supremacy. "The conduct of this nation's foreign affairs cannot be effectively managed on behalf of all of the nation's citizens if each of the many state and local governments pursue its own foreign policy",[56] the three judges stated in their 78-page opinion.

On 19 June 2000, the US Supreme Court upheld the appeals in their ruling. The Clinton administration admitted that the Massachusetts law had violated the US constitution by "impermissibly infringing upon the national government's exclusive authority to conduct foreign affairs".[57]

Unilateralism in trade policy has its costs whether practiced at the federal, state, or local level. Sovereign countries have the right to act against their own economic interest. A key question in this case is whether an individual state has the right to act against the economic and foreign policy interests of the US as a whole. The EC and Japan provided their *amicus curiae* briefs with the courts for the NFTC.

On 11 February 2000, the authority for establishment of the Panel lapsed. The *US – Government Procurement* case was settled by the US courts rather than the WTO courts. Within the international dispute settlement field, the *US – Government Procurement* resolved without litigation; whereas, at the national level, the *Massachusetts Burma Law 1996* was solved by a legal method.

In addition to *US – Government Procurement,* the GPA was invoked in quite a few cases, namely *Japan – Procurement of a Navigation Satellite* and *Korea – Government Procurement.* The former was notified as a mutually agreed solution by the EC through consultations that lasted four

55 See *National Foreign Trade Council, Plaintiff, Appellee v Andrew S. Natsios*, in his official capacity as Secretary of Administration and Finance of the Commonwealth of Massachusetts, and Philmore Anderson, III, in his official capacity as State Purchasing Agent for the Commonwealth of Massachusetts, Defendants, Appellants. (No. 98–2304), United States Court of Appeals, in http://www.law.berkeley.edu/faculty/yooj/courses/forrel/reserve/burma.htm last visited 11 July 2004.

56 *Ibid.*

57 See Lobe, J. Pro-Burmese Business Wins in US Court (June 21, 2000), in http://www.atimes.com/se–asia/BF21Ae02.html last visited 11 July 2004.

months.[58] The latter was resolved by the Panel ruling, which rejected the US claims.[59]

In general, situations such as the lapse of authority for the Panel establishment or no agreement on the Panellists, still led to disputes being factually all solved.

Helms-Burton Act and the Massachusetts Burma Law are the extraterritorial application of national legislations imposed by the US, which were characterised as unilateral sanctions against foreign countries in response to human rights practices.[60] The US allows these unilateralist

58 See WT/DS73/4, *Japan – Procurement of a Navigation Satellite* – Communication from the Chairman of the Panel.

59 See WT/DS163/R, *Korea – Measures Affecting Government Procurement* – Report of the Panel. This case involved the procurement practices of the Korea Airport Construction Authority (KOACA), which Korea asserted were not covered by its commitments under the GPA, but the US held different views. On 11 September 1998, in order to expedite the resolution of this important issue, the US requested the Committee on Government Procurement that Korea responded in writing to the list of questions relating to KOACA and its procurement practices. However, on 16 February 1999, the US requested consultations, claiming that practices relating to qualification for bidding as a prime contractor, domestic partnering and the absence of access to challenge procedures were inconsistent with Korea's obligation under the GPA. The US also contended that the KOACA was within the scope of Korea's list of central government entities covered by the GPA. The Panel concluded that the construction project was not covered in Korea's GPA Schedule because the entities responsible for procurement under the project were not 'covered entities' under GPA Article 1, and overturned the US claim with respect to non-violation as examined under VCLT article 48.

60 In the US, there are other national laws on this issue. The Federal Legislation invoked to impose unilateral sanctions and/or impose secondary boycott have included the Andean Trade Preference Act; the Anti-Terrorism and Effective Death Penalty Act, 1996 (Antiterrorism, 1996); The Arms Export Control Act (AECA); The Atomic Energy Act; the Cuban Democracy Act, 1992; The Cuban Liberty and Democratic Solidarity Act, 1996 (Helms-Burton or LIBERTAD Act); the Department of Commerce, Justice and State, the Judiciary, and Related Agencies Appropriations Act, 1990 (Commerce Appropriations, 1990); the Department of Defence Appropriations Act, 1987 (Defence Appropriations Act, 1987); The Export Administration Act; the Export-Import Bank Act ("E-Im"); The Fisherman's Protective Act, 1967; the Foreign Assistance Act (FAA); Foreign Relations Act; the Foreign Relations Authorisation Act; the Foreign Operations, Export, Financing, and Related Programmes Appropriation Act, 1995; the General System of Preferences Renewal Act (GSP); the High Seas Drift Net Fisheries Enforcement Act (Drift Net Act); the Internal Emergency Economic Powers Act (IEEPA); the Internal Revenue Code; the Internal Security and Development

laws to exist. Other countries, including their trading partners, have denounced these sanctions. Some countries, such as the EC, may challenge these unilateral legal provisions, especially those that impede their trade interests. Nevertheless, the US declines to change them with regard to its political and/or economic demands. It is unlikely that through international litigation the US could alter its policies, but it is possible through initiating domestic litigation (i.e. the *Massachusetts Burma* case). Thus, the feasible way is to seek common ground for the purpose of settlement through amicable negotiations on an international level.

As a matter of fact, these two categories have not come back until recently.[61] However, it is still necessary to stress the notification.

Co-operation Act, 1985 (ISDCA); the International Financial Institutions Act; the Iran-Iraq Non Proliferation Act, 1992; the Iran and Libya Sanctions Act, 1996; the Iraq Sanctions Act, 1990; the Marine Mammal Protection Act, 1972 (Marine Act); the Narcotics Control Trade Act; the National Defense Authorisation Act, 1996 (Defence Authorisation Act, 1996); the Nuclear Non-Proliferation Act, (NNPA) 1994; the Omnibus Appropriation Act, 1997 (1997 Omnibus); the Spoils of War Act, the Trade Act, 1974 (Trade Act); Trading with the Enemy Act (TWEA). Furthermore, there are lots of unilateral imposition of sanctions by Executive Orders and Presidential Determinations. For example, during 1997–1998 there are four instances of this sanctions, including Executive Order 13047 of 21 May 1997 invoking a prohibition on new investment in Burma (Myanmar); Executive Order 13067 of 3 November 1997, imposing a comprehensive trade embargo on Sudan; Presidential Determination No. 98–22 of 13 May 1997, prohibiting the sale of specific goods and technology and United States Bank loans to the Government of India, terminating sales of defence articles and design and construction equipment and services, and shutting down Export-Import Bank (Ex-Im), Overseas Private Investment Corporation (OPIC) and TDA; and Presidential Determination No. 98–XX of May 30, 1998, prohibiting the sale of specific goods and technology and United State Bank loans to the Government of Pakistan, terminating sales of defence articles and design and construction equipment and services, and shutting down Ex-Im, OPIC and TDA. In addition, some states in the US incline to establish their own measure against other countries. See Extra-Territorial Application of National Legislation: Sanctions Imposed against Third Parties, in http://www.aalco.org/etanlcairoIII.htm last visited 11 July 2004.

61 After the US-Government Procurement was concluded in 1999, there has been no dispute either under the category of no agreement on panellists or of the lapse of establishing the Panel.

c. *Settling Disputes before the Panel Composition*

There have been many disputes resolved under this category. The case study helps to disclose how the disputants solved the conflicts and whether these cases were settled by mutually agreed solutions or by the 'shadow of the law'.

(1) *US – Tax on Processed Orange and Grapefruit Products*

On 20 March 2002, the US received from Brazil a request for consultations pertaining to the Equalising Excise Tax (EET) imposed by the State of Florida through Section 601.155 Florida Statutes on processed orange and grapefruit products produced from citrus fruit grown outside the US. However, the statute by its terms exempted from the tax products "produced in whole or in part from citrus fruit grown within the US".[62]

Brazil claimed that the application of the tax to imported processed citrus products differed from the tax treatment of domestic citrus and citrus products in several respects, in violation of Article II:1(a), III:1 and III:2 of GATT 1994. Brazil further claimed that the proceeds of the tax were directed by the Florida statute to the promotion of Florida citrus and citrus products, with no promotion of imported citrus or citrus products, in violation of Article III: 1 and III:4 of GATT 1994. Since processed citrus products, principally in the form of frozen concentrated orange juice were among Brazil's most significant exports to the US, Brazil was of the view that the restraint on their importation by the State of Florida constituted a nullification and impairment of benefits accruing to Brazil.[63]

Consultations were held on 2 May 2002 and on 27 June 2002. Although consultations promoted an important exchange of information, the two parties could not reach a mutually agreed solution to the problems posed by the EET.

In April 2002, a state court in Florida ruled that this exemption for domestic juice was unconstitutional to the extent that it favoured juice made from citrus fruit grown in US states other than Florida. As a result, the law was amended on 1 July 2002, to eliminate the exemption for

62 See WT/DS250/1, *United States – Equalizing Excise tax Imposed by Florida on Processed Orange and Grapefruit Products* – Request for Consultations by Brazil.

63 *Ibid.*

juice produced in states other than Florida. Until 1 July 2002, the Florida EET contained an exemption for all citrus products produced from oranges and grapefruit grown in the US and only juice produced from oranges grown in Florida was exempt from the EET. Brazil was unsure as to whether the elimination of this exemption was permanent since the Florida court decision might be appealed and overturned on appeal or possibly lead to the reinstatement of the cited exemption. Therefore, on 16 August 2002, Brazil requested the establishment of a Panel.[64]

The DSB established a Panel at its meeting on 1 October 2002 after Brazil requested for a second time to establish the Panel. However, the Panel was not formally active as two parties had space to consult.

Following rounds of consultations between the two governments, and consultations between the Florida industry and the State of Florida, the Florida Legislature on 30 April 2004 passed SB 96, which amended provisions of section 601.155, Florida Statutes, concerning the EET. The Governor of Florida signed the amendment into law as Part 200436, Laws of Florida, on 12 May 2004.[65]

Based on these developments, Brazil agreed that a mutually satisfactory solution had been reached with the US. The course of solving the dispute is quite similar with the *US – Government Procurement* case by filing a lawsuit in the US against the Florida department of Citrus seeking to abolish the equalisation tax. The judge ruled that the Department of Citrus could not tax-exempt citrus products from other US states. Therefore, this Florida Statutes must be amended. However, legislation amendment cannot be worked out within a short period, but needs a longer due proceeding. This amended Act directly affects the outcome of the dispute.[66]

64 See WT/DS250/2, *United States – Equalizing Excise Tax Imposed by Florida on Processed Orange and Grapefruit Products* – Request for the Establishment of a Panel by Brazil.

65 See WT/DS250/3, *United States – Equalizing Excise tax Imposed by Florida on Processed Orange and Grapefruit Products* – Notification of Mutually Agreed Solution.

66 Any payment of the tax must be allowed without discretion as to the validity thereof and the person shall be granted the immediate right to elect not to pay two thirds of the applicable tax rate. This act takes effect on 1 July 2004. More information see Committee Substitute for Committee Substitute for Senate Bill No. 96, http://election.dos.state.fl.us/laws/04laws/ch_2004–036.pdf last visited 13 July 2004.

The international dispute settlement again was solved by a domestic court, in which domestic complainants gained 'aid' from foreign companies including Brazilian ones. The following governmental consultations speed up the amendment progress to some extent as it is unusual to completely put aside international relations.

(2) *Uruguay – Tax Treatment*

On 18 June 2002, Chile requested consultations with Uruguay with regard to Uruguay's Internal Specific Tax (IMESI) treatment on certain products, including, *inter alia*, beverages (alcoholic beverages, juices, and mineral water), tobacco and cigarettes, automobiles, lubricants and fuel.[67]

Chile contended that the fiscal framework for the IMESI would increase taxable income if compared to the real sales price, especially in the case of foreign goods. Chile claimed that the IMESI violated Article I and III of the GATT 1994, because it established a tax system based on the use of fictitious prices in order to determinetaxable income. Chile considered that this system discriminated between national and imported products and, in some cases, between imported products depending on their origin, among which for certain products this discrimination amounted in practice to an import prohibition. Chile further claimed that this alleged discrimination constituted a *de facto* import prohibition in case of certain products.

Chile recalled that this system was already questioned by the WTO in 1998, during the Trade Policy Review of Uruguay. This system was subject to some discussion and Uruguay indicated, at the time, that they were in the process of elaborating norms that ensured an equal treatment for all products regardless of their origin.

The consultations took place in Montevideo, Uruguay, on 23 July 2002. In Chile's view, consultations enabled the parties to acquire a better understanding of each other's position. Nonetheless, they did not lead to a mutually satisfactory solution. According to the comparison between

67 WT/DS261/1, *Uruguay – Tax Treatment on Certain Products* – Request for Consultations by Chile.

the request for the Panel and the request for consultations, thefact did not change, and there was no improvement on the divergences.[68]

On 3 April 2003, Chile decided to request the DSB to establish a Panel. In response to a second request by Chile, the DSB established a Panel, and composed it on 4 July 2003.

However, both parties jointly requested the Panel to suspend its work and jointly required extension of the suspension on 15 August 2003, 12 October 2003 and 11 December 2003 respectively in order to seek a positive and bilateral solution to the dispute.[69]

Finally, on 8 January 2004, thetwo parties notified the DSB that on 16 December 2003, the two countries had signed an *Agreement between the Eastern Republic of Uruguay and the Republic of Chile on Settlement of the WTO Dispute 'Uruguay – Tax Treatment on Certain Products'*.[70]

The Agreement contains six Articles. Essentially, it aimed to ensure that the regime for the assessment and payment of the Internal Specific Tax on cigarettes shall be in accordance with the principles and obligations of MFN and National Treatment (NT). In return, Chile promised it would immediately withdraw its request for the Panel.[71]

This case was solved with the outcome of removal of violating provisions between two developing countries, which are both the Member States of the MERCOSUR[72].

(3) *Peru – Tax Treatment*

On 22 April 2002, Chile requested consultations with Peru in respect of its tax treatment on imports of fresh fruits, vegetables, fish, milk, tea and

68 See WT/DS261/4, *Uruguay – Tax Treatment on Certain Products* – Request for the Establishment of a Panel by Chile.

69 See WT/DS261/6, WT/DS261/6/Add. 1 and Add. 2, *Uruguay – Tax Treatment on Certain Products* – Communication from the Chair of the Panel.

70 See WT/DS261/7, *Uruguay – Tax Treatment on Certain Products* – Notification of Mutually Agreed Solution.

71 *Ibid.*, Article 1 and 4, Agreement between the Eastern Republic of Uruguay and the Republic of Chile on Settlement of the WTO Dispute 'Uruguay – Tax Treatment on Certain Products'.

72 A free trade agreement signed on 26 March 1991 by several South American countries including Argentina, Bolivia, Brazil, Chile, Paraguay and Uruguay, creating a common market between them. Negotiations to grant full Membership to Mexico were scheduled to start on July 2004. The agreement also known as the Treaty of Asuncion, allows goods and services to circulate tariff free among Member States.

other natural products. In particular, Chile explained that, before the adoption of Law 27.614 published on 29 December 2001, both the sale in the Peruvian market and the importation into Peru of the products at issue had been exempt from sales taxes. After the adoption of Law 27.614, the importation into Peru of the products at issue was no longer exempt from sales tax (18%) while the sale of those products in the Peruvian market was still exempt from sales tax. Therefore, Chile considered that Peru violated Article III of the GATT 1994.[73]

Chile contended that the above measure prejudiced the competitiveness of Chile's exports to Peru of the said products, including apples, table grapes and peaches, which were natural goods and thus perishable. Chile was invoking the urgency consultation procedure under Article 4.8 of the DSU.[74]

The consultations were held in Lima, Peru on 9 May 2002. This allowed the parties to gain a better understanding of their respective positions, but the government of Peru did not promise to withdraw the measure. Hence, the process remained inconclusive. On 13 June 2002, Chile requested the establishment of a Panel.[75]

On 26 July 2002, Chile asked that its second request for the establishment of a Panel be withdrawn from the agenda of the DSB meeting on 29 July 2002.[76]

On 25 September 2002, Chile informed the DSB that it was withdrawing this complaint as Peru had repealed Article 2 of Law 27.614 and as a result the disputed measures had disappeared.[77]

The same occurred with the *Uruguay – tax treatment* case, between two developing South America countries, which ended with the violating party making full concessions.[78]

73 See WT/DS255/1, *Peru – Tax Treatment on Certain Imported Products* – Request for Consultations by Chile.

74 *Ibid.*

75 See WT/DS255/3, *Peru – Tax Treatment on Certain Imported Products* – Request for the Establishment of a Panel by Chile.

76 See WT/DS255/4, *Peru – Tax Treatment on Certain Imported Products* – Communication from Chile.

77 See WT/DS255/5, *Peru – Tax Treatment on Certain Imported Products* – Communication from Chile.

78 See above case study: (2) the *Uruguay – Tax Treatment*.

(4) *Romania – Wheat and Wheat Flour*

On 18 October 2001, Hungary requested consultations with Romania concerning Romania's Joint Decree of the Ministry of Agriculture, Food Industry and Forestry No. 119069, Ministry of Family and Health No. 495 and the National Consumer Protection Authority No. 1/3687 prohibiting the import of wheat and wheat flour which did not meet certain quality standards. Hungary claimed that the import prohibition had been imposed in a manner inconsistent with Romania's obligations under Article XI of the GATT 1994, and the introduction of the quality requirements was in breach of Article III of the GATT 1994 because domestically produced products were not subject to the same quality requirements.[79]

On 30 October 2001, Hungary requested consultations with Romania according to the urgency procedure provided in Article 4.8 of the DSU, with regard to the seasonal character of the products. Hungary asked to enter into consultations within a period of no more than 10 days after the date of receipt of the request, and required that if consultations failed within a period of 20 days after the date of receipt of the request, Hungary would request the establishment of a Panel.[80]

Hungary obviously took this matter seriously. Romania and Hungary held consultations on 10 November 2001. The consultations failed to settle the dispute. Thus, on 27 November 2001, Hungary requested the establishment of a Panel.[81]

On 19 December 2001, Romania informed Hungary that the Romanian Government had decided to abrogate the contentious measures as of 1 January 2002. Hungary therefore withdrew its second request contained in the letter of 10 December 2001 for the establishment of a Panel.[82]

Two disputes invoking Article 4.8 urgent proceeding of the DSU were resolved before establishing a Panel. First one involved two Latin

79 See WT/DS240/1, *Romania – Import Prohibition on Wheat and Wheat Flour* – Request for Consultations by Hungary.

80 See WT/DS240/1/Add.1, *Romania – Import Prohibition on Wheat and Wheat Flour* – Request for Consultations by Hungary – Addendum.

81 See WT/DS240/2, *Romania – Import Prohibition on Wheat and Wheat Flour* – Request for the Establishment of a Panel by Hungary.

82 See WT/DS240/3, *Romania – Import Prohibition on Wheat and Wheat Flour* – Withdrawal of the Request for the Establishment of a Panel by Hungary.

America countries and the last one was between two East European developing countries, which are Member States of the Central European Free Trade Agreement (CEFTA).

(5) *Turkey – Fresh Fruit*

On 31 August 2001, Ecuador requested a consultation with Turkey concerning import procedures known as Kontrol Belgesi for fresh fruits (particularly bananas). Ecuador alleged that this procedure applied by the Turkish authorities was a barrier to trade because an importer must obtain a Control Certificate (Kontrol Belgesi) issued by the Turkish Ministry of Agriculture and Rural Affairs to be able to seek the SPS clearance certificate (which is a prerequisite for presentation of goods for customs clearance). Ecuador noted that the Control Certificate was not an SPS clearance certificate but an administrative document, which allowed goods to be submitted to SPS control. Furthermore, Turkey failed to confirm that it imposed similar requirements and limitations on domestic production. Thus, Ecuador considered this procedure was inconsistent with Article III and XI of the GATT 1994, Article 2, 7 and 8 of the SPS Agreement, Article 1 of the Agreement on Import Licensing Procedures and Article 4 of the Agreement on Agriculture.[83]

The consultations were held in Geneva on 17 September 2001, achieving the goal of clarifying the facts of the situation, without any resolution of the dispute. On 13 June 2002, Ecuador requested the establishment of a Panel to examine Turkey's import procedures for fresh fruit and clarified the legal basis of this case.[84]

On 22 November 2002, the two parties notified the DSB that they had reached a mutually agreed solution. Turkey modified the application of the control certificate system and published Amending Communique (Number 2002/21) including the control certificates for the importation of bananas in the quantities requested by the importers and for the valid periods. Turkey further committed itself not to revert to practices of the

83 See WT/DS237/1, *Turkey – Certain Import Procedures for Fresh Fruit* – Request for Consultations by Ecuador.

84 See WT/DS237/3, *Turkey – Certain Import Procedures for Fresh Fruit* – Request for the Establishment of a Panel by Ecuador.

kind that gave rise to Ecuador's concerns. Ecuador therefore agreed to withdraw its complaint.[85]

So, two developing countries had resolved their dispute with full concessions from the violating state.

(6) *Peru – Taxes on Cigarettes*

On 1 March 2001, Chile requested consultations with Peru concerning the Peruvian Supreme Decree No. 15899EF of 25 September 1999 modifying appendices III and IV of the General Sales Tax and Selective Consumption Tax Law, which identify the goods subject to the selective consumption tax. Article 1B of the Supreme Decree amends the tax applied to cigarettes made of dark tobacco, standard cigarettes made of bright tobacco and premium cigarettes made of bright tobacco, setting a different specific tax for each one of these categories of cigarettes ranging from S/0.025 to S/0.100 per unit.[86]

Chile contended that the difference in the amount of the tax appears to be contingent only on the number of countries in which the different commercial brands were marketed – more than three of less than three – a criterion which is a source of concern for Chile, since it could signify discrimination against imported cigarettes, from Chile, for example, which, being marketed in more than three countries, were subject to a higher tax than local brand cigarettes. In Chile's view, this situation, which was damaging to Chilean cigarette exports to Peru, could constitute a violation of the GATT 1994.[87]

The consultations were held in Lima, Peru, on 20 April 2001, and enabled the parties to gain a better understanding of each other's positions, but did not give rise to a mutually satisfactory solution. On 3 May 2001, Chile requested the establishment of a Panel against Peru.[88]

At its meeting of 24 June 2001, the DSB established a Panel to further Chile's request. On 12 July 2001, Chile announced its withdrawal of the complaint on the grounds that the contested measure, i.e. the specific

85 See WT/DS237/4, *Turkey – Certain Import Procedures for Fresh Fruit* – Notification of Mutually Agreed Solution.

86 See WT/DS227/1, *Peru – Taxes on cigarettes* – Request for Consultations by Chile.

87 *Ibid.*

88 See WT/DS227/2, *Peru – Taxes on Cigarettes* – Request for the Establishment of a Panel by Chile.

selective consumption tax system applied to cigarettes by Peru, had been amended on 30 June 2001, which became effective on 1 July 2001. As from that date, cigarettes are subject to the common selective consumption tax system at a rate of 100%, regardless of their origin, price, type or quality of tobacco and/or the number of sales markets.[89]

This amendment in the tax regime applicable to cigarettes resulted from an unappealable ruling of the Constitutional Court of Peru on 19 June 2001. Following a request by the British American Tobacco (South America) Ltd, the Constitutional Court ruled that Supreme Decree No. 15899EF did not apply to that company, citing, among other reasons, that it established "an arbitrary classification, which granted preferential treatment to a category of cigarettes, favouring certain producers and/or marketers over others", thus violating the principle of equality before the law.[90]

Since the disputed measure disappeared through a domestic ruling, Chile terminated the Panel composition stage and formally withdrew the dispute. These two developing South America countries are another example of settling a dispute with a concession. However, this time the domestic court played a key role in resolving this international dispute.

(7) *Belgium – Customs Duties for Rice*

On 12 October 2000, the US requested consultations with the EC concerning the administration by Belgium of laws and regulations establishing the customs duties applicable to rice imported from the US. The US considered that:

> Belgium failed to administer the pertinent laws and regulations leading to the assessment of duties on rice imported from the US in excess of the bound rate of duty provided for the Schedule of Specific Commitments of the EC and their Member states LXXX, which was inconsistent with Belgium's commitments under GATT 1994 Article II. The rejection by Belgian customs authorities of the proffered transaction value based, *inter alia*, on the application of an unpublished interpretative memorandum addressing the value to be assigned to specific, limited product characteristics in breach of Article X, the GATT 1994. The EC advised Belgium imposing a penalty on the entries in question in the amount of 50 ECU per metric ton through Commission Regulation in breach of Article VIII and II of the said Agreement;

89 See WT/DS227/3, *Peru – Taxes on Cigarettes* – Communication from Chile.
90 *Ibid.*

> Belgian customs authorities rejected the use of the transaction values associated with certain shipments of rice when assessing duties. This was inconsistent with Articles 1–7, 14 and Annex I of the Customs Valuation Agreement. Furthermore, it disclosed confidential information without the specific permission of the party to whom the information pertained in breach of Article 10 of the said Agreement. In addition, it failed to administer its assessment of tariffs on imported rice in a transparent manner in writing as to how the customs value of the importer's goods were determined, which was inconsistent with Article 7.3 and 16 of the Agreement;
>
> The measure restricted imports of rice into Belgium violated Article I, X and XI of the GATT 1994 and Article 4 of the Agreement on Agriculture.
>
> The afore mentioned interpretative memorandum of April 1998 confined the category of product characteristics and the value to be assigned to such characteristics in establishing the customs value of the imports. This was in breach of Article 2 of the TBT Agreement.[91]

They held consultations on 30 November 2000. The consultations did not resolve the dispute. On 19 January 2001, the US requested the DSB to establish a Panel and increased some failure of Belgium.[92] After receiving a second request to establish a Panel by the US, the DSB established a Panel at its meeting of 12 March 2001. On 29 May 2001, the US requested the DG to determine the composition of the Panel. On 7 June 2001, the Panel was composed.

On 26 July, 27 September, 9 October, 1 November and 19 November 2001 respectively, the US requested the Panel to suspend its work in light of on-going consultations between the two parties.[93]

On 18 December 2001, the two Member States informed the DSB that on 16 November 2001 the Belgian authorities, acting under EC law, redetermining the duties on the basis of new evidence produced, had reached a mutually agreed solution.[94]

91 See WT/DS210/1, *Belgium – Administration of Measures Establishing Customs Duties for Rice* – Request for Consultations by the United States, and WT/DS210/2/Rev.1, *Belgium – Administration of Measures Establishing Customs Duties for Rice* – Request for the Establishment of a Panel by the United States – Revision.

92 See WT/DS210/2 *Belgium – Administration of Measures Establishing Customs Duties for Rice* – Request for the Establishment of a Panel by the United States.

93 See WT/DS210/4, WT/DS210/4/Add. 1–3 and WT/DS210/5, *Belgium – Administration of Measures Establishing Customs Duties for Rice* – Communications from the Chairman of the Panel.

94 See WT/DS210/6, *Belgium – Administration of Measures Establishing Customs Duties for Rice* – Notification of Mutually Agreed Solution.

The agricultural regimes of WTO Members have been challenged in a diverse number of disputes, particularly between the US and the EC. The agricultural sector is a sensitive one for many countries which do not find it easy to make concessions.

How did they do it in this case? It appeared that the purpose of the US complaint was rather to strengthen the position of a US company involved in a court case before a Belgian Court.[95] Similar tactics have been used by many countries, especially the US.

(8) *Brazil – Patent Protection*

On 30 May 2000, the US requested consultations with Brazil, with respect to those provisions of Brazil's 1996 industrial property law and other related measures, which establish a 'local working' requirement for the enjoyment of exclusive patent rights that can only be satisfied by the local production – and not the importation – of the patented subject matter.[96]

The US asserted that Article 68 of Brazil's 1996 industrial property law imposed a, 'local working' requirement, which stipulated that a patent should be subject to compulsory licensing if the subject matter of the patent is not 'worked' in the territory of Brazil. Specifically, a compulsory licence shall be granted on a patent if the patented product was not manufactured in Brazil or if the patented process was not used in Brazil. In addition, if a patent owner chose to exploit the patent through importation rather than 'local working', then Article 68 would allow others to import either the patented product or the product obtained from the patented process. The US considered that Article 68 discriminated against US owners of Brazilian patents whose products were imported into, but not locally produced in Brazil and curtailed the exclusive rights conferred on these owners by their patents. The US further noted that Brazil's local working requirements were inconsistent with its obligations

95 See EU/US News: A Review of Transatlantic Relations, Transatlantic Relations After 11 September from http://europa.eu.int/comm/external_relations/us/eu_us_news/8.pdf last visited 18 July 2004.

96 WT/DS199/1, *Brazil – Measures Affecting Patent Protection* – Request for Consultations by the United States.

under Article 27 and Article 28 of the TRIPS Agreement and Article III of the GATT 1994.[97]

The US and Brazil then held consultations in Geneva on 29 June 2000 and 1 December 2000, but failed to reach a mutually satisfactory resolution of the dispute. The US requested the establishment of a Panel and the DSB established one at its meeting on 1 February 2001.

The US insisted that the law was illegal, but Brazil maintained that its laws were acceptable under WTO rules. Brazil's ambassador told the DSB that Washington had not thought about the political implications of the move to challenge the laws. Although the rules apply to all products, aid agencies said they were mostly concerned about the effect on drugs used to treat HIV/AIDS. The Nobel Prize-winning charity, *Doctors Without Borders*, said the Brazilian government's programme allowed it to offer free treatment to more than 90,000 patients and this would be threatened if Brazil had to accept higher-priced imported drugs. The European Council of AIDS Service Organisations noted that 146,000 people had benefitted from this programme since 1996 because of the policy.[98]

However, the commitment of the US to TRIPS enforcement remains strong. The effective protection of all American intellectual property, including that of pharmaceuticals, is an essential US trade interest. Moreover, protection of these property interests is important to spur additional research and development of new pharmaceuticals that offer major opportunities to combat disease and ease human suffering. WTO dispute settlement is available in cases where US commercial interests are being seriously harmed by another Member's failure to comply with this agreement.[99]

The USTR on 25 June 2001 announced that the US and Brazil agreed to transfer their disagreement from WTO litigation to a newly created

97 WT/DS199/3, *Brazil – Measures Affecting Patent Protection* – Request for the Establishment of a Panel by the United States.

98 Associated Press: WTO to rule on US Complaint against Cut-Price AIDS Drugs in Brazil, for more see http://www.accessmedmsf.org/prod/publications.asp?scntid=2982001739218&contenttype=PARA& (1 February 2001), last visited 26 July 2004.

99 US and Brazil Agree to Use Newly Created Consultative Mechanism to Promote Co-operation on HIV/AIDS and Address WTO Patent Dispute, see http://www.ustr.gov/releases/2001/06/01-46.htm last visited 27 July 2004.

bilateral consultative mechanism. The agreement was a step forward both in the common fight against HIV/AIDS and the constructive handling of this patent dispute. It would permit more effective and less confrontational consideration of intellectual property issues and ensured that such discussions did not divert attention away from the shared goal of combating the spread of HIV/AIDS.

The US commented that litigation in this dispute before a WTO dispute Panel had not been the most constructive way to address their differences, especially since Brazil had never actually used the provision at issue. The Understanding was another step in the administration's flexible approach to health and intellectual property. The Bush Administration stated that the commitment of the US to a flexible approach that was sensitive to health crises and also protective of IPRs. The US would raise no obligation if Members availed themselves of the flexibility afforded by the TRIPS Agreement. This Understanding allowed Brazil to receive important pharmaceutical support for its HIV/AIDS programme.

Meanwhile, Brazil described the agreement between its country and the US as a 'victory for both sides', where they could work together in order to leave space for public policies to be made with a view to providing less expensive pharmaceutical products, which are necessary for the population. Brazil added that it would continue with its efforts to achieve the objective of lowering prices of pharmaceutical products, which are of special interests to developing countries.

Under the terms of the agreement, Brazil would provide 10 days notice to the US before utilising the provision. Therefore, if Brazil seeks to activate the provision there will be an adequate opportunity for consultations in the bilateral Consultative Mechanism. This will provide an early warning system to protect US interests.

In response to the United States WTO complaint, Brazil initiated a tit-for-tat complaint against US patent legislation, which it said discriminated against foreign producers. The Brazilian counter-complaint focuses on Article 204 and 209 of Title 35 of the US patent code. The Brazilian government said the complaint, which was in the consultation phase of WTO dispute settlement proceedings, would not be put on ice as a result of the US-Brazil agreement.[100]

The statement issued by USTR office noted that the US government would aggressively engage other countries that impose or maintain such a requirement and, if appropriate, pursue WTO dispute settlement. In addition, it said that resolving the dispute with Brazil would facilitate efforts by the two countries to work together towards addressing issues related to intellectual property rights in various forums.

On 5 July 2001 the US and Brazil notified the DSB that they had reached a mutually satisfactory solution. It is hard to tell whether the 'threat' isfrom tit-for-tat reaction, given that the US is in a similar situation, or from non-governmental organisations which strongly support the view that the success of the strategies led to universal access to HIV/AIDS medication in Brazil, or maybe from both sides. Brazil believed that the counter-complaint accomplished a final agreement, and the US maintained that it had been supportive of Brazil's bold and effective programme to fight HIV/AIDS and, therefore, adopted flexibility toward their shared goal of combating the spread of the HIV/AIDS virus. The Brazilian delegation held the view that this was a political dispute, rather than a legal one.

(9) *Chile – Transit and Importation of Swordfish*

On 19 April 2000, the EC requested consultations with Chile regarding its prohibition of the unloading of swordfish in Chilean ports, imposed on the basis of Article 165 of the Chilean Fishery Law. The EC asserted that fishing vessels operating in the South East Pacific were not allowed under Chilean legislation to unload their swordfish in Chilean ports, neither to land them for warehousing nor to tranship them onto other vessels. The EC considered that, as a result, Chile made transit through its ports impossible for swordfish and the prohibition rendered also impossible the importation of the affected catches into Chile. The EC

100 Pharmaceuticals: United States Drops WTO Case Against Brazil Over HIV/AIDS Patent Law, see http://www.cptech.org/ip/health/c/brazil/bna06262001.htm last visited 27 July 2004.

claimed that the measures were inconsistent with Article V and XI of GATT 1994 thereof.[101]

Chile activated the United Nations Convention on the Law of the Sea (UNCLOS) dispute settlement procedure, alleging a violation of UNCLOS norms relating to the protection of the marine environment. They filed this case to the International Tribunal for the Law of the Sea (ITLOS). However, the EC considered that questions relating to environmental concerns in a context of trade should be dealt with on a multilateral basis, and not by resorting to the use of discriminatory unilateral measures.

The EC remained hopeful that an amicable solution could be reached with the Chileans, without the need to proceed to a Panel. Furthermore, the EC remained open to continue the exchange of technical and scientific information within the framework of the EC-Chile Joint Technical Commission on swordfish with a view to assessing the stock of swordfish in the South Pacific.[102]

The consultations where held on 14 June 2000 in Geneva, allowing a better understanding of the respective position, but did not lead to a satisfactory resolution of the matter. On that occasion, the EC suggested that multilateral negotiations open to any interested party should start as soon as possible and be concluded within a pre-established timeframe. Moreover, a limited and regulated access to Chilean ports should be made available to EC vessels in parallel with the negotiating process. Chile refused to discuss any access to their ports by the EC vessels. A new settlement initiative was taken by Commissioner Lamy. It continued to be open to a settlement, which took into consideration both its WTO rights and the need for an effective conservation and management of swordfish resources in the South East Pacific; given the time which had elapsed and the entrenched Chilean position, the EC had no other option. Thus, on 6 November 2000, the EC requested the establishment of a WTO Panel.[103]

101 See WT/DS193/1, *Chile – Measures Affecting the Transit and Importation of Swordfish* – Request for Consultations by the European Communities.

102 EC to Request WTO Consultations with Chile over Prohibition of Unloading of Swordfish in Chilean Ports (IP/00/397), 18 April 2000, see http://tradeinfo.cec.eu.int/wtodispute/show.cfm?id=145&code=1 last visited 28 July 2004.

103 See WT/DS193/2, *Chile – Measures Affecting the Transit and Importation of Swordfish* – Request for the Establishment of a Panel by the European Communi-

While this request was desirable in order to safeguard the EC's trade interests under the WTO, Chile and the EC continued to explore alternative avenues to settle the dispute in a negotiated way, thereby avoiding the need for a Panel. The EC reiterated its call on Chile and other interested Members to launch negotiations and to resume in the shortest possible time scientific co-operation and exchange of data with the EC.

Lamy and Fisheries Commissioner Fischer played an active role in this dispute. They submitted a proposal,[104] which constituted a solid basis for reaching a satisfactory compromise for both sides. They believed that the package proposed reflected the priority the EC attached to environmental concerns linked to trade. They also believed it ensured that their fishermen were allowed to operate according to the rules of world trade.

---

ties. These Chilean restrictions dated back to 1991. Since then, this matter has been raised several times in bilateral meetings between the EC and Chile. The latest dispute took place before the WTO case in July 1998. A Spanish fishery association lodged a complaint pursuant to the Trade Barriers Regulation (TBR) claiming a violation of Chile's obligations under GATT 1994 and of several provisions of the UNCLOS. The investigation concluded that the Chilean ban violated the principle of freedom of transit under Article V of GATT 1994. Additionally, by making unloading in Chilean ports impossible for swordfish catches made by the EC vessels, the Chilean measures were contrary to Article XI of GATT 1994. The EC tried unsuccessfully for more than one year to find an amicable solution. To this effect, two meetings with the Chilean authorities took place in June and September 1999, which did not record any major progress, but helped understanding the respective positions. While these negotiations were ongoing, Chile reinforced its prohibition by adopting a new decree according to which any sanctions provided or that will be provided for the Chilean national vessels will be enforce against the EC vessels fishing swordfish anywhere on the high sea. Furthermore, Chile signed a framework agreement on the conservation of living resources in the high sea. It was striking because the EC were not invited to this negotiating table although the EC repeatedly showed its willingness to take part in a similar multilateral negotiating exercise. Instead, what Chile proposed to the EC was participation in a unilateral "take it or leave it" agreement. This clearly raised doubts on Chile willingness to enter into cooperative arrangements with EC. Under these circumstances, the EC initiated WTO dispute settlement proceedings with Chile. See EU Requests the Establishment of a WTO Panel against the Republic of Chile (MEMO/00/77), 10 November 2000, http://trade–info.cec.eu.int/wtodispute/show.cfm?id=145&code=1, last visited 28 July 2004.

104 This proposal envisaged a solution based on three main elements: strong bilateral technical and scientific co-operation on conservation of fish stocks, the creation of a genuinely multilateral organization to manage swordfish stocks in the Pacific, and the granting of limited access to Chilean ports for EC vessels.

The EC firmly believed that the most effective way to tackle international environmental issues such as the conservation of migratory stocks is a multilaterally negotiated agreement. This is the best guarantee against the use of discriminatory actions and of trade measures for protectionist purposes.[105]

After several rounds of intensive consultations on the basis of this proposal, the EC and Chile finally reached an amicable settlement. As a result and pending the ratification of the arrangement, the EC requested a suspension of Panel proceedings on 23 March 2001 and Chile suspended proceedings before the ITLOS.[106]

The settlement struck a balance between taking due account of the requirements of the multilateral trade system and an effective conservation and management of natural resources. This arrangement showed that it is possible to resolve disputes amicably by reconciling trade and environmental concerns.

Furthermore, the critical question of whether the ITLOS had the jurisdiction to hear the dispute, or whether it was prevented from doing so because of Article 282 UNCLOS has remained of interest.[107]

Indeed, it is legitimate to ask whether the issue of access to Chilean ports and services pending before the WTO and that of the preservation of the swordfish stock are the same. If they are, the ITLOS might have to defer to the dispute settlement procedures of the WTO in compliance with the exception of Article 282 of the UNCLOS. If not, however, then the possibility of parallel proceedings before the two for the same situa-

105 EU and Chile Reach an Amicable Settlement to End WTO/ITLOS Swordfish Dispute (IP/01/116), 25 January 2001, see http://trade-info.cec.eu.int/wtodispute/show. cfm?id=145&code=1 last visited 28 July 2004.

106 See WT/DS193/3, Dispute Settlement Body – *Chile – Measures Affecting the Transit and Importation of Swordfish* – Arrangement between the European Communities and Chile.

107 The original context of Article 282 is as follows: If the States Parties which are parties to a dispute concerning the interpretation or application of this Convention have agreed, through a general, regional or bilateral agreement or otherwise, that such dispute shall, at the request of any party to the dispute, be submitted to a procedure that entails a binding decision, that procedure shall apply in lieu of the procedures provided for in this Part, unless the parties to the dispute otherwise agree. See Article 282, Section 1 General Provisions, Part XV Settlement of Disputes, United Nations Convention on the Law of the Sea of 10 December 1982, http://www.un.org/Depts/los/convention_agreements/texts/unclos/part15.htm last visited 28 July 2004.

tion is real. It is not far-fetched to imagine that, by resorting to two different bodies of law, the two organisations could eventually come to antithetical conclusions, with the WTO Panel upholding the EC claims and the ITLOS upholding those of Chile – an awkward situation indeed – where the only real loser would be the unity of international law.

(10) *Argentina – Woven Fabric of Cotton and Cotton Mixtures*

On 29 July 1999, Argentina requested consultations with Brazil concerning transitional safeguard measures applied by Argentina against certain imports of woven fabrics of cotton and cotton mixtures originating in Brazil. The measures at issue were applied through the Resolution of the Ministry of the Economy and Public Works and Services of Argentina. The traditional safeguard measures were applied against five categories or groups of categories of textile imports from Brazil. The Argentina system of categories was notified by Argentina in document WT/L/276.[108]

Consultations were held in Geneva, on 8 September 1999, at which time it was not possible to reach a mutually agreed solution. Brazil then notified the TMB of the results of the consultations and referred the issue to the TMB. The TMB conducted a review of the measures implemented by Argentina.

The TMB examined the case category by category. On all categories except 613/617/627, the TMB could not find serious damage caused by imports. In the case of categories 613/617/627, the TMB was not able to reach the conclusion that imports were the primary cause of difficulties faced by the Argentina's domestic industry. The TMB, therefore, made a recommendation for Argentina to withdraw the safeguard measures.[109]

On 29 November 1999, Argentina notified the TMB that it considered itself unable to conform to the recommendations. In December, the TMB reviewed the case again, but was not able to reverse its previous finding.[110] Argentina communicated its continuing inability to comply. Brazil

108 See WT/DS190/1, *Argentina – Transitional Safeguard Measures on Certain Imports of Woven Fabrics of Cotton and Cotton Mixtures Originating in Brazil* – Request for the Establishment of a Panel by Brazil.

109 See G/TMB/20, Fifty-Ninth Meeting of the TMB – Note by the Chairman, 1999.

110 See G/TMB/21, Textiles Monitoring Body – Sixty-First Meeting of the TMB – Note by the Chairman, 1999.

then on 11 February 2000 requested the establishment of a DSB Panel without alternatives.

Before the Panel was established, the matter was resolved in favour of Brazil by an arbitration tribunal under the Brasilia Protocol, the dispute settlement mechanism for MERCOSUR. On 27 June 2000, Argentina and Brazil notified the DSB of their intention to suspend the dispute procedure, retaining the right to resume it in 12 months time.[111]

It is necessary to note that the Brasilia Protocol and the DSU are distinct legal entities. Thus, the MERCOSUR arbitral tribunal ruled only on the compatibility of the safeguard measure with MERCOSUR, not with the ATC.[112] Therefore, there has been no ruling by the DSB on Argentina's safeguard actions against Brazil.

We see in this case that, although the ATC temporarily became the victim of the asymmetric exchange rate regimes of MERCOSUR, the institutions of MERCOSUR were able to rise to the occasion and solved the matter.[113]

The ATC expired at the end of 2004. Interest in textile and clothing safeguard actions, however, will extend to 2008 under the provisions of China's accession to the WTO. Latin American countries have used ATC safeguard actions as a way to address macroeconomic and balance of payments issues. In this case, the TMB and MERCOSUR dispute settlement procedures were able to successfully address these issues. Although it is fair to say that this dispute was resolved by the regional trade agreement, the request to the DSB promoted the settlement. The consultations between two parties in MERCOSUR paralleled with the requests for the establishment of a Panel led to the final concessions,

111 See WT/DS190/2, *Argentina – Transitional Safeguard Measures on Certain Imports of Woven Fabrics of Cotton and Cotton Mixtures Originating in Brazil* – Notification of Mutually Agreed Solution.

112 See Dispute Settlement Body, Minutes of Meeting Held on 20 March 2000, WT/DSB/M/77, 17 April 2000. Under the DSU, Article 3.6 states that mutually agreed solutions to matters formally raised under the consultation and dispute settlement provisions of the covered agreements shall be notified to the DSB and the relevant Councils and Committees, where any Member may rise any point relating thereto.

113 See Kim, S. J., Reinert, K. A. & Rodrigo, G. C. The Agreement on Textiles and Clothing: Safeguard Actions From 1995 to 2001, see http://mason.gmu.edu/~kreinert/paperspdf/atcJ.I.E.L..pdf last visited 28 July 2004.

which withdrew the transitional safeguard measures by Argentina issued Regulation 265/2000.

(11) *Colombia – Plain Polyester Filaments*

The facts in this case are quite similar to those in the last one. On 28 and 29 September 1998, Colombia requested a consultation with Thailand, regarding imports of plain polyester filaments from Thailand. The consultations did not result in a mutual understanding as to whether the situation called for restraint on the said imports.[114]

On 6 November 1998, Colombia notified TMB that it had decided, on 26 October 1998, to apply transitional safeguard measures on imports of plain polyester filaments (tariff heading 54.02.43) from Korea and Thailand, for a period of one year. The TMB conducted an examination of the matter and, at its fiftieth meeting held on 16–19 November 1998, recommended that the measures introduced by Colombia on imports of plain polyester filaments from Thailand should be rescinded.[115]

Following this review, the TMB reviewed a communication made by Colombia's inability to conform to the above TMB recommendation. At its fifty-second meeting held on 18–20 January 1999, the TMB reviewed the matter and issued a further recommendation that the measures introduced by Colombia should be removed forthwith.[116]

In a communication dated 22 June 1999, Colombia informed the TMB that the safeguard applied to imports from Thailand was justified and it would maintain its safeguard measure.[117] The matter was not resolved. Consequently, Thailand requested the establishment of a Panel on 7 September 1999.

Before the DSB meeting on 27 October 1999, the Chairman consulted with Thailand and Colombia, since the measure in question had expired and was, therefore, no longer in force. In light of the confirmation made

114 See WT/DS181/1, *Colombia – Safeguard Measure on Imports of Plain Polyester Filaments from Thailand* – Request for the Establishment of a Panel by Thailand.

115 See G/TMB/R/49, Textiles Monitoring Body – Report of the Fiftieth Meeting.

116 See G/TMB/R/51, Textiles Monitoring Body – Report Fifty-Second Meeting.

117 See G/TMB/N/344, Textiles Monitoring Body – Agreement on Textiles and Clothing – Communication from Colombia.

by Colombia, Thailand withdrew its request for a Panel from the agenda.[118]

The dispute resolved itself as the safeguard measure had been terminated by its time limit without extension. In fact, this case could not be settled by a Panel with respect to the timing requirement of due proceedings in the WTO. It brings out an importantquestion: which method is proper and realistic to solve a dispute within such a 'short term'? The answer is obviously not through litigation.

(12) *Argentina – Footwear*

On 23 April 1998, Indonesia requested consultations with Argentina regarding the provisional and the definitive safeguard measures imposed by Argentina on imports of footwear. Argentina imposed a definitive safeguard measure in the form of minimum specific duties on imports of footwear. Indonesia maintained that these measures caused serious injury to the trade interests of Indonesia, which is a significant exporter of footwear.[119]

Consultations were held on 21 May and 7–8 September 1998 in Geneva, but did not lead to a satisfactory solution of the matter. On December 1998, Indonesia requested supplementary consultations with Argentina, regarding the tariff-rate quota (TRQ) that Argentina had imposed in November 1998. These consultations were held on 11 January and 2 February 1999 in Geneva, and also did not lead to a satisfactory resolution of the matter. Therefore, Indonesia requested a Panel on 15 April 1999.[120]

During the discussion of this matter at the meeting of the DSB, held on 28 April 1999, regarding developments in a related Panel proceeding, Indonesia reconsidered its decision based upon the intervention of the delegations of Argentina and the EC. Argentina noted that, with regard to the timing of the request, the safeguard measure on imports of footwear challenged by Indonesia was currently being examined by the

118 See WT/DSB/M/70, Dispute Settlement Body – Minutes of Meeting – Held in the Centre William Rappard on 27 October and 3 November 1999.

119 See WT/DS123/1, *Argentina – Safeguard Measures on Imports of Footwear –* Request for Consultations by Indonesia.

120 See WT/DS123/3, *Argentina – Safeguard Measures on Imports of Footwear –* Request for the Establishment of a Panel by Indonesia.

Panel established at the request of the EC and Indonesia, which was one of the third parties.[121] Repeated Panel proceedings could undermine the dispute settlement mechanism, in particular, when the respondent was a developing country with limited resources, although Argentina recognised Indonesia's right to request a Panel. The EC indicated that the modifications introduced by Argentina to the disputed measures had been considered by the Panel and its work would soon be completed. The EC believed that it would win the case. On 10 May 1999, Indonesia informed the DSB that it withdrew the request for the establishment of a Panel, but stated that if Indonesia should choose to include the request for establishment of a Panel as an item on the agenda of a future meeting of the DSB, the DSB would treat the agenda item as its second consideration of the request.[122]

The Panel report filed by the EC found that Argentina's measure was inconsistent with the Agreement on Safeguards. Argentina appealed, but the AB upheld the Panel's finding. Argentina informed the DSB on 11 February 2000 that the safeguard measure would remain in force until 25 February 2000, by which date, the measures, aimed at complying with the DSB's ruling, would be adopted.

This case filed by Indonesia was solved because of 'multilateralism' as a 'free-rider'. The consultation arguably gave a strong impression of bilateralism rather than multilateralism stressed by the WTO. Nevertheless, the court rulings could be relied upon by every Member state because of report publication.

Indonesia had participated as a third party in the Panel requested by the EC; however, under the existing DSU rules, it was not possible to inform third parties of the results of the Panel's work. As Indonesia had a strong trade interest, it referred the disputed measures to the Panel. In the case at hand, the Panel established at the request of the EC, was to be adopted by the DSB before the new proceedings requested by Indonesia were completed. Therefore, the Panel requested by Indonesia would become a moot case. It was wise of Indonesia that it opted for reservation of all rights under the DSU rather than repeated the Panel proceed-

121 See WT/DS121/R, *Argentina – Safeguard Measures on Imports of Footwear –* Report of the Panel.

122 See WT/DS123/4, *Argentina – Safeguard Measures on Imports of Footwear –* Communication from Indonesia and WT/DSB/M/60, Dispute Settlement Body – Minutes of Meeting – Held in the Centre William Rappard on 28 April 1999.

ings, which placed an excessive burden on the respondent and the complainant.

The above three disputes had mainly the same facts about textiles, regarding safeguard measures. All had been resolved during the 'consultation stage'; although the actual methods of settling disputes were not by consultations, they interlink each other under the DSU.[123]

(13) *US – Anti-dumping Duties on Colour Television Receivers*

On 10 July 1997, Korea requested consultations with the US in respect of the imposition of anti-dumping duties on imports of colour television receivers (CTVs) from Korea. Korea contended that the US had, for the past twelve years, maintained an anti-dumping order for Samsung's CTVs despite the absence of dumping and the cessation of exports from Korea, without examining the necessity of continuing to impose such duties.[124]

Consultations were held on 7 August 1997 and on 8 October 1997. However, no mutually satisfactory solution was reached. On 6 November 1997, Korea requested the establishment of a Panel.

The Korean government's experience of dispute settlement under the GATT system was fairly limited.[125] Korea was challenged twice as a respondent but had no experience of the disputes as a complainant. Under the WTO system, the Korean government had become far more active in asserting its rights through the dispute settlement mechanism.

Until 2001, Korean complaints in the WTO dispute settlement system focused primarily on US antidumping measures. Five out of six complains had been about antidumping matters, brought against the US. The trade deficit of Korea, with respect to the US, began in 1994 and remained throughout 1997, reaching 8.5 billion USD in 1997.[126]

While Korea had been challenged in the WTO dispute settlement system from a very early time, the country appeared reluctant to bring complaints against other WTO Member states. This dispute was the first one

123 See the following table.

124 See WT/DS89/1, *United States – Imposition of Anti–Dumping Duties on Imports of Colour Television Receivers from Korea* – Request for Consultations by Korea.

125 See Ahn, D. GATT/WTO Dispute Settlement and Korea: From Passivity to Aggression, CDAMS Discussion Paper O4/3E, Kobe University, April 2004, http://www.cdams.kobe-u.ac.jp/archive/dp04-3.pdf last visited 30 July 2004.

126 *Ibid.*

for which Korea began to use the WTO dispute settlement system as a complainant.

On 19 December 1997, the US Department of Commerce took measures relevant to this matter: termination of the anti-circumvention investigation initiated on 19 January 1996 and a preliminary determination to revoke the antidumping duty order with respect to Samsung Electronics Co., Ltd.[127]

In response to these measures, Korea withdrew its request for a Panel. On 27 August 1998, the US made a final drive to revoke the antidumping duty order, which had been imposed on Samsung CTVs since 1984. At the DSB meeting on 22 September 1998, Korea announced that it definitively withdrew the request for a Panel, because the imposition of anti-dumping duties had been restrained.[128]

So, as a complainant, Korea won its first dispute with US making concessions.

(14) *Turkey – Taxation of Foreign Film Revenues*

On 12 June 1996, the US requested consultations with Turkey concerning Turkey's taxation of revenues generated from the showing of foreign films in a manner less favourable than its taxation of revenues generated from the showing of domestic-origin films. The US claimed that Turkey imposed 25% discriminatory tax against foreign films under the Law No. 2464, in violation of Article III of the GATT 1994.[129]

Consultations were held on July 23, 1996, but did not result in a resolution of the dispute. Thus, on 9 January 1997 the US requested the establishment of a Panel. At its meeting on 25 February 1997 the DSB established a Panel.[130]

Turkey still hoped that a resolution could be found in consultation with the US. As a result of subsequent consultations, Turkey agreed to

127 See WT/DS89/8, *United States – Imposition of Anti-Dumping Duties on Imports of Colour Television Receivers from Korea* – Withdrawal of the Request for the Establishment of a Panel by Korea.

128 See WT/DS89/9, *United States – Imposition of Anti-Dumping Duties on Imports of Colour Television Receivers from Korea* – Communication from Korea.

129 See WT/DS43/1, *Turkey – Taxation of Foreign Film Revenues* – Request for Consultations by the US.

130 See WT/DS43/2, *Turkey – Taxation of Foreign Film Revenues* – Request for the Establishment of a Panel by the US.

equalise its tax on box office receipts from the showing of domestic and imported films as soon as reasonably possible. On 14 July 1997, both parties notified the DSB of a mutually agreed solution.[131] In late 1996, Turkey implemented the required changes to eliminate the discriminatory taxation of foreign films.

Turkey had been on the Special 301 Priority Watch List since 1992 for its failure to enact copyright reform and its lack of enforcement efforts to combat high levels of piracy. The US copyright industries experienced high losses due to copyright piracy in Turkey, losing more than $269 million (trade loss due to motion picture piracy was $59 million) in 1996, a major increase from the $159 million lost in 1995.

The US offers Turkey the status of Generalised System of Preferences (GSP) beneficiary developing country. From 1 June 1993, Turkey was under USTR review under the GSP Programme to withdraw Turkey's eligible beneficiary status for its failure to provide "adequate and effective protection" to US copyrights as required by the GSP statute. In a matter related to copyright industry issues, USTR initiated an investigation under Section 302 of the 1974 Trade Act, of Turkey's taxation of foreign films revenues. On 24 February 1997, USTR was required to suspend benefits and/or revoke Turkey's GSP status again by the US copyright industries.[132]

Under these circumstances, Turkey had to make concessions in order to keep the GSP statute. This was not a surprising result because of their 'special relationship'.

(15) *US – Tariff Increasing*

On 17 April 1996, the EC requested consultation with the US with respect to Presidential Proclamation No. 5759 of 24 December 1987, any implementing measures thereof and all other related measures, which were taken in response to the adoption of EC legislation on the use in livestock farming of certain substances having a hormonal action, and purport on unilaterally settle an issue without resorting to the mecha-

131 See WT/DS43/3, *Turkey – Taxation of Foreign Film Revenues* – Notification of Mutually Agreed Solution.

132 See Excerpt from the IIPA Special 301 Recommendations, February 24, 1997: Turkey, in http://www.iipa.com/rbc/1997/rbc_turkey_301_97.html last visited 31 July 2004.

nisms of the WTO. These measures increased the bound rates of duty on imports of certain products from the EC.[133]

Consultations were held in Geneva on 22 May 1996, during the course of which, it emerged from the information and the argumentation put forward by the US that the measures in question, including Section 301 of the 1974 Trade Act (as amended) and as applied in this case, apparently failed to ensure conformity of the US laws, regulations and administrative procedures with its obligations under the WTO. The consultations failed to settle the dispute, and, as a consequence, the EC requested the establishment of a Panel on 19 June 1996, after 60 days due proceeding of the consultation.[134]

On 15 July 1997, the US terminated the application of increased duties on certain products from the EC and applied the MFN rates on those products. The EC decided not to pursue its Panel request.[135]

(16) *Pakistan – Patent Protection*

On 30 April 1996, the US requested consultation with Pakistan, regarding the absence in Pakistan of either patent protection for pharmaceutical and agricultural chemical products or a system to permit the filing of an application for product patents and a system to grant exclusive marketing rights in such products (so-called 'mailbox system').[136]

Consultations were held on 30 May 1996, but did not result in a resolution of the dispute. Then, the US immediately requested the establishment of a Panel on 3 July 1996.[137]

The DSB considered the request at its meeting on 16 July 1996, but did not establish a Panel due to Pakistan's objection. Pakistan noted that it had responded positively and had invited the US to hold the consultations in Islamabad, due to financial difficulties preventing use of Ge-

133 See WT/DS39/1, *United States – Tariff Increases on Products from the European Communities* – Request for Consultations by the EC.

134 See WT/DS39/2, *United States – Tariff increases on products from the European Communities* – Request for the Establishment of a Panel by the EC.

135 See WT/DSB/M/21, Dispute Settlement Body – Minutes of Meeting – Held in the Centre William Rappard on 15 and 16 July 1996.

136 See WT/DS36/1, *Pakistan – Patent Protection for Pharmaceutical and Agricultural Chemical Products* – Request for Consultations by the US.

137 See WT/DS36/3, *Pakistan – Patent Protection for Pharmaceutical and Agricultural Chemical Products* – Request for the Establishment of a Panel by the US.

neva. Moreover, many policy-making officials were involved in the preparation of the annual budget and in trade policy matters. Pakistan was disappointed with the US decision to proceed to the Panel stage, though it still engaged in the process of consultations as it had assured the US that it was committed to fulfilling its obligations under the TRIPS agreement. The bill to amend its Patents and Designs Act to provide for the mailbox system had been before Parliament and was expected to be shortly enacted into law. Pakistan had responded to US concerns, positively and in good faith, and had informed the US in writing of its commitments. Three days after these assurances, the US had proceeded with its request for the Panel.[138]

This also raised important questions in relation to the DSU such as: (i) the real difficulties faced by developing countries on the insistence by a developed country that consultations be held only in Geneva; (ii) the meaning and significance of the consultations stage; (iii) whether a Member could decide unilaterally that consultations had been concluded since Article 12.10 of the DSU provided that "in the context of consultations involving a measure taken by a developing country Member, the parties may agree to extend the period established in paragraphs 7 and 8 of Article 4".[139] For all of these reasons, Pakistan could not agree to the establishment of a Panel requested by the US.[140] Therefore, the two parties decided to continue negotiations on this matter.

On 28 February 1997, both parties informed the DSB that they had reached a mutually satisfactory solution. As soon as possible after the date of this joint notification, Pakistan would issue regulations implementing the mailbox system under Presidential Ordinance.[141]

The US aggressively pushed Member States, particularly the developing Members, to implement obligations under the TRIPS Agreement in such a manner that its trade interests were not impeded by them. The

138 See WT/DSB/M/21, Dispute Settlement Body – Minutes of Meeting – Held in the Centre William Rappard on 15 and 16 July 1996.

139 Article 12.10 of the DSU.

140 See WT/DSB/M/21, Dispute Settlement Body – Minutes of Meeting – Held in the Centre William Rappard on 15 and 16 July 1996.

141 See WT/DS36/4, *Pakistan – Patent Protection for Pharmaceutical and Agricultural Chemical Products* – Notification of a Mutually Agreed Solution.

India – Patent Protection for Pharmaceutical and Agricultural Chemical Products case[142] supported this view.

(17) *Hungary – Agricultural Products*

On 27 March 1996, Argentina, Australia, Canada, New Zealand, Thailand and the US claimed that Hungary violated the Agreement on Agriculture by providing export subsidies in respect of agricultural products not specified in its schedule. Moreover, it provided agricultural export subsidies in excess of the budgetary outlay and quantity commitment levels specified in Hungary's Schedule.[143]

Consultations were held on 3 May 1996 between Hungary and these complainants and on several occasions thereafter, but did not result in a settlement of the dispute although Hungary acknowledged that its agricultural exports subsidy programme was inconsistent with its WTO export subsidy commitments. On 9 January 1997, Argentina, Australia, New Zealand and the US requested the establishment of a Panel.[144]

Hungary regretted that, despite its country's continuing efforts to find a mutually satisfactory solution, four complaining parties had decided to proceed with their request for the establishment of a Panel. Hungary believed that the establishment of a Panel was not a suitable way to provide a positive solution to a problem caused by errors in its Schedule.[145]

142 See WT/DS50, *India – Patent Protection for Pharmaceutical and Agricultural Chemical Products*. The whole proceedings began on 2 July 1996, ended on 15 April 1999 from the consultations to recourse to Article 21.5 of the DSU with India's full compliance.

143 See WT/DS35/1, *Hungary – Export Subsidies in Respect of Agricultural Products* – Request for Consultations by Argentina, Australia, Canada, New Zealand, Thailand and the United States.

144 See WT/DS35/4–7, *Hungary – Export Subsidies in respect of Agricultural Products* –Request for the Establishment of a Panel by Australia, New Zealand, the US and Argentina.

145 On 9 April 1996, Hungary informed WTO Members about the critical error that occurred when its export subsidy reduction commitments on agricultural products, as contained in its Schedule LXXI, were established. As a consequence of this error, the referred to section of Hungary's Schedule covered only a small fraction of the products subsidised and the amounts of subsidies in the base period of 1986–1990. The submitted schedule contained 16 narrowly defined products with an aggregate base outlay level of 22 billion Forints against the actual base period figures of some 720 subsidised products and over US$1 billion annual average export subsidies. See WT/L/144.

Since the protection of its national interests related to the preservation of agricultural activity was at stake, Hungary thought that a Panel was not appropriate. Due to unique conditions which lay at the root of the problem, it requested the complaining parties to hold consultations in order to take into account the exceptional circumstances outlined. Hungary was ready to make further efforts to find a mutually acceptable solution to this dispute outside the Panel procedure, which would enable Hungary to produce and export agricultural products, and to make the necessary adjustments in this sector under socially acceptable conditions.[146]

Consultations continued. At the DSB meeting on 30 July 1997, Australia, on behalf of all the complainants, notified the DSB that the parties to the dispute had reached a mutually agreed solution, which required Hungary to seek a waiver of certain of its WTO obligations.[147]

(18) *Australia – Salmonids*

This request for consultations dated 17 November 1995, concerned the same regulation alleged to be in violation of the WTO Agreements in WT/DS18, regarding the prohibition by Australia of the import of salmonids.[148]

Consultations were held on 13 December 1995, but failed to settle the dispute. On 11 May 1999, the US requested the establishment of a Panel. At the DSB meeting on 16 June 1999, it established a Panel.[149]

At the request of the US, the Panel had suspended its work three times until 17 July 2000 since the proceeding requested by Canada in WT/DS18 was ongoing and the US was waiting for implementation within a reasonable period of time.[150]

146 See WT/DSB/M/29, Dispute Settlement Body – Minutes of Meeting – Held in the Centre William Rappard 25 February 1997.

147 See WT/DSB/M/36, Dispute Settlement Body – Minutes of Meeting – Held in the Centre William Rappard on 30 July 1997.

148 See WT/DS21/1, *Australia – Measures affecting the Importation of Salmonids –* Request for Consultations by the United States.

149 See WT/DS21/4, *Australia – Measures affecting the Importation of Salmonids –* Request for the Establishment of a Panel by the United States.

150 See WT/DS21/7–9, *Australia – Measures Affecting the Importation of Salmonids –* Communication from the Chairman of the Panel.

On 27 October 2000, the parties to the dispute notified a mutually satisfactory solution, involving the amendments to Australia's July 1999 quarantine policies.[151]

This was the third dispute resolved after the ruling of another case sharing the same complaint with the same factual matters. In this dispute, the Panel requested by Canada, issued the report on 18 February 2000 that Australia should bring its measures into conformity with its obligations under the DSU and the SPS Agreement.

Furthermore, in this case, Australia raised important due process concerns with regard to the US Panel request. It noted that the US request for a Panel went beyond the scope of the consultations. The US sought to extinguish Australia's legal right before consultation, as well as asked the DSB to exceed its legal authority by establishing a Panel with terms of reference covering matters including Article 7 and 8 of the SPS Agreement not previously raised in consultations.[152]

(19) *EC – Duties on Imports of Grains*

On 18 July 1995, the US requested consultations with the EC regarding the application of tariffs to grains, including wheat, corn, barley and rice, which had broader product coverage than the case brought by Canada (WT/DS9) on 10 July 1995, but otherwise, concerned the same issues.[153]

Consultations were held on 13 September 1995, but failed to settle the dispute; accordingly, on 28 September, the US requested the establishment of a Panel, which Canada had previously asked foron 14 September.[154]

In November 1995, the EC and US reached a settlement. This took the form of an exchange of letters which provided for a number of undertakings on the part of the EC to be implemented by the EC, including EC's market access commitments on grains, reducing import charges on rice and providing for consultations on the EC's 'reference price sys-

151 See WT/DS21/10, *Australia – Measures Affecting the Importation of Salmonids* – Notification of Mutually Agreed Solution.

152 See WT/DSB/M/64, Dispute Settlement Body – Minutes of Meeting – Held in the Centre William Rappard on 16 June 1999.

153 See WT/DS13/1, *European Communities – Duties on Imports of Grains* – Request for Consultations by the US.

154 See WT/DS13/2, *European Communities – Duties on Imports of Grains* –Request for the Establishment of a Panel by the US.

tem'. The exchange had also stated the US would withdraw its request for a Panel. Therefore, the EC informed the DSB that they had solved the dispute on 30 November 1996.[155]

However, the US on 20 December 1996 noted that the EC had not implemented its commitments in that agreement. The US renewed its request for a Panel on 13 February, unless the EC immediately took steps to implement the settlement agreement.[156]

The EC challenged that the US request was premature since consultations were under way to find a solution to this matter, which should allow negotiations within a period of adequate time, at least until April. The EC claimed that it had drafted a regulation and waited for a response from the US. The EC also explained that this was not a case of unwillingness by one party, but a case in which both parties had difficulties in making progress.[157]

Finally, on 30 April 1997, the US withdrew all requests for the establishment of a Panel as the EC adopted regulations to implement the provisions of that agreement.[158]

The US in this case, not only pursued the proceedings settling dispute, but also enhanced it to the stage of implementation, although it was arguably beyond the scope of consultations.

(20) *Malaysia – Polyethylene and Polypropylene*

On 10 January 1995, Singapore requested to consult with Malaysia concerning the prohibition of imports of polyethylene (PE) and polypropylene (PP) instituted and maintained by the Malaysian Government under

155 See WT/DS13/3, *European Communities – Duties on Imports of Grains* – Communication from the EC.

156 See WT/DS13/4, *European Communities – Duties on Imports of Grains* – Communication from the US, and WT/DS13/5, *European Communities – Duties on Imports of Grains* – Request for the Establishment of a Panel by the US.

157 See WT/DSB/M/29, Dispute Settlement Body – Minutes of Meeting – Held in the Centre William Rappard on 25 February 1997.

158 See WT/DS13/8, *European Communities – Duties on Imports of Grains* – Communication from the US.

the Customs Order 1994. This order formalised its restrictive policies through the imposition of import prohibitions on PE and PP.[159]

Singapore held consultations with Malaysia on 13–15 February 1995 and on 8–9 March 1995, but failed to settle the dispute. Therefore, on 16 March 1995, Singapore submitted a request for the establishment of a Panel.[160]

After one week, Malaysia informed Singapore that the existing import licensing procedure would be modified to that of automatic licensing, whereby approved permits would be issued freely, irrespective of the grade and quantity to be imported. The automatic licensing mechanism was necessary for the purpose of close monitoring of imports of both items. Licences would be issued freely to all bona fide importers who were eligible to apply for the import licence. Import licences would be issued for imports on a MFN basis. On 29 March 1995, Malaysia notified the DSB and the Committee on Import Licensing Procedures that it had modified the import restrictions on PE and PP into an automatic import licensing procedure. On 10 April, Singapore withdrew the complaint.[161]

This, the first dispute under the WTO dispute settlement procedures, was settled with Singapore's withdrawal of the Panel request. According to the statement by Mr Kenyon, Chairman of the DSB, the greater predictability and automaticity in the DSU rules is encouraging the early settlement of disputes and this is clearly consistent with the intent of the new rules.[162]

159 See WT/DS1/1, *Malaysia – Prohibition of Imports of Polyethylene and Polypropylene* – Request for Consultations under Article XXIII:1 of the GATT 1994 by Singapore.

160 See WT/DS1/2, *Malaysia – Prohibition of Imports of Polyethylene and Polypropylene* – Request by Singapore for Establishment of Panel under Article XXIII:2 of the GATT 1994 and the Understanding on Rules and Procedures Governing the Settlement of Disputes.

161 See WT/DS1/3, *Malaysia – Prohibition of Imports of Polyethylene and Polypropylene* – Communication from Malaysia, and WT/DSB/M/6, Dispute Settlement Body – Minutes of Meeting – Held in the Centre William Rappard on 19 July 1995.

162 See WT/DSB (96)/ST/1, Statement by H. E. Mr D Kenyon (Australia), Chairman of the Dispute Settlement Body.

This case took place between two countries from the Association of Southeast Asian Nations (ASEAN).[163] The Introduction of this thesis reviewed Asian attitudes to law and to the dispute settlement. There have been few disputes between two Asian countries, but in general, these have been settled after the Panel.[164]

2. *Before the Final Panel Reports*

Two cases (four disputes) were settled after the constitution of the Panel, but before the final Panel report, namely the *EC – Scallops* (WT/DS7, WT/DS12 and WT/DS14) and the *EC – Butter* (WT/DS72). The Panels issued legal reports. The key issue is how the disputants reached mutually agreed results through the method of consultations.

a. *EC – Scallops*

On 19 May 1995, Canada requested consultations with the EC, following Peru and Chile raised same requirement, concerning the French Order and its amendments relevant to the official names and permitted trade descriptions of scallops in France. These requests were made pursuant to Article XXII:1 of the GATT, Article 14.1 of the TBT and Article 4 of the DSU.

Governments frequently regulate labelling policies for the sake of providing the consumer with accurate information. The challenge for WTO law is to distinguish between policies that legitimately regulate labelling policies and those that act as trade barriers. A report by Oxfam placed the EC at the top of their list for holding double standards with its trade barriers against agricultural imports from non-EC Members. Label-

163 The ASEAN was established on 8 August 1967 in Bangkok by the five original Member countries, namely, Indonesia, Malaysia, Philippines, Singapore, and Thailand. Brunei Darussalam joined on 8 January 1984, Vietnam on 28 July 1995, Laos and Myanmar on 23 July 1997, and Cambodia on 30 April 1999. See http://www.aseansec.org/64.htm last visited 3 August 2004.

164 There have been only four different cases between two Asian countries, namely *Indonesia – Certain Measures Affecting the Automobile Industry* (WT/DS54, 55, 59, and 64), *Philippines – Anti-Dumping Measures Regarding Polypropylene Resins* from Korea (WT/DS215), *India – Anti-Dumping Measure on Batteries* from Bangladesh (WT/DS306), and *Korea – Anti-dumping Duties on Imports of Certain Paper* from Indonesia (WT/DS312). There was only one case (*Indonesia – Automobile*) after the Panel.

ling policies represent one kind of non-tariff barrier that could be used to discriminate, such as by reserving the common marketable name for domestic products.

The regulation of the EC prohibited Canada from marketing its particular species of scallops under the description 'noix de coquille Saint Jacques', by which name scallops are traditionally known in France. Instead, Canadian scallops were designated to be labelled simply as 'petoncles', a less esteemed word used for scallops. Canadian exporters reported a substantial decrease in the volume of exports after the labelling change went into effect.[165]

The Canadian government had negotiated a temporary solution in bilateral talks, but France subsequently annulled this agreement, and therefore, Canada formally requested consultations under the rules of the DSU. Canada stated that Canadian scallops were being given less favourable treatment than the national product with the result that Canada suffered nullification of its rights under the WTO agreement; it also claimed the French measure was inconsistent with the TBT agreement. This agreement stipulates that technical regulations should not have the effect of creating unnecessary obstacles to international trade, as in Article 2.2.[166]

Peru and Chile closely followed Canada and initiated independent requests for consultations. As with Canada, no compromise was found during consultations with the EC. Peru and Chile could assume that the Canadian delegation had evaluated the legal case and determined it was strong enough to justify raising the issue during the Panel stage.

After formal consultations had failed to settle the dispute, Canada, Peru and Chile requested a Panel on 7 July, 18 September and 25 September 1995, respectively.

At the meeting on 11 October 1995, the DSB established a single Panel according to Article 9 of the DSU. The Panel met the four parties on 11 December 1995 and on 5 February 1996. During this stage, there was little room for negotiation as each side presented its legal case. Panellists were expected to determine the legal status of the policy as judges rather than to mediate a compromise solution.

165 The Financial Times, 21 July 1995.

166 See WT/DS7/1, *European Committee – Trade Description of Scallops* – Request for Consultations by Canada.

The Panel issued an interim report on 14 March 1996. Afterwards, it opened the period for comments by the participants on the ruling before it was made public. The period between the Interim Ruling and its public release represents an opportunity for a return to negotiation among the parties. The idea behind keeping the interim report confidential is to give parties one last chance, having seen how the Panel would resolve the issue.

On 16, 19 and 29 April and 2 May 1996 the parties requested the Panel to postpone issue of the final report, then on 10 May 1996 further requested the Panel to suspend the Panel proceedings. On 5 July 1996, they notified the DSB and the relevant Council and Committees that they had reached a mutually agreed solution.

The announced solution included an exchange of letters in which the EC representative said the French government order would be replaced by a new order that would allow marketing of scallops under the name 'noix de coquilles Saint Jacques' as long as the scientific name of the species and country of origin were also indicated.[167] A new draft order was included with these texts and would take effect within two months.

According to a Peruvian negotiator's word, early settlement was possible because the interim ruling favoured Canada, Peru and Chile, so the EC completely gave in. Since this was the first case regarding the TBT agreement, EC officials may have been "reluctant to have a precedent set with broader implication for other policies that contained potential violations of the TBT".[168]

Why the mutually agreed solution took place after the release of the interim report, rather than during the initial negotiation, was obviously an emerging question afterwards. The French government had made concession on the earlier bilateral settlement with the Canadians and the EC had refused compromise during consultations with Canada, Peru and Chile when it faced the certain initiation of a Panel. Canada, Peru and Chile understood that this was simply a disguised effort by Europe to

167 See WT/DS12/12 and WT/DS14/11, *European Communities – Trade Description of Scallops* – Notification of Mutually Agreed Solution.

168 Davis, C. L. Do WTO Rules Create a Level Playing Field For Developing Countries in Papers Prepared for a Conference on Developing Countries and the Trade Negotiation Process, Geneva: UNCTAD, 2003, pp. 8–11. These observations were based on a telephone interview by the author with an official of Peru's delegation in Geneva.

protect its local fishermen not limited to those of France but to protect consumers and avoid confusion.[169]

In this case, fisheries represent a sensitive sector. Member states, such as France, had scallops producers who competed with Canada, Peru and Chile, and thus could be expected to oppose the change.

The implications of the case are much broader than just about scallops or even food labelling. The threat of a Panel report clearly gave impetus to complainants to find a solution; however, it depends on political realism within the community, whether or not the threat of a Panel report will be sufficient. The 'shadow of the law' worked in this case as the EC might think the public release of a negative ruling would be politically worse than settling this dispute before the ruling.

Food labelling involves domestic regulations with legitimate concerns about consumer information and opportunities for hidden protectionism. More and more countries try to use geographical indicators or quality distinctions to maintain advantages for local producers. Reduction of tariffs, quotas, and subsidies that long protected sensitive primary goods sectors leave labelling regulations as one of the hidden barriers under the name of TBT Agreement in the WTO.

There were twenty disputes after and two disputes before the *Scallops,* all of which were relevant to this issue.[170] Sixteen disputes were about agriculture and fishery, out of which eleven were against the EC. As these difficult trade disputes continue to occur, it will be important for both sides to engage in negotiations based on common standards rather than escalating the conflicts. Most disputes were solved during consultations or remained inactive, except for the *EC – Sardine*

169 Davis 2003; 12.

170 The 22 disputes are listed as follows: WT/DS3 and WT/DS41 *Korea – Inspection of Agricultural Products*, WT/DS5 *Korea – Shelf*, WT/DS20 *Korea – Bottle Water*, WT/DS26 and WT/DS48 *EC – Hormones*, WT/DS77 *Argentina – Textiles and Clothing*, WT/DS85 *US – Textiles and Apparel Products*, WT/DS100 *US – Poultry*, WT/DS134 *EC – Rice*, WT/DS137 *EC – Wood of Conifers*, WT/DS144 *US – Cattle, Swine and Grain*, WT/DS210 *Belgium – Rice*, WT/DS231 *EC – Sardines*, WT/DS232 *Mexico – Match*, WT/DS233 *Argentina – Pharmaceutical Products*, WT/DS263 *EC – Wine*, WT/DS279 *India – Export and Import Policy 2002–2007*, WT/DS290 *EC – Trademarks and Geographical Indications for Agricultural Products and Foodstuffs*, WT/DS291, WT/DS292 and WT/DS293 *EC – Biotech Products*.

(WT/DS231), which the EC lost finally.[171] However, recently it seems that this co-operative method cannot be accepted because of the Panel constitutions of the *EC – Geographical Indication* and *EC – Biotech Products* cases.[172] The defendant is the EC again. It is too early to say whether these two cases can be implemented after the Panel reports.

On the whole, the consultation on the issue of labelling works quite well, except with regard to the *EC – Sardine*. This indicates that early settlement in tough disputes is promising.

b. *EC – Butter*

In June 1996, the EC ruled that New Zealand butter manufactured by the AMMIX and spreadable butter-making processes was not eligible for New Zealand's country-specific tariff quota (CSTQ) for butter established by the EC's WTO schedule, because it believed that these butter products were not manufactured directly from milk or cream (one of the conditions of the CSTQ). The practical effect of the decision was that these two products would be levied by the EC at the much higher out-of-quota tariff rate. New Zealand disagreed with the EC ruling.[173]

171 According to Davis's article, this case could be solved before the Panel. She interviewed an official of the WTO secretariat, who said from the beginning it was clear that the EC regulation was a trade barrier and it was a surprising this case went to a Panel. Spain, France and Portugal had sardine producers. Another reason is the major exporter of sardines to the EC markets competed with Peru was Morocco, which stands as a beneficiary of special economic relations with the EC. As a result of political difficulty to compromise on these interests, the EC continued to uphold its position that the name sardines must be reserved for the one species. Furthermore, Davis observed that the EC might think Peru would not go beyond the consultation since Peru was the only country to file a compliant and if Peru invoked the Panel, it would be first time Peruvian as a claimant to use WTO dispute settlement independently. The ruling as expected upheld the complainant. The EC drew support from external power (WTO Panel ruling) to change internal regulation (Member States' policies) and to release pressure when negotiating with partner (Morocco). "Political opposition made early concessions difficult, but the ruling strengthened the argument that change was necessary". See Davis 2003; 11–15.

172 These two cases are reminiscent of the *EC – Banana* and *EC – Hormones* cases.

173 See The New Zealand Ministry of Foreign Affairs & Trade: Legal Division–Dispute Index Page, http://www.mfat.govt.nz/support/legal/disputes/disputespeech.html last visited 5 July 2004.

After extensive bilateral negotiations on this issue, the EC confirmed that it would not alter its position. New Zealand opted for the WTO dispute settlement mechanism.

On 24 March 1997, New Zealand requested consultations with the EC, pursuant to Article 4 of the DSU, Article 14 of the TBT, Article 6 of the Agreement on Import Licensing Procedures and Article XXII:1 of the GATT 1994. The measures of the EC and the United Kingdom (UK)'s Customs and Excise Department were challenged by NZ, since it perceived them to be in violation of the above referred to provisions.[174]

The formal consultations were held between the EC and New Zealand on 29 April 1997, but did not lead to resolution of the dispute. After consultations failed to reach mutual agreement, New Zealand, on 6 November 1997, required the establishment of a Panel and on 13 January 1998 the Panel was composed.[175]

On 18 February 1998, New Zealand requested a six-week suspension of the work of the Panel. As New Zealand Dairy Board's subsidiaries in the UK initiated the proceedings before the UK Value Added Tax & Duties Tribunal, New Zealand explored whether it would be possible to reach a mutually agreed solution with the EC on the basis of the Tribunal's decision.[176] However, no progress was made.

The Panel resumed its work on 30 March 1998, meeting with the disputants twice on 10 June 1998 and 15 July 1998. The Panel in December 1998 submitted its interim report, and on 23 December 1998 submitted the final report.

On 24 February 1999, New Zealand requested the Panel to suspend its work until 25 March. Thereafter, New Zealand requested five extensions of the suspension until 24 November.[177] This time the negotiations were fruitful and made improvements.

174 See WT/DS72/1, *European Communities – Measures Affecting Butter Products –* Request for Consultations by New Zealand.

175 See WT/DS72/2, *European Communities – Measures Affecting Butter Products –* Request for the Establishment of a Panel by New Zealand, and WT/DS72/3, *European Communities – Measures Affecting Butter Products –* Constitution of the Panel Established at the Request of New Zealand – Note by the Secretariat.

176 See WT/DS72/R, *European Communities – Measures Affecting Butter Products –* Report of the Panel.

177 See WT/DS72/6, *European Communities – Measures Affecting Butter Products –* Communication from the Chairman of the Panel, as well as WT/DS72/6/Add.1–Add.5.

On 11 November 1999, the disputants notified the DSB and the relevant councils and committees that they had reached a mutually agreed solution:

1. The EC adopted new regulation on 22 October 1999 specified that the meaning of the requirement in the New Zealand CSTQ 'manufactured directly from milk or cream' does not exclude butter manufactured from milk or cream, without the use of stored materials, in a single, self-contained and uninterrupted process which may involve the cream passing through a stage of concentrated milk-fat and/or the fractionation of such milk-fat.
2. The EC will not take any action which has the direct or indirect purpose or effect of undermining or offsetting the basis of the settlement, New Zealand accordingly agrees to terminate the Panel proceedings.[178]

The Panel concluded its work by reporting that a mutually agreed solution to this dispute had been reached between the parties, rather than issuing a public ruling.

Settlement negotiations were eventually successful, after there had, in fact, been the full sets of Panel hearings and detailed written and oral submissions had been made. Finally, the EC accepted the eligibility of the spreadable and AMMIX butter under the CSTQ.

In this case, New Zealand was an only plaintiff against one Member of the so-called 'Quad', the term used to refer to the four major economic players in the world, namely the US, the EC, Canada and Japan. The important implication of this case is how New Zealand successfully used the WTO dispute settlement in an effort to ensure that the big players made concessions.

The WTO process brought compliance by how it influenced the view of the alternative to a negotiable settlement. Within the WTO dispute settlement system, the EC had to be concerned about a ruling that would set a precedent.

From the perspective of the complainant, a negotiated settlement may mean that remedial action is to be put in place much earlier than would be the case even with a successful Panel outcome. This is because, invariably, a WTO violating Member found to be in breach of its obligations would be given extra time to comply. In some cases, this means another 15 months or more are allowed. From the perspective of a re-

178 See WT/DS72/7, *European Communities – Measures Affecting Butter Products –* Notification of Mutually Agreed Solution.

spondent, a settlement avoids the unpalatable prospect of another defeat. In addition, in some cases, it is clear that respondents may see a real incentive in settling cases before the Panel has issued a ruling given that the implications of the ruling could have adverse consequences for other aspects of their trade regime. In this regard, New Zealand concerns every stage including the consultation.[179]

According to New Zealand's summary of its six disputes, the decision to initiate formal dispute settlement, which is highly resource-intensive, is never taken lightly. The preparation of a case requires painstaking legal and factual analysis, and a commitment to remain fully engaged in several-stage process, which, in exceptional cases, may last several years (i.e. *US – Steel Safeguard*). New Zealand's track record to date indicates that the commitment has been worthwhile. Meanwhile, New Zealand highlights the fact that the resources need to prosecute or defend a case are considerable and, from this perspective alone, a settlement at a fairly early stage of a dispute is an attractive alternative.[180]

3. *Observations*

The above 26 disputes are summarised in the following table:

179 As a matter of fact, New Zealand won all disputes both on the court and out of the court surprisingly, and without as a respondent in one dispute. It pursued six principal party dispute settlement complaints to date.Three cases were settled before the Panel, namely *Hungary – Agricultural Products* (WT/DS35), *EC – Butter*, and *India – Agricultural, Textile and Industrial Products* (WT/DS93). Another three cases were solved through litigation, including *Canada – Milk and Dairy Products* (WT/DS113), *US – Lamb* (WT/DS177) and *US – Steel Safeguard* (WT/DS258). New Zealand and New Zealanders have had a high profile in the operation of the dispute settlement system since its outset. A New Zealand international lawyer, Chris Beeby, served on the AB for four years and played a significant role in shaping some of the WTO jurisprudence developed over that time. In additional to that, two of New Zealand's Ambassadors had chaired for a year at a time the DSB which oversees the operation of the DSU. Furthermore, many New Zealanders continue to serve on WTO Panels. According to latest Panellists, Canada, New Zealand, Australia and Switzerland have provided the most, between 12 and 15 of each country. In details of New Zealand's practical ways to different disputes, see Ministry of Foreign Affairs and Trade: Legal Division-Dispute Index, http://www.mfat.govt.nz/support/legal/disputes/disputespeech.html last visited 5 July 2004.

180 *Ibid.*, Ministry of Foreign Affairs and Trade: Legal Division-Dispute Index.

Table 3.23. Overview of 26 cases

No	*Dispute No.*	*Complainant (Respondent)*	*Agreements (Products)*	*RTA*	*Outcomes*	*Methods*	*Length (Months)*
1	DS1	Malaysia (Singapore)	GATT and Licensing (PE, PP)	ASEAN	Malaysia modified	Consultations	10/01/95–10/04/95 (3)
2	DS7	Canada, Peru, and Chile (EC)	GATT and TBT (Scallops)	/	Replaced by a new Order	Consultations (interim report issued)	19/05/95–05/07/96 (13)
3	DS9	Canada (EC)	Customs and GATT (Wheat)	/	EC adopted its import rule	Consultations	30/06/95–22/12/95 (6)
4	DS13	US (EC)	GATT and Customs (Gains)	/	EC implemented	Consultations	09/07/95–30/04/97 (22)
5	DS21	US (Australia)	GATT and SPS (Salmonids)	/	Australia implemented	Ruling of DS18	17/11/95–27/10/00 (59)
6	DS35	Argentina, Australia, NZ and US (Hungary)	Agriculture	/	Seek a waiver	Consultations (errors in Hungary's Schedule)	27/03/96–30/07/97 (16)
7	DS36	US (Pakistan)	TRIPS (Pharmaceutical and agricultural chemical products)	/	Pakistan implemented	Consultations	30/04/96–28/02/97 (10)
8	DS38	EC (US)	GATT (goods) and GATS (Transition)	/	Created an Agreement	Consultations	03/05/96–11/04/97 (11)
9	DS39	EC (US)	GATT (certain products)	/	US terminated the application	Consultations	17/04/96–15/07/97 (15)

No	*Dispute No.*	*Complainant (Respondent)*	*Agreements (Products)*	*RTA*	*Outcomes*	*Methods*	*Length (Months)*
10	DS43	US (Turkey)	GATT (Film)	/	Turkey eliminated discriminatory taxation	Consultations (under the shadow of GSP statute)	12/06/96–14/07/97 (13)
11	DS72	New Zealand (EC)	GATT, Licensing, and TBT (butter)	/	EC adopted a new Regulation	Consultations (interim report issued)	24/03/97–11/11/99 (32)
12	DS77	EC (Argentina)	ATC and GATT (textiles, clothing and footwear)	/	Argentina implemented	Ruling of DS56	24/04/97–26/05/99 (25)
13	DS88	EC (US)	GPA (goods and services)	/	US implemented	Ruling of a US' court	20/06/97–11/02/00 (32)
14	DS89	Korea (US)	AD and GATT (TV)	/	US terminated the measures	Consultations	10/07/97–05/01/98 (6)
15	DS123	Indonesia (Argentina)	GATT and Safeguard (Footwear)	/	Argentina complied	Ruling of DS121	22/04/98–25/02/00 (22)
16	DS181	Thailand (Colombia)	ATC (Plain Polyester Filaments)	/	The measure expired	/	08/09/98–27/10/99 (13)
17	DS190	Brazil (Argentina)	ATC (Woven Fabric of Cotton and Cotton Mixtures)	MERCOSUR	Argentina withdrew the measures	Ruling by MERCOSUR	29/07/99–27/06/00 (11)
18	DS193	EC (Chile)	GATT (Swordfish)	/	A multilaterally negotiated agreement	Consultations and Chile filed the same dispute to the ITLOS	06/11/00–23/03/01 (5)

No	*Dispute No.*	*Complainant (Respondent)*	*Agreements (Products)*	*RTA*	*Outcomes*	*Methods*	*Length (Months)*
19	DS199	US (Brazil)	TRIPS (pharmaceutical products)	/	Created a bilateral consultative mechanism	Consultations (Supported by NGO and filed a tit-for-tat complaint against US)	30/05/00–05/07/01 (13)
20	DS210	US (Belgium)	Customs, GATT, and TBT (rice)	/	Belgium acted in line with EC law	Ruling of a Belgian court	12/10/00–18/12/01 (14)
21	DS227	Chile (Peru)	GATT (cigarettes)	/	Peru amended law	Ruling of Peruvian court	01/03/01–12/07/01 (4)
22	DS237	Ecuador (Turkey)	Agriculture, GATT, Licensing, and SPS (banana)	/	Turkey modified	Consultations	31/08/01–22/11/02 (15)
23	DS240	Hungary (Romania)	GATT (wheat and wheat flour)	CEFTA	Romania abrogated the measures	Consultations	18/10/01–20/12/01 (2)
24	DS250	Brazil (US)	GATT (processed orange and grapefruit products)	/	US amended its legislation	Ruling of the US' court	20/03/02–28/05/04 (26)
25	DS255	Chile (Peru)	GATT (fresh fruit, vegetable, fish, milk, tea and other natural products)	/	Chile amended discriminatory taxation	Consultations	22/04/02–25/09/02 (5)

No	*Dispute No.*	*Complainant (Respondent)*	*Agreements (Products)*	*RTA*	*Outcomes*	*Methods*	*Length (Months)*
26	DS261	Chile (Uruguay)	GATT (beverages, tobacco and cigarettes)	MERCOSUR	Signed an agreement	Consultations	18/06/02–08/01/04 (18)

These disputes were solved, after the request for establishment of a Panel, but before the final report by the Panel. Eight of them were solved by different rulings, including those of domestic courts (four disputes), of other Panels sharing similar matters (three disputes) and of an RTA's tribunal; one dispute was settled by itself as the measure expired. These cases were not resolved by means of consultations under the DSU. However, it is hard to evaluate whether there existed any influence by requests for consultations and for the establishment of a Panel on the final outcome in the WTO because of its increasingly important effect.

17 disputes were settled at the consultations stage, among them two using 'counter-filing' – the first one filed a similar case to another international court and the second initiated a 'tit-for-tat' complaint. It may be argued that these two disputes were settled under the 'shadow of the law'. However, the consultative atmosphere must be stronger than the litigious atmosphere, since the complainants involved in these two disputes were the EC and the US respectively.[181]

It can be observed that (1) the more equal power the countries have, the more 'real consultation' they hold. Otherwise, the weak Members have to apply tactics such as 'counter-filing' or make concessions without any alternatives (i.e. DS35 and DS43); (2) under most circumstances the consultations last from three to 18 months. When the time frame is longer than 18 months, the outcomes transfer from the consultations to the rulings of the court with the exception of the *EC – Butter* case; (3) the applicants successfully solving the disputes between a request for establishment of a Panel and the final Panel report changed from devel-

181 As two big players in the WTO, they would not hesitate to go to the court against countries like Chile and Brazil.

oped Members to developing Members;[182] (4) the products involved changed from diversified items to solely agricultural products.

D. *Two Possible Chances for Consultation Stage*

Legal reforms may present an opportunity for consultations to be based on the theory of the 'shadow of the law'. That is to say, the rule-oriented DSU can promote the resolution of disputes at the consultation stage. Furthermore, as the law itself is incomplete, there is no doubt that diplomatic methods can supplement and be interactive.

While the WTO dispute settlement system generally works fairly well, there are many proposals to be submitted to improve the DSU.[183] The concern with making the WTO dispute settlement more legalistic is largely based on a concern that emphasises litigation as a means of solving disputes rather than letting them escalate.

The Chairman's text contains a sufficiently high level of support for some prevailing views of Member states. These substantial issues include the enhancement of third-party rights, both at the Panel and Appellate stage, as well as improved conditions for Members seeking to join consultations,the introduction of an interim review stage and remand at the Appellate stage, clarification and improvement of the sequence and details of procedures at the implementation stage, enhancement of compensation; strengthening of notification requirements for mutually agreed solutions and strengthening of SDT for developing countries at various stages of the proceedings.[184]

182 From 2001, the developed complaints settled disputes either before the request for establishment of a Panel or through the litigation method regardless the pending disputes as of 31 January 2006.

183 See documents TN/DS/W/1–, Contributions towards the Improvement of the WTO Dispute Settlement Understanding from each delegation, from 13 March 2002, and TN/DS/9, Special Sessions of the Dispute Settlement Body: Report by the Chairman, Ambassador Peter Balas, to the Trade Negotiations Committee, 6 June 2003. http://docsonline.wto.org/ last visited 19 April 2005.

184 See TN/DS/9, 6 June 2003, DSB Special Session: Special Session of the Dispute Settlement Body: Report by the Chairman, Ambassador Peter Balas, to the Trade Negotiations Committee.

With regard to the improvement of the Panel stage, one can analyse whether there is any chance for the consultation to 'remedy' inherent legal disadvantages.

1. *Time Disadvantage*

According to Davey's empirical research, the establishment of a Panel to the adoption of a report takes roughly 15–16 months. The length of Panel proceedings is an important component of the overall dispute settlement timeframe. While the main reasons for delay lie between Panel composition and implementation, particularly the length of the reasonable period of time for implementation,[185] it is crucial for the reputation of the WTO dispute settlement system.

It is not easy to distinguish the desirable or undesirable legal methods to resolve disputes, but some abusive practices should be controlled (i.e. the *US – Steel Safeguard* case). The solution is to balance due process and over-legalisation, or to balance the application of the consultation and of the Panel.

It is necessary to respect the legal texts of the DSU, but the DSU should not be used to delay unnecessarily the dispute resolution. It should be remembered that the need to preserve the right of defence is not equivalent to a need to facilitate or encourage procedural delays.[186]

In general, the time frame for resolution of disputes through consultations is less than the litigation time under complicated DSU procedure(s). In most cases, the statistics show that consultations solved disputes in two to 12 months. The disputes, which took longer time during

185 The average reasonable period of time has fallen to nine months rather than 15 months years ago. It is now clearly accepted that the 15 months referred to as a guide for arbitration rather than a minimum or standard time. For instance, the US Gasoline is 15 months, Japan Alcohol Tax is 15 months, the Canada Periodical is 15 months, and the EC Hormones is 15 months and a half; while the Canada Pharmaceutical Patent is six months, the Australia Salmon is eight months, and the Korea Alcoholic Tax is 11 months. Unfortunately, the biggest player, the US insists around 15 months basically, for instance, the US-Hot-Rolled Steel is 15 months, the Byrd Amendment is 11 months, the Irish Music 12 months, and the US-Act 1916 is 10 months, even worse, there is no any implementation except the first one.

186 See Davey, W. J. WTO Dispute Settlement: Segregating the Useful Political Aspects and Avoiding 'Over-Legalization', in Bronckers, M. & Quick, R. (ed.), New Direction in International Economic Law: Essays in Honour of John H. Jackson, The Hague: Kluwer Law International 2000; 307.

the consultation stage, involved either the US or the EC, especially the disputes between the US and the EC.[187]

2. *Remedies*

As with time delay section, remedies in the WTO system are a challenge to the credibility of the WTO.[188] Remedies in the WTO are in the form of compensation or retaliation. As of 30 April 2005, there are seven retaliation and one compensation cases to be realised, and one case is in the process of being completed.[189] Moreover, 12 cases have led to the adoption of Article 21.5 compliance Panel reports and eight cases to the adoption of Article 21.5 AB reports. Thus, the argument for the implementation stage becomes much more eye-catching than before.[190]

However, law is a double-edged sword. The current problems are: (1) if retaliation is authorised, a lower level of or no trade liberalisation will be agreed to and there will be no compliance, a basic WTO obligation, (at least in theory); (2) the *Banana* and the *Hormones* cases demonstrated that retaliation is not always effective, (at least not immediately). Its inefficacy and the unfavourable position in which it leaves developing countries, may soon diminish the credibility of the DSU for in its litigation status.[191]

187 For instance, in the Denmark Intellectual Property Rights case, the US notified mutually agreed solution after four years from the date of require for consultations. See WT/DS83, *Denmark – Measures affecting the Enforcement of Intellectual Property Rights*.

188 It may not be a case at present because this is a small number.

189 One compensation case is *US – Section 110 (5)* (WT/DS160); seven retaliation disputes are: *EC – Banana* (the US and Ecuador) (WT/DS27); *EC – Hormones* (the US and Canada) (WT/DS26 and WT/DS48); *Brazil – Aircraft* (WT/DS46); *US – FSC* (WT/DS108); and *Canada – Aircraft* (WT/DS222); and the on–process retaliation case is *US – Byrd Amendment* (WT/DS217 and WT/DS234).

190 Davey on World Trade Forum 2004 concluded his evaluation to dispute settlement mechanism within these 10 years that generally the DSU works quite well except the US non-implementation. See also Davey, W. J. Implementation in WTO Dispute Settlement: An Introduction to the Problem and Possible Solution (Draft, December 22, 2004), in MILE 5, Bern: WTI, 2005. He argued a significant part of the problem is the failure to ensure prompt implementation.

191 See Davey, W. J. Dispute Settlement in GATT, 11 Fordham International Law Journal 51, 1987; 99.

Compensation is, arguably, a remedy to buy the way out of the legal obligation of compliance. Another problem related to compensation is the disparity in fine-payment ability among Members. If a poor Member has no financial ability to pay a fine, but finally undertakes compliance, the question would be whether it fulfils its obligations or not. The dilemma is: rich states can pay without compliance, while poor states can comply but cannot pay. The *EC – Banana* case is a good example that Ecuador has hesitated to retaliate against the EC, unlike the US, who made recourse to Article 22.7 of the DSU in a maximum amount of US$191.4 million per year to retaliate against the EC without any hesitation.[192]

Although the purpose of remedies is to prevent further violations of the law, (or to rescue injured parties, thus inducing compliance), the infringement in general was restored after entire legal procedures which do not imply that it is the fault of law, butthat law cannot guarantee to solve all disputes. The fact is that disputants still have to go back to the negotiation table in order to reach agreement.

The contribution of law to solve the dispute is undoubted, but is not always guaranteed. The consultation is an auto-remedy through a co-operative method. The recent popular Genetically Modified Organisms (GMO) restrictions in the EC are good examples. The EC, after the *Hormones* case, criticised WTO jurisprudence and stated that the WTO is not an appropriate international forum for resolving the GMO issues raised by complainants. However, Member states kept challenging this issue. In the EC's view, these Members preferred to start a litigation based on flawed premises than to promote international co-operation as a method to build a sound international framework for addressing the GMO issues. The WTO is not the place for determining the legitimacy and legality of a country's decision to exercise its right to reject GMOs. The EC, therefore, requires international co-operation.[193]

If, in the course of some disputes (i.e. the *Banana* and the *Hormones* cases), one party realises that early settlement is better than further escalation, it is successful co-operation within the international trade community rather than a risk of the failure of law.

192 See WT/DS27/49, *European Communities – Regime for the Importation, Sale and Distribution of Banana* – Recourse by the United States to Article 22.7 of the DSU.

193 See http://www.iuf.org/cgi–bin/editorials/db.cgi?db=default&ww=1&uid=default&ID=206&viewrecords=1&en=1 last visited 1 July 2004.

The consultation as a political method has been criticised as a non-binding method that leads to a 'non-potential position'. Nevertheless, there are always complaints of enforcement of law at the same time. In other words, judicial decision-making is a binding decision, but implementation relies on the co-operation of the violating party.[194]

Moreover, the improvement of law always lags behind social development.

3. *Alternative Functions of the Consultation*

The consultation is an alternative way to solve disputes, since it is a part of the DSU. Meanwhile, it has many functions other than settlement.

First, consultation as a prerequisite is a very important means of focusing the dispute and setting up the case to facilitate the Panel's work, similar to the role of pre-trial conferences between parties to domestic litigation.[195]

Second, it provides a chance to settle in the manner that maximises party control by negotiation, resolves the uncertainties about the scope and nature of the measures at issue, eliminates fruitless or invalid claims as the exchange of information,[196] makes it possible to present a case in shape for a Panel or the further AB to do its work, assists the judicial process by refining opposing views and revealing significant facts and legal theories,[197] and therefore makes the judicial procedure easier.[198]

194 There are seven so-called failed cases with reference to Davey's empirical study in this field, namely, *US – Anti-Dumping Act of 1916* (WT/DS136, WT/DS162), *US – Tax Treatment for 'Foreign Sales Corporations'*, Recourse by the European Communities to Article 21.5 (WT/DS108), *Canada – Export Credits and Loan Guarantees for Regional Aircraft* (WT/DS222), *European Communities – Measures Affecting Livestock and Meat* (Hormones) (WT/DS48, WT/DS26), *Brazil – Export Financing Programme for Aircraft*, Second Recourse by Canada to Article 21.5 (WT/DS46), *US – Section 110(5) of US Copyright Act* (WT/DS160), *US – Final Dumping Determination on Softwood Lumber from Canada* (Byrd) (WT/DS264).

195 See Davey, W. J. & Porges, A. Performance of the System I: Consultations & Deterrence, 32 Int'l Law 1998; 696: from WESTLAW.

196 For example, the EU as a third party in the *US – Shrimp/Turtle* case (WT/DS58) had access to the arguments by the US arguments that the EU could use to defend itself against likely US charges in its dispute over the EU ban on furs caught leg-hold traps.

197 See WT/DS78/1, *US – Safeguard Measure Against Imports of Corn Broom* – Request for Consultations by Colombia.

Among these, the real exchange of factual information can be more useful for settlement either during consultation phase or judicial phase. For instance, in the *Canada – Certain Measures Concerning Periodicals* case, the exporting Member knew how imports were treated, but might not know how domestic interests are treated.[199]

Third, it brings the case to public attention and might attract other countries having similar problems to participate in the case.[200] For instance, in the consultation of the *US – Steel Safeguard* case with the EU, at the end of April 2002, BBC News claimed a pair of comparative statistics: there are 175,000 employee in the U.S. steel industry, among which 20,000 jobs have been lost in the past four years; in the EU there are 299,600 employee, 22,200 lost their jobs; in the UK there are 26,500 employee, 10,000 lost their jobs.[201] The other media outlets within the EU gave detailed reports on this case as well. In the meantime, the US media reported that 30% of US steel-making capacity have filed for bankruptcy and domestic steel prices in the last quarter of 2001 were at their lowest levels in 20 years.[202] Obviously, the media reports evoked public indignation. The reports relating to this case about an individual country's loss appeared at the head of newspaper. After the EC required consultations with the US, the formal requests to participate consultations were delivered by Korea, China, Switzerland and Norway.

Fourth, consultations are sometimes not even reported to the GATT/WTO until after they are concluded; this gives disputants more latitude to strike a deal, latitude that may be especially important for

---

198 See Davey, W. J. & Porges, A. Performance of the System I: Consultations & Deterrence, 32 Int'l Law1998; 695: from WESTLAW, Horlick, G. N. Consultation Phase of WTO Dispute Resolution: A Private Practitioner's View, 32 Intl Law 1998; 685: from WESTLAW, Wethington, O. J. Commentary on consultation Mechanism under the WTO Dispute Settlement Understanding During Its First Five Years, 31(3–4) L.P.I.B. 2000; 583.

199 WT/DS31, *Canada – Certain Measures Concerning Periodicals.*

200 See Bulter, M. & Hauser, H. The WTO Dispute Settlement: A First Assessment from An Economic Perspective, 16 J.L.econ.Org 2000; 503: from WESTLAW.

201 See www.bbc.co.uk/hi/english/business/newsid_1881000/1881821.stm last visited 31 December 2004.

202 See www.Whitehouse.gov/news/releases/2002/03/20020305–8.html last visited 31 December 2004.

democracies, given their greater accountability to domestic constituents.[203]

Fifth, consultations can serve as 'action forcing events' for the involved governments to rethink the merits of their cases and the desirability of moving.[204] In some cases, settlements can occur at any time not just in pre-Panel consultations. The *EU – Trade Description of Scallops* is an example. As soon as the interim report came out, the losing party in effect conceded as long as the report was kept secret.

All the above functions can be shared by either developing or developed Member states. Furthermore, there are some other advantages in dealing with cases involving developing countries or LDCs.

As a matter of fact, the developed Members do not consider the consultation to be a meaningless stage. Busch gave us some interesting findings that pairs of highly democratic countries (eg, the US, Canada) are up to 21% more likely to settle their disputes co-operatively during consultation stage, compared to pairs with one or more states that are not fully democratic (eg, Mexico, Guatemala). In addition, pairs of democratic states are no more likely than non-democratic ones to resolve their disputes co-operatively after a Panel has been established.[205]

Since judicial means are satisfactory and diplomatic means are not unsatisfactory, it is useful to research their interwoven relationship in order to solve disputes fairly and efficiently.

203 See Wethington, O. J. Commentary on consultation Mechanism under the WTO Dispute Settlement Understanding During Its First Five Years, 31(3–4) L.P.I.B. 2000; 31(3–4): 583, Busch, M. L. & Reinhardt, E. Bargaining in the Shadow of the Law: Early Settlement in GATT/WTO Disputes, 24 FDM.I.L.J.158: from WESTLAW.

204 Horlick, G. N. Consultation Phase of WTO Dispute Resolution: A Private Practitioner's View, 32 Intl Law 1998; 685: from WESTLAW.

205 Busch, M. L. & Reinhardt, E. Bargaining in the Shadow of the Law: Early Settlement in GATT/WTO Disputes, 24 FDM.I.L.J; 158: from WESTLAW.

IV. Balance between Consultations and Judicial Means

The WTO legal framework has corrected some of the GATT defects and created a more rule-oriented dispute settlement procedure, but some problems remain. These defects could be corrected by the improvement of rule-based resolutions, but it is argued that they could be solved by resorting to other means (such as consultations). Thinking carefully, one cannot rely on merely a single means to solve all.

First, since the WTO agreements are umbrella agreements, which involve large amount of contexts or fields, they unavoidably overlap with other treaties. To some extent, those treaties may produce unpredictable results through judicial means. For instance, in the *Shrimp/Turtle* case, the AB quoted several international treaties including the Convention on International Trade in Endangered Species of Wild Fauna and Flora of 1973 (CITES), UN Treaty for the Law of the Sea of 1982, Biological Varieties Act of 1992, 21st Century Agenda of 1992, and Wildlife Preservation Act of 1992 in order to prove that the turtle is an exhaustible natural resource.[206] Alternatively, the Member involved can take advantage of the consultation stage to discuss these treaties so as to make preparation or make the cases more predictable.

Second, the cases have become more and more complicated given the background of continuous social change, and influenced by many other factors, such as environmental issues and human rights. Thus, legal means may not be able to do as much as it would like to. To some extent, consultations can supplement some places where judicial method hardly works. Law cannot overcome this barrier itself, so it needs other means to make up in theory, as well as in practice.

Third, though Member states consider consultations useless in some non-negotiable cases, in practice they do not give up every effort to solve disputes to maintain good relationships. Also, the further the procedures go through, the more time they have to spend and the more money they have to pay.

206 See WT/DS58/23, *United States – Import Prohibition of Certain Shrimp and Shrimp Products* – Appellate Body Report and Panel Report pursuant to Article 21.5 of the DSU – Action by the Dispute Settlement Body

Fourth, judicial means may prove hard to sustain the burden of proof, which in some cases is impossible or almost so, and which falls on the party invoking the exceptional Article. It may either override the provision or produce a blank. For example, in the *Hormones* case, the problem raised was whether use of hormones had potential risk. Although this case was solved, the problem remains.

Fifth, in some cases, disputants applied to the DSB merely for indignation. If, presumably, at the first stage, they go directly to the Panel, it would make a mutual relationship much worse. Consultations give two parties more time to cool down and create possibilities for future negotiations. As consultations are confidential, and do not affect any Members' rights in further proceedings, Members involved can communicate freely, and take this opportunity to look for common ground. Additionally, what they say is off the record.[207]

Sixth, the dispute settlement system reflects an "ecological balance between settlement values and enforcement values".[208] Settlement values support either the complainant or the respondent who wants to have a private discussion, not intervened by onlookers such as a judge, and enforcement values support the quasi-working party approach of plurilateral consultations.[209]

Seventh, the role of courts in international trade regulation and the globalisation ofeconomic relations as much as trade regulation in general, is a matter still in its infancy, so we cannot rely on the experience of trial and error.[210] In other words, consultations should be one of the alternative and important venues to solve disputes since the WTO legal system is included in the international trade law system and therefore it also needs more time to mature.

Eighth, the numerous WTO guarantees of private access to domestic courts have given rise to an increasing number of parallel or successive dispute settlement proceedings in domestic courts, before WTO dispute settlement bodies, which often lead to conflicting or otherwise inconsistent decisions entailing legal insecurity and challenges to the legitimacy

207 See Davey, W. J. & Porges, A. Performance of the System I: Consultations & Deterrence, 32 Int'l Law 1998; 696: from WESTLAW.

208 *Ibid.*

209 *Ibid.*

210 See Cottier, T. Dispute Settlement in the WTO: Characteristics and Structural Implications for the European Union, 35 C.M.L.Rev 1998; 325:337.

of intergovernmental WTO rules. In contrast within litigation, the consultation can offer important advantages such as taking into account goals.[211]

In general, the judicial means is undoubtedly vital, but it is not a good idea to rely on one method, and, logically, it is impossible to expect that law can deal with all disputes. Law can never be complete.

Moreover, it should be remembered that law is a final weapon rather than the only one. Therefore, the consultation, particularly in the DSU, is a venue to balance judicial methods. The outlook for the WTO dispute settlement system is positive if such a balance is struck between the legal nature of the system and the political nature of the organisation within which it is operating.[212] Dispute settlement in the WTO today is to deal with its "carefully crafted balance of law and policy".[213]

It has been pointed out that institutional reforms were moving too quickly in the direction of legalism.[214] Then, as a possible solution, Prescatore proposed to return from genuine dispute settlement to mere conciliation.[215]

Reforms on consultations are discussed in the context of the overall reform proposals under the Doha Agenda in the Conclusion below.

211 Petersmann, E. Proliferation and Fragmentation of Dispute Settlement in International Trade: WTO Dispute Settlement Procedures and Alternative Dispute Resolution Mechanisms, in Lacarte, J. & Granados, J. (ed.), Inter-Governmental Trade Dispute Settlement: Multilateral and Regional Approaches, London: Cameron May, 2004; 425.

212 See Clough, M. The WTO Dispute Settlement System – A Practitioner Perspective, 24 FDM.I.L.J. 2000; 252: from WESTLAW.

213 See Cottier, T. Dispute Settlement in the WTO: Characteristics and Structural Implications for the European Union, 35 C.M.L.Rev 1998; 325.

214 Hudec, R. E. Forum: Taiwan and the GATT and the Developing Countries, C.B.L.Rev 1992; 67: from WESTLAW.

215 See Pescatore, P. The GATT Dispute Settlement Mechanism: Its Present Situation and Its Prospects, (1993) J. I. A. 1993; 10, and Stiles, K. Negotiating Institutional Reform: The Uruguay Round, the GATT, and the WTO, 2 Global Governance 1996; 119.

V. Conclusion

This section is about the process from the consultation to the Panel, but it does not arrive at issuing the final Panel report stage. Whenever the disputes resolve during this course, they are regarded as a consultative settlement, although some of them are likely resolved under the 'shadow of the law'. In fact, it does not change the rationale that they basically use the diplomatic method of bargaining through consultations to reach a mutually-agreed solution.

Disputes are a fact of life. When addressing legitimate improvements of the DSU, it is always desirable to consider consultations, which make disputes less complicated and pressing on the one hand, and more amicable and easily acceptable on the other.

Whichever method Member States apply, solving the dispute is the most important goal. This mantra has been solidified by the practice of the dispute settlement mechanism in the WTO. It is preferable to solidify the judicial mechanism, but not at the expense of weakening diplomatic methods. However, the stronger and more legitimate the process is, the better the consultation will work and fewer judicial procedures will be initiated.

From practice to theory (and then back to practice), many subjects, scholars and much data build a constructive framework for the field of consultations.

The consultation is the primary stage of the entire dispute settlement proceeding. Although the domain of the DSM shifts from 'power-orientation' to 'rule-orientation' in the WTO, the diplomatic approach is an alternative method to solve disputes. The WTO has evolved from being a diplomatic instrument to an increasingly legalised one; governments are still free to use diplomacy to settle their disputes.

The WTO's procedures for solving trade disputes under the DSU are significant for enforcing the rules and, therefore, ensuring that trade flows smoothly. Whichever means of dispute settlement Member states choose, the ultimate responsibility for settling disputes lies with member governments through the DSB. The dispute settlement system will "survive and flourish only if all (or at least a vast majority) of its Members feel that they have the ability to adequately protect their WTO rights".[216]

Both legal and diplomatic methods have their own advantages and disadvantages. What we could do is to remedy the weaknesses by exploiting the strengths. As an efficient way to solve disputes, the consultation cannot and should not be neglected. If one focuses too much on adjudication, the whole legal framework will be impeded. We need diplomatic means to act as a supplement to the system and *détente* between the disputing parties. The possibility of judicial dispute settlement facilitates negotiation.

Judicial means are important and effective ways to solve disputes. However, beforejudicial methods, alternative methods of solving disputes should be tried. The function of these diplomatic methods could be to make preparation for future judicial settlement, apart from resolving the disputes. Of course, our expectations of consultations should be modest and objective.

216 Parlin, C. C. Operation of Consultations, Deterrence and Mediation, 31(3–4) L.P.I.B. 2000; 565:572 from WESTLAW.

Conclusion

I. Challenges and Reform

Requests for consultations should be sufficiently clear to ensure efficiency and that the responding party is fully able to prepare for, and respond to, the request. The Panel shall limit in its jurisdiction if issues are raised before it which were not the subject of the consultation stage, as the consultation is a precondition to a Panel's establishment. It is also important to ensure that overly legalistic requirements as to the ambit or detail of the consultation should be avoided in order to preserve diplomacy through flexibility.

The principle of 'free choice of means' posits that no one method of dispute settlement is privileged over any other. The principle further states that, in the event of discordant preferences between the disputing parties, a measure of agreement is required between the parties over which means to apply. How far there can be said to be a general legal duty to agree on choice of means is doubtful. Such a duty, if it exists, would have to be a derivative of a general legal duty to settle disputes.

Any given case may require a shift from prevention to settlement and back again.

A. *Proposals for Reform*

Some WTO Members complain that the consultation process is not useful, or at least not as useful as it could or should be. This is mainly because some disputing parties have treated it as an ancillary procedure due to the ineffectual results of some consultations in resolving the dispute. This is obviously true under certain situations. Nevertheless, it is not warranted to assert that the consultation requirement is entirely undesirable. Rather, it highlights that there are some provisions of Article 4 that need to be improved for better results in the future.

1. *Notification*

It has been put forward that the DSU could include a provision enabling a Member to formally withdraw a request of consultation; and, if there is no further request for establishment of a Panel within a certain time frame, it should address the issue of consultation.[1]

The EC allows Members to clean dormant cases, which are still technically open, but where parties do not want to proceed any further.[2] For the sake of many consultations pending on the DSB statistics list, this may help solving the confusion for WTO Member states, as well as confusion among academics on this issue.[3]

In addition, the EC proposed that, as a way to make early settlement more attractive, it would provide that compliance with mutually agreed solutions can be examined via the Article 21.5 and 22 DSU, to the extent that they have been notified in full to the DSB.[4]

According to most Member states' proposal, the Chairman's text can be summarised as follows:

> A request for consultations may no longer serve as a basis for a request for the establishment of a panel if the complaining party has not submitted such a request within 18 months after the date of circulation of the request for consultations. This shall not apply if the complaining party notifies the party complained against and the DSB, before the expiry of the 18-month period, of its objection to the lapse. In such case, the request for consultation may serve as a basis for a request for the establishment a panel for a further period of 18 months. Further extensions may take place for the same duration in the same manner.[5]

The purpose of this new paragraph is to be strict with the notification framework for the consultation, especially given the lapse of the authority for establishment of the Panel and no agreement on panellists.

1 Otherwise, it could be considered formally withdrawn upon the lapse of a special period. See TN/DS/W/43, Jordan's Contributions Towards the Improvement and Clarification of the WTO Dispute Settlement Understanding, 28 January 2003.
2 See TN/DS/W/1, Contribution of the EC and its Member States to the Improvement of the WTO Dispute Settlement Understanding, 13 March 2002.
3 As of 7 April 2005, there have been 116 cases pending on the DSB list. The fact is most of them already dropped. See Annex II.
4 *Supra note* 2.
5 See TN/DS/9, Special Sessions of the Dispute Settlement Body: Report by the Chairman, Ambassador Peter Balas, to the Trade Negotiations Committee, 6 June 2003.

2. *Third Parties*

This one is the most popular item among proposals. Member states, developed, developing countries and LDCs, are keen on this issue.

Taiwan's position is that substantial trade interests should continue to be a requirement for third-party participation. This is to ensure that "the necessary space and simplicity for the disputing parties is retained in the consultation stage, and that consultation is preserved as an important method of settling trade disputes".[6]

3. *SDT*

China proposed explicit SDT provisions applicable to all developing Members. For example, China raised the issue of limitation of cases: developed countries shall exercise due restraint in cases against developing countries. Developed Members shall not bring more than two cases to the DSB against a particular developing Member in one calendar year.[7]

China held that the improvement of the current DSU should facilitate the parties to a dispute in finding mutually acceptable solutions to fully honour the obligations under the WTO Agreements. This is particularly important for developing countries.

China structured its traditionally oriental thoughts into the proposal. As one of the largest trading nations and a constructive member of the WTO, China wishes to play a positive role in the formulation of multilateral trade rules. In particular, China propounds the interests of developing countries, since it is the largest developing country in the world.

In the Chairman's report, it suggested that Article 4(10) should be amended to:

> The developing countries prior to the expiry of the relevant period request the chairman of the DSB to extend the relevant period. After consultations with the parties, the Chairman of the DSB shall decide whether to extend the relevant period and if so, for how long. [A guideline for the Chairman of the DSB shall be that

6 See TN/DS/W/25, 27 November 2002, Contribution by the Separate Customs Territory of Taiwan, Penghu, Kinmen and Matsu to the Doha Mandated Review of the Dispute Settlement Understanding.

7 See TN/DS/W/57, 19 May 2003, DSB Special Session: Responses to Questions on the Specific Input of China, Communication from China.

> such extension should normally not exceed 15 days from the date of expiry of the relevant period.][8]

Proposals from Haiti, the LDC and African groups put forward a pragmatic suggestion to overcome the financial shortcomings of these particular Members. "Where a LDC is involved in the consultations, due consideration should be given to the possibility of holding such consultations and other meetings in the capitals of LDCs".[9] This has its operational significance with regard to the present situation of LDCs.

Some developing countries make efforts to strengthen the SDT at every stage of the proceedings. However worthy, these proposals would be hard to apply, if they were accepted.

For instance, it was proposed that, during consultations, Members shouldl give special attention to the particular problems and interests of any developing country Members. It is easy to change the word 'should to 'shall'. Practically, this seems to be a minor change since there is no substantial clarification of the difference between them. If there is no substantive context for this paragraph, the sentence is practically meaningless.

It is understandable that developing Members aim to participate more actively in the dispute settlement system by stressing their 'developing' status. Nevertheless, only feasible proposals enrich the SDT. They can effectuate progress for the SDT rather than leaving an ill-deserved reputation for playing word-changing games, since many developing countries complain that the SDT provisions are rarely efficient in practice.

"The WTO can function optimally, with adequate protection of procedural rights, but without suffocating itself in the name of due process".[10]

China believes that the value of the WTO dispute settlement mechanism does not depend on the number of cases or the number of panels established, but rather, lies in the goodwill and trust among its Members.

8 See TN/DS/9, *supra note* 5.

9 See TN/DS/W/17, 9 October 2002, Dispute Settlement Body – Special Session – Negotiations on the Dispute Settlement Understanding – Proposal by the LDC Group.

10 Davey, W. J. WTO Dispute Settlement: Segregating the Useful Political Aspects and Avoiding "Over-Legalization", in Bronckers, M. & Quick, R. (ed.), New Direction in International Economic Law: Essays in Honour of John H. Jackson, The Hague: Kluwer Law International, 2000; 293.

Since the establishment of the WTO, many trade disputes have been resolved through consultations rather than through panel proceedings, not to mention those even more successfully resolve through bilateral channels. Thus, such limitation will not affect the value of this mechanism.[11]

Even though the whole dispute settlement mechanism is working properly, including the consultation phase, improvement is still desirable. Some delegations have actively proposed preliminary plans for reform of the DSU. Other missions have kept quiet for certain reasons.

The WTO provides a mechanism equipped with various facilities. Nevertheless, it depends on the Member States which facility they choose, how they operate these facilities and what expectation they have of the facility. There is no alternative on this point except full participation.

II. Usefulness of Consultations

First, most sophisticated legal systems offer various methodologies, from informal bilateral negotiations (consultations) at one end of the spectrum, to binding adjudication at the other.

Second, the experience of GATT alerts us to the fact that the real settlement is likely to be found in the pre-ruling stage.

Third, the basic aim of dispute settlement in the WTO is to settle disputes. In addition, the first objective of the dispute settlement mechanism is usually to secure the withdrawal of the measures concerned. Therefore, the ideal method in the DSU is only consultations because of its functions of dispute settlement and dispute prevention. This is obviously the most important function of the consultation.

Fourth, disputing parties often continue to consult bilaterally while the Panel is conducting its activities. There are no specific controls over such informal consultations within the WTO system.

Fifth, a request for consultations is an indication of the seriousness with which the complaining country views an issue.

11 See TN/DS/W/57, *supra note* 7.

Sixth, it brings the case to public attention and might attract other countries having similar problems to participate into the case.

Seventh, in the case of the consultation and panel request, the obligation is on the claimant to present the claim clearly so as to give the challenged member an opportunity to understand the substance of the dispute.

Eighth, the requests for consultation help to frame terms of reference for the Panel and provide a chance for other Member states to determine whether they wish to participate as third parties or as co-complainants.

Ninth, a political perspective, besides finding a fair way to solve disputes, governments would like constituents to know that they are trying their best to strive for the rights of their countries. Since the WTO is an intergovernmental organisation, it reflects governmental interests.

Tenth, under certain circumstances, litigation cannot solve disputes such as the *DISC* and *FSC* cases. Therefore, disputing parties have to come back to the consultation if they want to seek a result.

In the absence of application of other diplomatic methods, the consultation is a highly important phase that should be taken seriously by the disputants.

III. Methods to Improve Consultations

A role of the consultation proceeding in the DSU of the WTO highlights two categories of disputants: disputes between the US and the EC, and those involving developing countries, which have frequently been on the list of the DSB. Strengthening the significance of consultations could play a positive role for setting up the credibility of the entire dispute settlement mechanism.

A. *US-EC Disputes*

The EC and US are parties to the largest two-way trade in the world. Thus, trade disputes are not unexpected. In order to build a smoother relationship, Brussels and Washington may have to resolve these disputes. Some of the efforts at dispute resolution have led to escalation and 'tit-for-tat' retaliation with the potential to harm the multilateral trading system.[12] Some conflicts stem, primarily, from traditional demands from producers or vested interests for protection or state aid.[13] Other conflicts arise when the US or the EC initiate actions or measures to protect or promote their political and economic interests.[14] Still, other conflicts are rooted in an array of regulations that deal mostly with issues that are considered domestic policy such as the *Hormones* case.

According to the statistics from the WTO website, from 1 January 1995 to 30 April 2005, six disputes (five cases) were authorised to the level of suspension, among them three disputes between the EC and US. More seriously, three disputes (two cases) have been imposed the retaliations, among them, two disputes have been initiated by the US against the EC.[15]

Furthermore, there have been other seven disputes (five cases) on the list of status reports on progress in the implementation of the DSB's

12 Ahearn, R. J. US-European Union Trade Relations: Issues and Policy Challenges (March 21, 2003), http://www.ncseonline.org/nle/crsreports/03May/IB10087.pdf last visited 1 June 2004.

13 For example, in *US – Steel Safeguard* case, Bush Administration imposed temporary tariffs of up to 30% on approximately 8 billion USD in steel imports in order to protect domestic steel industry. In detail for background see Cooney, S., Steel Industry and Trade Issues, http://www.ncseonline.org/NLE/CRSreports/02Dec/RS21152.pdf last visited1 June 2004.

14 For example, in the *FSC* case, while the FSC was enacted in 1984, the EC did not challenge the provision until November 1997. Many on the US side suspect that the challenge had much to do with an attempt by the EC to gain negotiating leverage over the US, as well as with getting even for US pressures over beef and bananas. The fact that few European companies were complaining about the FSC as disadvantaging them commercially further suggests a calculated political motive for launching the case. For further arguments see Ahearn, R. J. US–EC Trade Tensions: Causes, Consequences, and Possible Cures, http://fpc.state.gov/documents/organization/10922.pdf last visited 1 June 2004.

15 The detailed status of these seven disputes and level of suspension authorized are as follows: *EC – Bananas III* by the US (WT/DS27), USD191.4 million/year, initiated; *EC – Bananas III* by Ecuador (WT/DS27), USD201.6 million per year, not initiated yet; *EC – Hormones* (WT/DS26), USD116.8 million annually, initiated; *EC – Hormones* (WT/DS48), CAND11.3 million/year, initiated; *Brazil – Aircraft* (WT/DS46), CAND344.2 million per year, not initiated; *US – FSC* (WT/DS108), USD4, 043 million annually, not initiated yet; and *Canada – Aircraft* (WT/DS222), total amount of USD247,797,000, not initiated.

rulings. Among them, three different cases were brought by the EC against the US.[16] Additionally, *United States – Section 110(5) of the US Copyright Act* (WT/DS160), from the EC, is still pending on the implementation stage.[17]

Polls indicate in the US and the EC that trade disputes are "likely have some effect on public attitudes, contributing to a perception of each other as inward-looking, egotistical, and hypocritical free traders".[18] Trade tensions may also make co-operation in other areas more difficult. These include efforts to settle other trade disputes if media and public pressures provide encouragement.[19]

The most serious consequence of escalating trade tensions may impede the improvement of the DSU itself. The reason is obvious, since the EC and the US are the WTO's two biggest parties, their relationship and examples are critical for the smooth functioning of the multilateral trading system. When either of these two parties does not comply with WTO obligations, acts unilaterally, or uses the authorisations through Article

16 These five cases are: *US – Anti-Dumping Act of 1916* (WT/DS136 from the EC, and WT/DS162), on February 24, 2004, the arbitrator issued its award in the arbitration under Article 22.6 of the DSU: "The EC may suspend obligations under GATT 1994 and the AD Agreement against imports from the U S. The E C must ensure that the application of this suspension is quantified, and does not exceed the quantified level of nullification or impairment it has sustained as a result of the 1916 Act" (WT/DS136/ARB, *United States – Anti-Dumping Act of 1916* – (Original Complaint by the European Communities) – Recourse to Arbitration by the United States under Article 22.6 – Decision by the Arbitrators); *US – Section 211 Omnibus Appropriations Act of 1998* (WT/DS176 from the EC); *US – Anti-Dumping Measures on Certain Hot–Rolled Steel Products* (WT/DS176), *US – Continued Dumping and Subsidy Offset Act of 2000* ("Byrd Amendment" WT/DS217 from the EC, and WT/DS234); *Chile – Price Band System and Safeguard Measures Relating to Certain Agricultural Products* (WT/DS207).

17 On June 23, 2003, the US and the EC notified the WTO a mutually satisfactory temporary arrangement regarding the disputes. Pursuant to this arrangement, the US made a lump-sum payment of USD3.3 million to the EC, to a fund established to finance activities of general interest to music copyright holders, in particular awareness-rising campaigns at the national and international level and activities to combat piracy in the digital network. The arrangement covered the three-year period ending December 21, 2004. See: http://www.ustr.gov/enforcement/update.pdf last visited 2 June 2004.

18 Parlin 2000; 571.

19 *Ibid.*, p. 572.

22 of the DSU to retaliate against each other to satisfy their political pressures, the WTO multilateral trading system surely suffers.

To deal with these problems, one alternative is to apply the diplomatic method, namely the consultation, as opposed to legal solutions to disputes. To show good faith and to move towards negotiations, it is not only good for the EC-US trade relationship, but also good for the improvement of the DSU.

In fact, according to Busch and Reinhardt's empirical studies, about 58% of US-EC disputes had been solved during consultations or Panel deliberations.

However, there are some negative facets, some unsolved disputes or failed cases. It is noteworthy that most of these failed cases are between the US and EC.

The way out is to forge into the consciousness of all Members the desire for co-operative settlement. Litigation should be applied only after exhaustive efforts within the consultation phrase. The US and the EC are of roughly equal economic strength, and neither side has the ability to impose concessions on the other. Some disputes involve clashes in domestic values and priorities, (i.e. *Hormones* case)[20] where the law itself is unable to help under such circumstances or inadequate to provide a basis for effective and timely dispute resolution. Several of the disputes may be resolved and new potential disputes avoided through consultations. Moreover, the procedure on the bilateral level could provide a foundation for the two trading giants to make progress in efforts to begin the process of multilateral trade negotiation.

The EU, after losing the *Banana* and *Hormones* cases, thought that the binding nature of the DSU encouraged the settlement of disputes through consultations.[21] From the US perspective, the new dispute set-

20 The EC justified the ban to protect the health and safety of consumers, but several WTO dispute settlement panels subsequently ruled that the ban was inconsistent with the SPS Agreement. Although the Panels concluded that the EC ban lacked a scientific justification, the EC refused to remove the ban primarily out of concern that European consumers were opposed to having this kind of meat in the marketplace.

21 Horlick, G. N. & Butterton, G. R. A Problem of Process in WTO Jurisprudence: Identifying Disputed Issues in Panels and Consultations, L.P.I.B. 2000; 31(3–4): 573, from WESTLAW.

tlement rules often makes it possible to enforce WTO obligations without ever having to reach a panel decision.[22]

B. *Disputes between Developing Countries: Special Needs*

There is an argument that it is a waste of time and money for developing countries to invoke the WTO's dispute settlement procedure against industrial countries. In fact, WTO law does not give weaker counties the same protection that well-developed domestic legal systems usually afford their weaker citizens. One said it has nothing to do with the utility of the dispute settlement procedure for a developing country complainant.[23] Then, the problem arises as to how developing countries can overcome this legal disadvantage.

First, developing countries need more access to information on the WTO-legality of the measures employed by their major trade partners. This information is vital, not only in thinking about how to prosecute a case, but also as to whether a case should be prosecuted. To close the early settlement gap, developing Members need to bridge the important communication with some institutions like Advisory Centre on WTO Law, particularly with respect to evaluating the merits of a case before it is filed in Geneva, and articulating a negotiating strategy to win concessions before a legal verdict is issued.

A proposal made by the African Group in the WTO suggested the establishment of a permanent fund, financed by WTO Members, to help developing countries overcome their shortage of human and financial resources in using the complex WTO dispute settlement procedures. Alternatively, as dispute settlement proceedings were expensive in terms of both financial and human resources, effective consultations or skilful negotiation could also be beneficial for developing countries.

22 U.S.T.R., Report on Trade Expansion Priories Pursuant to Executive Order 12901 (Super 301), 62 Fed. Reg. 52, 604–611 (1997), from Horlick, G. N. Consultation Phase of WTO Dispute Resolution: A Private Practitioner's View, 32 INTL LAW 1998; 685.

23 Hudec, R. E. The Adequacy of WTO Dispute Settlement Remedies: A Developing Country Perspective, in Hoekman, B. (ed.), Development, Trade and the WTO: A Handbook, Washington: World Bank, 2002; 81–90.

Capacity building through legal assistance is the best solution for developing countries in the field of dispute settlement proceedings.

Second, developing Members need to forge alliances with foreign trade associations, since these organisations have a strong incentive to keep track of practices on behalf of their constituents, and often have information that governments need to monitor compliance. This, to some extent, remedies the shortage of resources problem.

This research elucidates what we understand and what we should do accordingly to remedy present problems. Throughout the research journey, I have attempted to take a position, which could explain existing problems, and articulate solutions based on Member states' experiences.

Compared with most other dispute settlement mechanisms, the DSU has established a relatively well-founded system and infrastructure. The system is evolving, and many factors, (sometimes, competing demands), are shaping the configuration of the system. The challenge confronting each government is to find a balanced approach among these issues. The DSU is no exception.

To meet the challenge, one must ensure that the DSU framework is neither under, nor over legitimate from the Chinese perspective. Overly stringent legitimacy would not only hinder trade growth, but it would also increase the costs of implementation, which may eventually create unfair competition, where only big players could afford to go through a costly regulatory process, and small or developing stakeholders would simply be screened out of a dispute. However, a lack of adjudication would also restrict trade. This could undermine the overriding goals of dispute settlement that litigation helps to achieve.

The unique features of the consultation make it flexible enough to quickly reach an agreement with a win-win situation. This achieves the goal of dispute settlement, and gains can be made on both sides. Moreover, bilateral understandings are appreciable and desirable and the main point of effective dispute settlement.

Promotion of the consultation, (i.e. maximising its benefits to achieve the goal of mutually agreed resolution), does not necessarily contradict improvement of the adjudicative process. The right approach for all Member states is to develop a balanced, whole DSU framework that is robust across areas of concern. Member states' experiences and theoretical analyses in the management of the dispute settlement system demonstrate that, consultations cannot be addressed in isolation.

According to ancient Chinese philosophy, to win the case is not a goal, but an expectation under the circumstance of unavoidable conflicts. The consultation can ease tensions between Member states and, therefore, achieve the result of a win-win situation. The achievement of valuable reforms should be applauded by all disputants. Furthermore, negotiations that implement the good faith principle during the consultation stage, benefit the later litigations phase(s) as well. This quest for a reconstruction of the consultation stage is not only necessary, but also crucial.

As the currents of globalisation have caused the east and west to converge, non-litigation methods have exponentially increased in importance in the Member-driven world trading system. The Consultation is the most Eastern of tactics within that system, and should be enhanced, not only for its effectiveness, but also for its origins.

Bibliography

Agreements, Laws and Treaties

Article VIII, Agreement of the IMF: http://www.imf.org/external/pubs/ft/aa/aa08.htm#6

Article I, Canada-United States: Agreement Regarding the Application of Their Competition and Deceptive Marketing Practices Laws, ILM 1996; 35:309.

Article 2 (2), Charter of the United Nations: http://www.un.org/aboutun/charter/

Article 142 (2), Convention on the Law of the Sea, UN Doc. A/CONF 1982; 62:122.

Article 2.1, 3.2, 4, 5.3, 6.1, 7.1, 8.5, 8.7, 16.4, 17.5, 17.14 of the DSU.

Article XXII and XXIII of GATT 1947.

Article 3, International Convention Relating to Invention on the High Seas in Cases of Oil Pollution Casualties, Nov. 29, 1969, 26 U.S.T. 765, T.I.A.S. No. 8086.

Article 5, The 1979 Geneva Convention on Long-range Transboundary Air Pollution: http://www.unece.org/env/lrtap/lrtap_h1.htm

Article 7, The 1961 Resolution on the Utilisation of Non-Maritime International Waters, AJIL 1962; 56:737.

Article 100, Treaty Establishing the European Community, Consolidated version of the EC Treaty: http://www.europa.eu.int/abc/obj/treaties/en/entoc05.htm

Article 26, 31 (1) and 46 (1), Vienna Convention on the Law of Treaties (VCLT): http://www.unog.ch/archives/vienna/

Canada-EU Agreements and Joint Statements: Exchange of Letters Between the EC and Canada on the Conclusion of Negotiations under GATT Article: http://www.dfait-maeci.gc.ca/canadaeuropa/caneu/ eu23-en.pdf

Declaration on Principles of International Law Concerning Friendly Relations and Co-operation among States in General Assembly in resolution 2625 (XXV), 1970: http://www.jur.ku.dk/Folkeret/materialesamling/Kilde%202%20UN%20GENERAL%20ASSEMBLY%20RESOLUTION%202625.doc

Libertad Act 1996: http://www.ustreas.gov/offices/eotffc/ofac/legal/statutes/libertad.pdf

Resolution 1135 on the implications for Europe and world of Helms-Burton Act of the US Congress: http://assembly.coe.int/Documents/AdoptedText/TA97/eres1135.htm

Treaty between the Federal Republic of Germany and Denmark, 10 ILM 1971; 10:603.Treaty between the Netherlands and the Federal Republic of Germany, ILM 1971; 10:607.

United Nations Convention on the Law of the Sea (UNCLOS) of 10 December 1982: http://www.un.org/Depts/los/convention_agreements/texts/unclos/part15.htm

Documents and Reports

Council of Europe Doc. EXP/Air (73) 2, Report of Committee of Experts on Air Pollution, Procedures for Consultation at National and International Level Prior to the Setting Up of Polluting Plant in Border Areas, at 4 (1973).

NATO Information Service, NATO Facts and Figures 308 (1976), Report of the Committee of Three on Non-military Co-operation in NATO, Dec. 13, 1956.

UN Doc. A/CONF. 48/14 (1972), Action Plan for the Human Environment, Recommendation 70, 11 ILM 1421(1972).

UN Pub.DPI/1247, Boutros-Ghali, B.: An Agenda for Peace, 1997.

US, the State of Florida, Committee Substitute for Senate Bill No. 96: http://election.dos.state.fl.us/laws/04laws/ch_2004-036.pdf

WTO, G/TMB/20, Fifty-Ninth Meeting of the TMB – Note by the Chairman, 29 October 1999.

WTO, G/TMB/21, Textiles Monitoring Body – Sixty-First Meeting of the TMB – Note by the Chairman, 17 December 1999.

WTO, G/TMB/N/344, Textiles Monitoring Body – Agreement on Textiles and Clothing – Communication from Colombia, 28 June 1999.

WTO, G/TMB/R/49, Textiles Monitoring Body – Report of the Fiftieth Meeting, 21 December 1998.

WTO, G/TMB/R/51, Textiles Monitoring Body – Report Fifty-Second Meeting, 11 February 1999.

WTO, Information on Recourse to WTO Dispute Settlement Procedures (1 January 1995–31 October 2003) Background Note by the Secretariat, 11 December 2003.

WTO, JOB (03) 225, WTO Special Session of the Dispute Settlement Body: Statistical

WTO, TN/DS/9, Special Sessions of the Dispute Settlement Body: Report by the Chairman, Ambassador Peter Balas, to the Trade Negotiations Committee, 6 June 2003.

WTO, TN/DS/W/1, Contribution of the EC and its Member States to the Improvement of the WTO Dispute Settlement Understanding, 13 March 2002.

WTO, TN/DS/W/21, Contribution by Jamaica to the Doha Mandated Review of the DSU, 10 October 2002.

WTO, TN/DS/W/25, Contribution by the Separate Customs Territory of Taiwan, Penghu, Kinmen and Matsu to the Doha Mandated Review of the Dispute Settlement Understanding, 27 November 2002.

WTO, TN/DS/W/43, Jordan's Contributions Towards the Improvement and Clarification of the WTO Dispute Settlement Understanding, 28 January 2003.

WTO, TN/DS/W/57, DSB Special Session: Responses to Questions on the Specific Input of China, Communication from China, 19 May 2003.

WTO, WT/DSB/M/6, Dispute Settlement Body – Minutes of Meeting Held in the Centre William Rappard on 19 July 1995.

WTO, WT/DSB/M/21, Dispute Settlement Body – Minutes of Meeting Held in the Centre William Rappard on 15 and 16 July 1996.

WTO, WT/DSB/M/29, Dispute Settlement Body – Minutes of Meeting Held in the Centre William Rappard on 25 February 1997.

WTO, WT/DSB/M/36, Dispute Settlement Body – Minutes of Meeting Held in the Centre William Rappard on 30 July 1997.

WTO, WT/DSB/M/60, Dispute Settlement Body – Minutes of Meeting Held in the Centre William Rappard on 28 April 1999.

WTO, WT/DSB/M/64, Dispute Settlement Body – Minutes of Meeting Held in the Centre William Rappard on 16 June 1999.

WTO, WT/DSB/M/70, Dispute Settlement Body – Minutes of Meeting Held in the Centre William Rappard on 27 October and 3 November 1999.

WTO, WT/DSB/M/77, Dispute Settlement Body, Minutes of Meeting Held on 20 March 2000, 17 April 2000.

WTO, WT/DSB/M/106, Dispute Settlement Body – Minutes of Meeting Held in the Centre William Rappard on 20 June 2001.

WTO, WT/DSB/M/129, Dispute Settlement Body – Minutes of Meeting Held in the Centre William Rappard on 8 July 2002.

WTO, WT/DSB (96)/ST/1, Statement by H. E. Mr D. Kenyon (Australia), Chairman of the Dispute Settlement Body.

WTO, WT/GC/66 and Add. 1, General Council – Request for Mediation by the Philippines, Thailand and the European Communities – Communication from the Director, 2002.

WTO, WT/GC/71, General Council – Request for Mediation by the Philippines, Thailand and the European Communities – Joint Communication from the European Communities, Thailand and the Philippines, 1 August 2003.

WTO, WT/L/432, Protocol on the Accession of the People's Republic of China, Decision of 10 November 2001.

Books

Bilder, R. B. An Overview of International Dispute Settlement in O'Connell, M. E. (ed.), *International Dispute Settlement*, Ashgate: Dartmouth, 2003.

Busch, M. L. & Reinhardt, E. Transatlantic Trade Conflicts and GATT/WTO Dispute Settlement in Petersmann, E. (ed.), *Dispute Prevention and Dispute Settlement in the Transatlantic Partnership,* Florence: EUI, 2002.

Busch, M. L. & Reinhardt, E. Testing International Trade Law: Empirical Studies of GATT/WTO Dispute Settlement in Kennedy, D. L. M. & Southwick, J. D. (ed.), *The Political Economy of International Trade Law: Essays in Honour of Robert E Hudec*, Cambridge: CUP, 2002.

Cheng, B. *General Principles of Law as Applied by International Courts and Tribunals*, London: Steven & Sons, 1953.

Cheng, B. Dispute Settlement in Bilateral Air Transport Agreements in Bockstiegel, K. (ed.), *Settlement of Space Law Disputes: the Present State of the Law and Perspectives of Further Development, Proceedings of an International Colloquium*, Munich 13 and 14 September 1979, Bonn: Carl Heymanns Verlag, 1980.

Chinkin, C. Alternative Dispute Resolution under International Law in O'Connell, M. E. (ed.), *International Dispute Settlement*, Ashgate: Dartmouth, 2003.

Cooper, R. M. *American Consultation in World Affairs: For the Preservation of Peace*, New York: MacMillan, 1934.

Dam, K. W. *The GATT Law and International Economic Organisation*, Chicago: University of Chicago Press, 1970.

Davey, W. J. WTO Dispute Settlement: Segregating the Useful Political Aspects and Avoiding "Over-Legalization" in Bronckers, M. & Quick, R. (ed.), *New Direction in International Economic Law: Essays in Honour of John H. Jackson*, The Hague: Kluwer Law International, 2000.

Davis, C. L. *Do WTO Rules Create a Level Playing Field For Developing Countries in Papers Prepared for a Conference on Developing Countries and the Trade Negotiation Process*, Geneva: UNCTAD, 2003.

Fombad, C. M. Consultation and Negotiation in the Pacific Settlement of International Disputes in O'Connell, M. E. (ed.), *International Dispute Settlement*, Ashgate: Dartmouth, 2003.

Gallagher, P. *Guide to the WTO and Developing Countries*, The Hague: Kluwer Law International, 2000.

Garner, B. A. *Black's Law Dictionary* (7th ed.), St Paul, Minn: West Group, 1999.

Goode, W. *World Trade Organisation: Dictionary of Trade Policy Terms* (4th ed.), Cambridge: CUP, 2003.

Gould W. *An Introduction to International Law*, New York: Harper Brothers, 1957.

Gulliver, P. H. *Disputes and Negotiations: A Cross-Cultural Perspective*, New York: Academic Press, 1979.

Hart, H. M. Jr. & Sacks, A. M. *The Legal Process: Basic Problems in the Making and Application of Law*, New York: Foundation, 1994.

Hudec, R. E. *The GATT Legal System and World Trade Diplomacy*, London: Praeger, 1975.

Hudec, R. E. *Enforcing International Trade Law: The Evolution of the Modern GATT Legal System*, New Hamshire: Butterworth, 1993.

Hudec, R. E. The Adequacy of WTO Dispute Settlement Remedies: A Developing Country Perspective in Hoekman, B. (ed.), *Development, Trade and the WTO: A Handbook*, Washington: World Bank, 2002.

Jackson, J. H. *Restructuring the GATT System*, London: Royal Institute of International Affairs, 1990.

Jackson, J. H. *The World Trading System: Law and Policy of International Economic Relations*, MIT: Cambridge, 1992.

Jackson, J. H., Davey, W. J. & Sykes, A. O. *Legal Problems of International Economic Relations* (3rd ed.), St Paul, Minn: West Publishing, 1995.

Jackson, J. H. *The World Organisation*, London: Royal Institute of International Affairs, 1998.

Jansen, M. Scope of Jurisdiction in GATT/WTO Dispute Settlement: Consultation and Panel Requests in Weiss, F. (ed.), *Improving WTO Dispute Settlement Procedures: Issues and Lessons from the Practice of Other International Courts and Tribunals*, London: Cameron May, 2000.

Jenks, C. W. *The Common Law of Mankind*, London: Stevens, 1958.

Jennings, R. & Watts, A. (ed.), *Oppenheim's International Law* (9th ed.), London: Longman, 1996.

Jessup, P. C. *International Security: The American Role in Collective Action for Peace*, New York: Council on Foreign Relations, 1935.

Keller, P. (ed.), *Chinese Law and Legal Theory*, Burlington: Ashgate, 2001.

Kelsen, H. *General Theory of Law and State*, Cambridge: CUP, 1946.

Kirgis, F. L. Jr., *Prior Consultation in International Law: A Study of State Practice*, Charlottesville: University Press of Virginia, 1983.

Lauterpacht H. (ed.), *Oppenheim's International Law, Vol. II Dispute, War and Neutrality* (7th ed.), London: Longman, 1952.

Merrills, J. G. *International Dispute Settlement* (3rd ed.), Cambridge: CUP, 1998.

O'Connell, M. E. (ed.), *International Dispute Settlement*, Aldershot: Dartmouth, 2003.

Petersmann, E. Proliferation and Fragmentation of Dispute Settlement in International Trade: WTO Dispute Settlement Procedures and Alternative Dispute Resolution Mechanisms in Lacarte, J & Granados, J. (ed.), *Inter-Governmental Trade Dispute Settlement: Multilateral and Regional Approaches*, London: Cameron May, 2004.

Qureshi, A. H. *International Economic Law*, London: Sweet & Maxwell, 1996.

Saner, R. *The Expert Negotiator*, The Hague: Kluwer Law International, 2000.

Schachter, O. *Sharing the World's Resources*, New York: Columbia University Press, 1977.

Serensen M. (ed.), *Manual of Public International Law*, London: MacMillan, 1968.

Shaw, M. N. *International Law* (5th ed.), Cambridge: CUP, 2003.

Sohn, L. The Future of Dispute Resolution in MacDonald, R. St. J. & Johnston, D. M. (ed.), *The Structure and Process of International Law: Essays in Legal Philosophy, Doctrine and Theory*, Boston, MA: Nijhoff Publishers, 1983.

Trebilcock, M. J. & Howse, R. *The Regulation of International Trade*, London: Routledge, 1995.

Van den Bossche, P. *United Nations Conference on Trade and Development: Course on Dispute Settlement World Trade Organization – 3.2 Panels*, New York and Geneva: UNCTAD, 2003.

Waincymer, J. *WTO Litigation: Procedural Aspects of Formal Dispute Settlement*, London: Cameron May, 2002.

Wang, G. G. *Law and Punishment: the Western and the traditional Chinese "Legal Mind"*, Oxford: Clarendon Press, 1986.

Wang, G. G. *Chinese Law*, The Hague: Kluwer Law International, 1999.

Zartman, I. W. & Berman, M. R. *The Practical Negotiator*, New Haven and London: Yale University Press, 1982.

Journals

Bilder, R. B. The Settlement of Disputes in the Field of the International Law of the Environment, Hague Recueil 1975.

Bourgeois, J. H. J. Some Reflections on the WTO Dispute Settlement System from a Practitioner's Perspective, J.I.E.L. 2001; 4(1):145.

Bourne, C. B. Procedure in the Development of International Drainage Basins: the Duty to Consult and to Negotiate, Canada Year Book of International Law 1972; 212.

Busch, M. L. & Reinhardt, E. Bargaining in the Shadow of the Law: Early Settlement in GATT/WTO Disputes, FDM.I.L.J. 2000; 24: 158.

Busch, M. L. & Reinhardt, E. Developing Countries and General Agreement on Tariffs and Trade/WTO Dispute Settlement, JWT 2003; 37(4): 719.

Buetler, M. & Hauser, H. The WTO Dispute Settlement System: A First Assessment from an Economic Perspective, Journal of Law, Economics, and Organisation 2000; 16(2): 503.

Campbell, B. R. The Canada-United States Antitrust Notification and Consultation Procedure, Canada Bar Review 1978; 56: 459.

Cheng, B. The Role of Consultation in Bilateral International Air Services Agreements, as Exemplified by Bermuda I and II, Columbia Journal of Transnational Law 1981; 19.

Clough, M. The WTO Dispute Settlement System – A Practitioner Perspective, 24 FDM.I.L.J. 252 (2000).

Cottier, T. The WTO Dispute Settlement System: New Horizons, 92 A.S.I.L.PROC 86 (1998).

Cottier, T. Dispute Settlement in the World Trade Organization: Characteristics and Structural Implications for the European Union, 35(2) C.M.L.Rev (1998) 325.

Davey, W. J., Dispute Settlement in GATT, *Fordham International Law Journal* 51 1987;11: 99.

Davey, W. J. & Porges, A. Performance of the System I: Consultations & Deterrence, Intl Law 1998; 32: 696.

Feeney, S. P. The Dispute Settlement Understanding of the WTO Agreement: An Inadequate Mechanism for the Resolution of International Trade Disputes, PEPD.R.L.J. 2002; 2: 99.

Green, C. J. APEC and Trans-Pacific Dispute Management, 26 LPIB 1995; 26: 719.

Horlick, G. N. Consultation Phase of WTO Dispute Resolution: A Private Practitioner's View, Intl Law 1998; 32: 685.

Horlick, G. N. & Butterton, G. R. A Problem of Process in WTO Jurisprudence: Identifying Disputed Issues in Panels and Consultations, 31(3–4) L.P.I.B. 2000; 31(3–4): 573.

Hudec, R. E. Transcending the Ostensible: Some Reflections on the Nature of Litigation Between Governments, Minn. L. Rev. 1987; 72: 211.

Hudec, R. E. Forum: Taiwan and the GATT and the Developing Countries, C.B.L.Rev 1992; 67.

Hudec, R. E. International Economic Law: The Political Theatre Dimension, U. Pa. J. Int'l Econ. L. 1996; 17: 9.

Irvin J. The Role of Law in the Negotiated Settlement of International Disputes, Vanderbilt International 1969; 3.

Jackson, J. H. International Economic Law in Times That Are Interesting, J.I.E.L. 2000; 3(1).

Jackson, J. Afterword: The Linkage Problem-Comments on Five Texts, AJIL 2002; 96(1): 118.
Leitner, S. & Lester, K. WTO Dispute Settlement 1995–2002: A Statistical Analysis, J.I.E.L. 2003; 6(1).
Leitner, S. & Lester, K. WTO Dispute Settlement 1995–2003: A Statistical Analysis, J.I.E.L. 2004; 7(1).
Lennard, M. Navigation by the Stars: Interpreting the WTO Agreements, J.I.E.L. 2002; 5(1).
Lichtenbaum, P. Dispute Settlement and Institutional Issues, J.I.E.L. 2000; 3(1).
Mather, L. & Yngvesson, B. Language, Audience and the Transformation of Dispute, Law & Society Review 1981; 15: 775.
Miller, R. E. & Sarat, A. Grievances, Claims and Disputes: Assessing the Adversary Culture, Law *& Society Review* 1981; 15: 527.
Palmeter, D. The WTO Appellate Body Needs Remand Authority, J.W.T. 1998; 32(1).
Park, Y. D. & Umbricht, G. C. WTO Dispute Settlement 1995–2000: A Statistical Analysis, J.I.E.L. 2001; 4(1).
Park, Y. D. & Panizzon, M. WTO Dispute Settlement 1995–2001: A Statistical Analysis, J.I.E.L. 2002; 5(1).
Parlin, C. C. Operation of Consultations, Deterrence and Mediation, L.P.I.B. 2000; 31(3–4): 565.
Peng, S. Y. The WTO Legalistic Approach and East Asia: from the Legal Culture Perspective, Asian-Pacific Law & Policy Journal 2000; 13: 1.
Pescatore, P. The GATT Dispute Settlement Mechanism: Its Present Situation and Its Prospects, J.I.A. 1993; 10.
Petersmann, E. U. The Dispute Settlement System Of the World Trade Organisation and the Evolution of the GATT Dispute Settlement System Since 1948, C.M.L.Rev. 1994; 31(6).
Reinisch, A. Widening the US Embargo Against Cuba Extraterritorially: A Few Comments on the Cuba Liberty and Democratic Solidarity (LIBERTAD) Act of 1996, EJIL 4 1996; 7: 545.
Shell, G. R. The Trade Stakeholders Model and Participation by Nonstate Parties in the World Trade Organisation, University of Pennsylvania Journal of International Economic Law 1996; 17: 359.
Steger, D. P. Afterward: The "Trade And..." Conundrum – A Commentary, 96 A.M.J.I.L. 2002; 96: 135.
Stewart, T. P. & Karpel, A. A. Review of the Dispute Settlement Understanding: Operation of Panels, L.P.I.B. 2000; 31(3–4): 593.
Stiles, K. Negotiating Institutional Reform: The Uruguay Round, the GATT, and the WTO, Global Governance 1996; 2: 119.
Trachtman, J. P. The Domain of WTO Dispute Resolution, Harvard International Law Journal 1999; 40: 333.
Wethington, O. J. Commentary on consultation Mechanism under the WTO Dispute Settlement Understanding During Its First Five Years, L.P.I.B. 2000; 31(3–4): 583.
Yu, X. Z. Legal Pragmatism in the People's Republic of China, Journal of Chinese Law, 1989; 3: 29.

Others

Panizzon, M., *Good Faith and Legitimate Expectations in WTO Adjudication: Integrating a General Principle of Law into the WTO Acquis* (PhD Dissertation), Bern: IEW, 2003.

World Trade Institute, Course Materials for Master of International Law and Economics Class, Bern: WTI, 2004

Websites

Advisory Centre on WTO Law, *Trade and Development Centre, Agreement Establishing the Advisory Centre on WTO Law,* www.itd.org/links/char1611.doc

Ahearn, R. J., *US-EC Trade Tensions: Causes, Consequences, and Possible Cures,* http://fpc.state.gov/documents/organization/10922.pdf

Ahearn, R. J., *US-European Union Trade Relations: Issues and Policy Challenges,* 21 March 2003, http://www.ncseonline.org/nle/crsreports/03May/IB10087.pdf

Ahn, D. *GATT/WTO Dispute Settlement and Korea: From Passivity to Aggression*, CDAMS Discussion Paper O4/3E, Kobe University, April 2004, http://www.cdams.kobe-u.ac.jp/archive/dp04-3.pdf

ASEAN: http://www.aseansec.org/64.htm

Asian Africa Legal Consultative Organisation, *Extra-Territorial Application of National Legislation: Sanctions Imposed against Third Parties*, in http://www.aalco.org/etanlcairoIII.htm

Associated Press: WTO to rule on US Complaint against Cut-Price AIDS Drugs in Brazil, 1 February 2001, http://www.accessmed-msf.org/prod/publications.asp?scntid=2982001739218&contenttype=PARA&

Becker, E. *US Files A Complaint Against China At the W.T.O.*, 19 March 2004, http://query.nytimes.com/gst/abstract.html?res=F20D10F738550C7A8DDDAA0894DC404482

Busch, M. L. & Reinhardt, E. *The WTO Dispute Settlement Mechanism and Developing Countries*, from http://userwww.service.emory.edu/~erein/research/SIDA.pdf

Consumer Project on Technology, Pharmaceuticals: United States Drops WTO Case Against Brazil Over HIV/AIDS Patent *Law,* 26 June 2001, http://www.cptech.org/ip/health/c/brazil/bna06262001.htm

Cooney, S. *Steel Industry and Trade Issues*, http://www.ncseonline.org/NLE/CRSreports/02Dec/RS21152.pdf

EC, *EC to Request WTO Consultations with Chile over Prohibition of Unloading of Swordfish in Chilean Ports* (IP/00/397), 18 April 2000: http://trade-info.cec.eu.int/wtodispute/show.cfm?id=145&code=1

EU, EU and Chile Reach an Amicable Settlement to End WTO/ITLOS Swordfish Dispute (IP/01/116), 25 January 2001: http://trade-info.cec.eu.int/wtodispute/show.cfm?id=145&code=1

EU, *EU Requests the Establishment of a WTO Panel against the Republic of Chile* (MEMO/00/77), 10 November 2000: http://trade-info.cec.eu.int/wtodispute/show.cfm?id=145&code=1

EU, EU/US News: A Review of Transatlantic Relations, Transatlantic Relations After 11 *September* from http://europa.eu.int/comm/external_relations/us/eu_us_news/8.pdf

EU, *WTO Dispute Settlement, Case Involving the EU* in http://trade-info.cec.eu.int/wtodispute/show.cfm?id=166&code=1

Global Policy Forum, *Multinationals win US Court Victory over Activists*, 24 June 1999, http://www.globalpolicy.org/socecon/tncs/court99.htm

International Intellectual Property Alliance, *Excerpt from the IIPA Special 301 Recommendations, February 24, 1997: Turkey*, in http://www.iipa.com/rbc/1997/rbc_turkey_301_97.html

Jackson, J. H. & Lowenfeld, A. F. *Helms-Burton, the US, and the WTO*, http://www.asil.org/insights/insight7.htm

Jackson, J. H. *Perceptions About the WTO Trade Institutions Inauguration Ceremony for the Advisory Centre for WTO Law Keynote Address*, 5 October 2001, http://www.acwl.ch/e/tools/news_detailsphoto_e.aspx?id=7192a684-8dac-4d91-974d-4f4f9ed3a682

Kim, S. J., Reinert, K. A. & Rodrigo, G. C. *The Agreement on Textiles and Clothing: Safeguard Actions From 1995 to 2001*, http://mason.gmu.edu/~kreinert/paperspdf/atcJ.I.E.L..pdf

Lobe, J. *Pro-Burmese Business Wins in US Court* (21 June 2000), http://www.atimes.com/se-asia/BF21Ae02.html

Mike Moore, *WTO's Unique System of Settling Dispute Nears 200 Cases in 2000*, Press Release (5 June 2000), http://www.wto.org/english/news_e/pres00_e/pr180_e.htm

Mills, R. & Moorjani, N. *US, China Settle Dispute Over Semiconductor Tax Refunds: China to Stop Refunds Favouring China-Designed Circuits*, 8 July 2004, http://hongkong.usconsulate.gov/uscn/trade/general/ustr/2004/070801.htm and *China Will Formula New Policies for Supporting the Production of IC Industry*, 10 July 004, in http://tech.sina.com.cn/it/2004-07-10/0743385876.shtml

Morrison, W. M. *China-US Trade Agreements: Compliance Issues*, http://www.usc.cuhk.edu.hk/wk_wzdetails.asp?id=3142

Steel safeguard case websites:
http://www.metalcenternews.com/2002/April/
www.ustr.gov/releases/2002/04/02-47.htm
www.asil.org/insights/insigh84.htm
www.europa.eu.int/comm/trade/goods/steel/pr_270302.htm
www.whitehouse.gov/news/release/2002/03/20020305-8.html
www.globalpolicy.org/socecon/bwi-wto/wto/2002/0307.htm
www.bbc.co.uk/hi/english/business/newsid_1881000/1881821.stm

Sun Tsu, III-Attack by Stratagem in *The Art of War* (Original Title: Sun Zi Bing Fa, ca. 490 B.C.), http://www.chinapage.com/sunzi-e.html#03

Synder, S. *The Insatiable Sino-Korean Economic Relationship: Too Much for Seoul to Swallow?,* July-September 2000, http://www.csis.org/pacfor/cc/003Qchina_skorea.html

The New Zealand Ministry of Foreign Affairs & Trade: Legal Division-Dispute Index Page: http://www.mfat.govt.nz/support/legal/disputes/disputespeech.html

The Thirty-Six Strategies in Ancient China (Original Title: 36 Ji, ca. 489-537B.C), http://www.chinastrategies.com/intro.htm

UN, *The Criteria for the identification of the LDCs*: http://www.un.org/special-rep/ohrlls/ldc/ldc%20criteria.htm

UN, *List of SIDS*, http://www.un.org/special-rep/ohrlls/sid/list.htm and *List of LLDCs*, http://www.un.org/special-rep/ohrlls/lldc/list.htm

US Department of State, Eizenstat Announces US/EU Understanding on Cuba (EU suspends challenge to Helms-*Burton in WTO)* on April 11th 1997, http://usinfo.state.gov/regional/ar/us-cuba/eizen.htm

USTR, *Database on Update Enforcement of the WTO*, March 2004, http://www.ustr.gov/enforcement/update.pdf

USTR, *US and Brazil Agree to Use Newly Created Consultative Mechanism to Promote Cooperation on HIV/AIDS and Address WTO Patent Dispute*, 1 June 2001, http://www.ustr.gov/releases/2001/06/01-46.htm

Wen, Y. *Trade Conflict between China and the US Upgrades and China Feels Surprised*, 20 March 2004, http://tech.sina.com.cn/other/2004-03-20/0928336599.shtml

Yang, G. H. *Analysis consultations in the WTO Dispute Settlement Mechanism*, 2003, http://chinalawinfo.com/research/academy/details.asp?lid=3525

Table of Cases

Public International Law

Mavromattis Palestine Concessions (Greece v. U.K.), 1924 P.C.I.J. Ser. A No. 2 (Judgment of Aug. 13)

The *German Interests in Polish Upper Silesia* case (Jurisdiction), 1925, P.C.I.J. Series A. No. 6

Factory at Chorzow (Merits) 1928, P.C.I.J. Series A No. 17

The *South West Africa* Cases (Ethiopia v South Africa; Liberia v South Africa) (Preliminary Objections) ICJ Reports (1962) 319

North Sea Continental Shelf Cases, ICJ (1969) 3

Agriculture Board v Aylesbury Mushrooms [1974] 1 WLR 190, 194–195

The *Nuclear Test* cases, ICJ Reports 253 (1974)

The *France/ US Air Transport Arbitration* Award of 1978, 54 ILR (1979)

The *Applicability of the Obligation to Arbitrate under Sect. 21 of the UN Headquarters Agreement* case, ICJ Reports (1988)

ICJ Decision *Gabcikovo-Nagymaros Project* (Hungary/Slovakia), 1994

GATT

The Netherlands v. Cuba Consular Tax, GATT/CP.2/9 or BISD 11/12 (1948)

The UK v. Greece Increase on Import Duties on Products Included in Schedule XXV, BISD 1S/51 (1953)

Brazilian Internal Taxes case, BISD 11/181 (1961)

The US v. the EEC Panel on Poultry in 1963, BISD 12S/65 (1963)

The EEC v. the US Income Tax Legislation (DISC) BISD 23S/98 (1977)

The EEC v. the US Programme of Minimum Import Price (MIPS), Licences, and Surety Deposits for Certain Processed Fruits and Vegetables, BISD 25S/68, (1978)

The US v. the EEC Measures on Animal Feed Proteins BISD 25S/49 (1979)

The EC v. Japan Customs Duties, Taxes, and Labelling Practices on Imported Wines and Alcoholic Beverages BISD 34S/83 (1988)

The EEC v. Japan Regulation on Imports of Parts and Components, BISD 37S/132 (1991)

WTO

WT/DS1/1, *Malaysia – Prohibition of Imports of Polyethylene and Polypropylene*, 1995

WT/DS3, *Korea-Measures Concerning the Testing and Inspection of Agricultural Products*, 1995

WT/DS4/2, *United States-Standards for Reformulated and Conventional Gasoline*, 1995

WT/DS7, WT/DS12 and WT/DS14 *European Communities-Trade Description of Scallops*, 1995

WT/DS8/R, WT/DS10/R and WT/DS11/R, Panel Report of *Tax on Japan-Alcoholic Beverages*, 1996

WT/DS9/1, *European Communities – Duties on Imports of Cereals*, 1995

WT/DS13/1, *European Communities – Duties on Imports of Grains*, 1995

WT/DS14, *European Communities – Trade Description of Scallops*, 1995

WT/DS21/1, *AUSTRALIA – MEASURES AFFECTING THE IMPORTATION OF SALMONIDS*, 1995

WT/DS22/R, Panel report of *Brazil – Measures Affecting Desiccated Coconut*, 1996

WT/DS24/R, Panel Report on *United States – Restrictions on Imports of Cotton and Man-Made Fibre Underwear*, 1996

WT/DS27AB/R, *WTO Appellate Body Report on EC-Regime for the Importation, Sale and Distribution of Bananas*, 1997

WT/DS33/R, *United States – Measure Affecting Imports of Woven Wool Shirts and Blouses from India* – Report of the Panel, 1997

WT/DS34/R, Panel Report on *Turkey – Restrictions on Imports of Textile and Clothing Products*, 1999

WT/DS35/1, *Hungary – Export Subsidies in Respect of Agricultural Products*, 1996

WT/DS36/1, *Pakistan – Patent Protection for Pharmaceutical and Agricultural Chemical Products*, 1996

WT/DS38/1, *United States – The Cuban Liberty and Democratic Solidarity Act*, 1996

WT/DS39/1, *United States – Tariff Increases on Products from the European Communities*, 1996

WT/DS43/1, *Turkey – Taxation of Foreign Film Revenues*, 1996

WT/DS46/AB/R, *Brazil – Export Financing Programme for Aircraft* – Report of the Appellate Body, 1999

WT/DS50/AB/R, *WTO Appellate Body Report on India-Patents Protection for Pharmaceutical and Agricultural Chemical Products,* 1997

WT/DS56/R, Panel Report on *Argentina – Measures Affecting Imports of Footwear, Textiles, Apparel and other Items*, 1997

WT/DS58/R, Panel Report on *US-Import Prohibition of Certain Shrimp and Shrimp Products*, 1998

WT/DS70, *Canada – Measures Affecting the Export of Civilian Aircraft*, 1997

WT/DS72/R, *European Communities-Measure Affecting Butter Products*, 1999

WT/DS73/4, *Japan – Procurement of a Navigation Satellite*, 1997

WT/DS75/R and WT/DS84/R, *Panel Report on Korea-Taxes on Alcoholic Beverages*, 1998

WT/DS77/1, *Argentina – Measures Affecting Textiles, Clothing and Footwear*, 1997

WT/DS88/1, *United States – Measure Affecting Government Procurement*, 1997

WT/DS89/1, *United States – Imposition of Anti-Dumping Duties on Imports of Colour Television Receivers from Korea*, 1997

WT/DS108/AB/R, AB Report on the *US-Tax Treatment for "Foreign Sales Corporations"*, 2000

WT/DS114/R, *Panel Report on Canada – Patent Protection of Pharmaceutical Products*, 2000

WT/DS120, *India – Measures Affecting Export of Certain Commodities,* 1998

WT/DS123/1, *Argentina – Safeguard Measures on Imports of Footwear*, 1998

WT/DS126/R, Panel Report on *Australia – Subsidies Provided to Producers and Exports of Automotive Leather*, 1999

WT/DS132/AB/RW, Appellate Body Report on *Mexico – Anti-Dumping Investigation of High-Fructose Corn Syrup (HFCS) from the United States*, 2000

WT/DS160/ARB25/1, *United States-Section 110(5) of US Copy right Act*, 2001

WT/DS163/R, *Korea – Measures Affecting Government Procurement*, 2000

WT/DS165/AB/R, Appellate Report on *United States – Import Measures on Certain Products from the European Communities*, 2000

WT/DS181/1, *Colombia – Safeguard Measure on Imports of Plain Polyester Filaments from Thailand*, 1998

WT/DS190/1, *Argentina – Transitional Safeguard Measures on Certain Imports of Woven Fabrics of Cotton and Cotton Mixtures Originating in Brazil*, 2000

WT/DS193/1, *Chile – Measures Affecting the Transit and Importation of Swordfish*, 2000

WT/DS195/4, *Philippines – Measures Affecting Trade and Investment in the Motor Vehicle Sector*, 2000

WT/DS199/1, *Brazil – Measures Affecting Patent Protection* – Request for Consultations by the United States, 2000

WT/DS200/13, *United States – Section 306 of the Trade Act of 1974 and Amendments Thereto*, 2000

WT/DS210/1, *Belgium – Administration of Measures Establishing Customs Duties for Rice*, 2000

WT/DS222, *Canada – Export Credits and Loan Guarantees for Regional Aircraft*, 2001
WT/DS227/1, *Peru – Taxes on cigarettes* – Request for Consultations by Chile, 2001
WT/DS237/1, *Turkey – Certain Import Procedures for Fresh Fruit*, 2001
WT/DS240, *Romania – Import Prohibition on Wheat and Wheat Flour*, 2001
WT/DS250/1, *United States – Equalizing Excise tax Imposed by Florida on Processed Orange and Grapefruit Products*, 2002
WT/DS252/1, *United States – Definitive Safeguard Measures on Imports of Certain Steel Products*, 2002
WT/DS255, *Peru – Tax Treatment on Certain Imported Products*, 2002
WT/DS258, *United States – Definitive Safeguard Measures on Imports of Certain Steel Products*, 2002
WT/DS261/1, *Uruguay – Tax Treatment on Certain Products*, 2002
WT/DS267/AB/R, Appellate Body Report on *United States-Subsidies on Upland Cotton*, 2005
WT/DS285/1, *US-Measures Affecting the Cross-border Supply of Gambling and Betting Services*, 2003
WT/DS305/1, *Egypt – Measures Affecting Imports of Textile and Apparel Products*, 2004
WT/DS307/1, *European Communities – Aid for Commercial Vessels*, 2004
WT/DS309/1, *China – Value-Added Tax on Integrated Circuits*, 2004

Annex (I)

Reference Questions

1. How many informal negotiations do you conduct before formal consultations are announced and taken up?
2. Do you think the formal consultation is useful or merely a proceeding burden as there were several informal negotiations held before?
3. Does the request of establishing a Panel increase the pressure to find an amicable solution?
4. If consultations are at a deadlock, does a complainant usually require the DSB to immediately establish a Panel or does he try to find negotiable issues to break the ice?
5. Who is involved during the consultation stage? Are there any changes of personnel in the informal negotiations and the formal consultations?
6. How are concessions made during the consultation?
7. Is there any impact from third parties?
8. How do you deal with potential third party's interests during the consultations?
9. How do you think to make consultations 'meaningful'? If consultations fail, as you go to the Panel stage, will you usually use the information obtained during the consultations in the Panel stage? How do you use the information?
10. Do you think that, during the consultations, the political impact is stronger than the legal influence?
11. Are there any other factors (such as media) affecting the outcome of the consultation?
12. What improvements could be made to the present consultation procedures in the DSU (reform package)?

Annex (II)

The Status of All Disputes

The disputes listed below are in reverse chronological order (the newest appear first) and they are grouped according to the years they were first brought to the WTO as of 31 January 2006:

WT/DS335 United States – Anti-Dumping Measure on Shrimp from Ecuador – Request for Consultations.

WT/DS334 Turkey – Measures Affecting the Importation of Rice – Request for Consultations by United States.

WT/DS333 Dominican Republic – Foreign Exchange Fee Affecting Imports from Costa Rica – Request for Consultations.

WT/DS332 Brazil – Measures Affecting Imports of Retreated Tyres – MAS.

WT/DS331 Mexico – Anti-Dumping Duties on Steel Pipes and Tubes from Guatemala – Request for Consultations.

WT/DS330 Argentina – Countervailing Duties on Olive Oil, Wheat Gluten and Peaches – Request for Consultations by the European Communities.

WT/DS329 Panama – Tariff Classification of Certain Milk Products – Request for Consultations by Mexico.

WT/DS328 European Communities – Definitive Safeguard Measure on Salmon – inactive.

WT/DS327 Egypt – Anti-Dumping Duties on Matches from Pakistan – Panels established by DSB.

WT/DS326 European Communities – Definitive Safeguard Measure on Salmon – inactive.

WT/DS325 United States – Anti-Dumping Determinations Regarding Stainless Steel from Mexico – Request for Consultations by Mexico.

WT/DS324 United States – Provisional Anti-Dumping Measures on Shrimp from Thailand – Request for Consultations by Thailand.

WT/DS323 Japan – Import quotas on dried laver and seasoned laver Brought by Korea – MAS.

WT/DS322 United States – Measures Relating to Zeroing and Sunset Reviews – Constitution of the Panel Established at the Request of Japan.

WT/DS321 Canada – Continued suspension of obligations in the EC – Hormones dispute Brought by EC – Request for the Establishment of a Panel by the European Communities.

WT/DS320 United States – Continued suspension of obligations in the EC – Hormones dispute Brought by EC – Request for the Establishment of a Panel by the European Communities.

WT/DS319 United States – Section 776 of the Tariff Act of 1930 Brought by EC – Request for Consultations by the European Communities.

WT/DS318 India – Anti-dumping measures on certain products from the Separate Customs Territory of Taiwan, Penghu, Kinmen and Matsu – Request for Consultations.

WT/DS317 United States – Measures affecting trade in large civil aircraft Brought by EC – Panels established by DSB.

WT/DS316 European Communities and certain Member States – Measures affecting trade in large civil aircraft Brought by United States – Panels established by DSB.

WT/DS315 European Communities – Selected Customs Matters – Request for the Establishment of a Panel by the United States.

WT/DS314 Mexico – Provisional Countervailing Measures on Olive oil from the European Communities – Request for Consultations by the European Communities.

WT/DS313 European Communities – Anti-dumping Duties on Certain Flat Rolled Iron or Non-alloy Steel Products from India – MAS.

WT/DS312 Korea – Anti-dumping Duties on Imports of Certain Paper from Indonesia – Panel Reports Adopted.

WT/DS311 United States – Reviews of Countervailing Duty on Softwood Lumber from Canada – Request for Consultations by Canada.

WT/DS310 United States – Determination of the International Trade Commission in Hard Red Spring Wheat from Canada – Request for the Establishment of a Panel by Canada.

WT/DS309 China – Value-Added Tax on Integrated Circuits – MAS.

WT/DS308 Mexico – Tax Measures on Soft Drinks and Other Beverages – On Appeal.

WT/DS307 European Communities – Aid for Commercial Vessels – Request for Consultations by Korea.

WT/DS306 India – Anti-Dumping Measure on Batteries from Bangladesh – MAS.

WT/DS305 Egypt – measures affecting imports of textile and apparel products – Removed measures.

WT/DS304 India – Anti-dumping Measures on Imports of Certain Products from the European Communities and/or Member States – Request for Consultations by the European Communities.

WT/DS303 Ecuador – Definitive Safeguard Measure on Imports of Medium Density Fibreboard – Inactive.

WT/DS302 Dominican Republic – Measures Affecting the Importation and Internal Sale of Cigarettes – On Implementation after Article 21.3 (c) Arbitration Report.

WT/DS301 European Communities – Measures Affecting Trade in Commercial Vessels – Implemented after the Panel Report.

WT/DS300 Dominican Republic – Measures Affecting the Importation of Cigarettes – Dead because of the new request of DS302.

WT/DS299 European Communities – Countervailing Measures on Dynamic Random Access Memory Chips from Korea – RTP Extended to 3 April 2006.

WT/DS298 Mexico – Certain Pricing Measures for Customs Valuation and Other Purposes – MAS.

WT/DS297 Croatia – Measure Affecting Imports of Live Animals and Meat Products – MAS in February 2004.

WT/DS296 United States – Countervailing Duty Investigation on Dynamic Random Access Memory Semiconductors (DRAMS) from Korea – RTP to 8 March 2006.

WT/DS295 Mexico – Definitive Anti-Dumping Measures on Beef and Rice – AB and Panel Reports adopted.

WT/DS294 United States – Laws, Regulations and Methodology for Calculating Dumping Margins (zeroing) – Panel Reports Adopted.

WT/DS291, WT/DS292, WT/DS293 European Communities – Measures Affecting the Approval and Marketing of Biotech Products – Constitution of the Panel.

WT/DS174, WT/DS290 European Communities – Protection of Trademarks and Geographical Indications for Agricultural Products and Food stuff – RTP to 3 April 2006.

WT/DS289 Czech Republic – Additional Duty on Imports of Pig-Meat from Poland – Cancelled.

WT/DS288 South Africa – Definitive Anti-Dumping Measures on Blanketing from Turkey – Dead.

WT/DS287 Australia – Quarantine Regime for Imports – Inactive.

WT/DS286, WT/DS269 European Communities – Customs Classification of Frozen Boneless Chicken Cuts – On Implementation.

WT/DS285 United States – Measures Affecting the Cross-Border Supply of Gambling and Betting Services – RTP to 3 April 2006.

WT/DS284 Mexico – Certain Measures Preventing the Importation of Black Beans from Nicaragua – Withdrawal.

WT/DS283, WT/DS265, WT/DS266 European Communities – Export Subsidies on Sugar – RTP to 22 May 2006.

WT/DS282 United States – Anti-dumping Measures on oil Country Tubular Goods (OCTG) from Mexico – AB and Panel Reports Adopted.

WT/DS281 United States – Anti-Dumping Measures on Cement from Mexico – Constitution of the Panel.

WT/DS280 United States – Countervailing Duties on Steel Plate from Mexico – Request for the Establishment of a Panel.

WT/DS279 India – Import Restrictions Maintained under the Export and Import Policy 2002–2007 – Inactive.

WT/DS278 Chile – Definitive Safeguard Measure on Imports of Fructose – Withdrawal.

WT/DS277 United States – Investigation of the International Trade Commission in Softwood Lumber from Canada – Implemented after Article 21.5 of the DSU.

WT/DS276 Canada – Measures Relating to Exports of Wheat and Treatment of Imported Grain – Implemented.

WT/DS275 Venezuela – Import Licensing Measures on Certain Agricultural Products – Inactive.

WT/DS274 United States – Definitive Safeguard Measures on Imports of Certain Steel Products – Withdrawal.

WT/DS273 Korea – Measures Affecting Trade in Commercial Vessels – Panel Report adopted.
WT/DS272 Peru – Provisional Anti-Dumping Duties on Vegetable Oils from Argentina – Inactive.
WT/DS271 Australia – Certain Measures Affecting the Importation of Fresh Pineapple – Inactive.
WT/DS270 Australia – Certain Measures Affecting the Importation of Fresh Fruit and Vegetables – Inactive.
WT/DS268 United States – Sunset Reviews of Anti-Dumping Measures on Oil Country Tubular Goods From Argentina – RTP to 17 December 2005.
WT/DS267 United States – Subsidies on Upland Cotton – Article 22.6 Arbitration.
WT/DS264 United States – Final Dumping Determination on Softwood Lumber from Canada – Reached agreement after AB report.
WT/DS263 European Communities – Measures Affecting Imports of Wine – Request for Consultations by Argentina – Inactive.
WT/DS262 United States – Sunset Reviews of Anti-Dumping and Countervailing Duties on Certain Steel Products from France and Germany – Withdrawal.
WT/DS261 Uruguay – Tax Treatment on Certain Products – MAS.
WT/DS260 European Communities – Provisional Safeguard Measures on Imports of Certain Steel Products – Dead.
WT/DS248, WT/DS249, WT/DS251, WT/DS252, WT/DS253, WT/DS254, WT/DS258, and WT/DS259 United States – Definitive Safeguard Measures on Imports of Certain Steel Products – US withdrawal after AB report.
WT/DS257 United States – Final Countervailing Duty Determination With Respect to Certain Softwood Lumber from Canada – Article 21.5 AB Report Circulated.
WT/DS256 Turkey – Import ban on Pet Food from Hungary – MAS.
WT/DS255 Peru – Tax Treatment on Certain Imported Products – Withdrawal. WT/DS250 United States – Equalising Excise Tax Imposed by Florida on Processed Orange and Grapefruit Products – MAS.
WT/DS247 United States – Provisional Anti-Dumping Measure on Imports of Certain Softwood Lumber from Canada – Withdrawal.
WT/DS246 European Communities – Conditions for the Granting of Tariff Preferences to Developing Countries – Arbitration Report Issued and Implemented.
WT/DS245 Japan – Measures Affecting the Importation of Apples – MAS after Article 21.5 of the DSU.
WT/DS244 United States – Sunset Review of Anti-Dumping Duties on Corrosion-resistant Carbon Steel Flat Products from Japan – Appellate Body Report: the US won.
WT/DS243 United States – Rules of Origin for Textiles and Apparel Products – Panel Report: the US won.
WT/DS242 European Communities – Generalised System of Preferences – Not pending.
WT/DS241 Argentina – Definitive Anti-Dumping Duties on Poultry from Brazil – Panel Report – Implemented after Panel report.
WT/DS240 Romania – Import Prohibition on Wheat and Wheat Flour – Withdrawal.

WT/DS239 United States – Certain Measures Regarding Anti-Dumping Methodology – Withdrawal.
WT/DS238 Argentina – Definitive Safeguard Measure on Imports of Preserved Peaches – Agreement under Article 21.3(b) of the DSU.
WT/DS237 Turkey – Certain Import Procedures for Fresh Fruit – MAS.
WT/DS236 United States – Preliminary Determinations with Respect to Certain Softwood Lumber from Canada – Implemented after Panel report.
WT/DS235 Slovakia – Safeguard Measure on Imports of Sugar – MAS.
WT/DS234, WT/DS217 United States – Continued Dumping and Subsidy Offset Act of 2000 (Byrd Amendment) – Retaliation authorised by DSB.
WT/DS233 Argentina – Measures Affecting the Import of Pharmaceutical Products – Request for Consultations by India – Inactive.
WT/DS232 Mexico – Measures Affecting the Import of Matches – Withdrawal.
WT/DS231 European Communities – Trade Description of Sardines – Notification of MAS According to Art. 21.3 after the AB and the Panel Reports.
WT/DS230, WT/DS/228 Chile – Safeguard Measures and Modification of Schedules Regarding Sugar – Removed.
WT/DS229 Brazil – Anti-Dumping Duties on Jute Bags from India – Inactive.
WT/DS227 Peru – Taxes on Cigarettes – Withdrawal.
WT/DS226 Chile Provisional Safeguard Measure on Mixtures of Edible Oils – Measures elapsed.
WT/DS225 United States – Anti-Dumping Duties on Imports of Seamless Pipe from Italy – Inactive.
WT/DS224 United States – US Patents Code – Withdrawal.
WT/DS223 European Communities – Tariff-Rate Quota on Corn Gluten Feed from the United States – Removed.
WT/DS222 Canada – Export Credits and Loan Guarantees for Regional Aircraft – No retaliation imposed.
WT/DS221 United States – Section 129(c)(1) of the Uruguay Round Agreements Act – Panel Report: US won.
WT/DS220 Chile – Price Band System and Safeguard Measures Relating to Certain Agricultural Products – MAS.
WT/DS219 European Communities – Anti-dumping Duties on Malleable Cast Iron Tube or Pipe Fittings from Brazil – Complied with the DSB rulings after AB report.
WT/DS218 United States – Countervailing Duties on Certain Carbon Steel Products from Brazil – Inactive.
WT/DS216 Mexico – Provisional Anti-dumping Measure on Electric Transformers – Measure expired.
WT/DS215 Philippines – Anti-Dumping Measures Regarding Polypropylene Resins from Korea – MAS.
WT/DS214 United States –Definitive Safeguard Measures on Imports of Steel Wire Rod and Circular Welded Quality Line Pipe – Inactive.
WT/DS213 United States – Countervailing Duties on Certain Corrosion-Resistant Carbon Steel Flat Products from Germany – Implemented after Appellate Body and Panel Report.

WT/DS212 United States – Countervailing Measures Concerning Certain Products from the European Communities – On Implementation after Article 21.5 of the DSU.

WT/DS211 Egypt – Definitive Anti-Dumping Measures on Steel Rebar from Turkey – Implemented Panel's recommendations.

WT/DS210 Belgium – Administration of Measures Establishing Customs Duties for Rice – MAS.

WT/DS209 European Communities – Measures Affecting Soluble Coffee – Inactive.

WT/DS208 Turkey – Anti-Dumping Duty on Steel and Iron Pipe Fittings – Inactive.

WT/DS207 Chile – Price Band System and Safeguard Measures Relating to Certain Agricultural Products – Implemented after Articles 21 and 22 of the DSU.

WT/DS206 United States – Anti-Dumping and Countervailing Measures on Steel Plate from India – Understanding between India and the United States Regarding Procedures Articles 21 and 22 of the DSU.

WT/DS205 Egypt – Import Prohibition on Canned Tuna with Soybean Oil – MAS.

WT/DS204 Mexico – Measures Affecting Telecommunications Services – Implemented Panel Report.

WT/DS203 Mexico – Measures Affecting Trade in Live Swine – MAS.

WT/DS202 United States – Definitive Safeguard Measures on Imports of Circular Welded Carbon Quality Line Pipe from Korea – Agreement under Article 21.3(b) of the DSU.

WT/DS201 Nicaragua – Measures Affecting Imports from Honduras and Colombia – Solved bilaterally and measures were removed.

WT/DS200 United States –Section 306 of the Trade Act of 1974 and Amendments Thereto – m/ina.

WT/DS199 Brazil – Measures Affecting Patent Protection – MAS.

WT/DS198 Romania – Measures on Minimum Import Prices – MAS.

WT/DS197 Brazil – Measures on Minimum Import Prices – Inactive.

WT/DS196, WT/DS171 Argentina – Certain Measures on the Protection of Patents and Test Data – MAS.

WT/DS195 Philippines – Measures Affecting Trade and Investment in the Motor Vehicle Sector – MAS.

WT/DS194 United States – Measures Treating Export Restraints as Subsidies – Panel Report: the US won.

WT/DS193 Chile – Measures Affecting the Transit and Importation of Swordfish – MAS.

WT/DS192, United States – Transitional Safeguard Measure on Combed Cotton Yarn from Pakistan – implemented after AB report.

WT/DS191 Ecuador – Definitive Anti-Dumping Measure on Cement from Mexico – measure expired.

WT/DS190 Argentina – Transitional Safeguard Measures on Certain Imports of Woven Fabrics of Cotton and Cotton Mixtures Originating in Brazil – MAS.

WT/DS189 Argentina – Definitive Anti-Dumping Measures on Imports of Ceramic Floor Tiles from Italy – implemented after Article 21.3(b) of the DSU.

WT/DS188 Nicaragua – Measures Affecting Imports from Honduras and Colombia – Solved.

WT/DS187 Trinidad and Tobago – Provisional Anti-Dumping Measure on Imports of Macaroni and Spaghetti from Costa Rica – MAS.

WT/DS186 United States – Section 337 of the Tariff Act of 1930 and Amendments Thereto – m/ina.

WT/DS185 Trinidad and Tobago – Certain Measures Affecting Imports of Pasta from Costa Rica – MAS.

WT/DS184 United States – Anti-Dumping Measures on Certain Hot-Rolled Steel Products from Japan – RPT extended to 31 July 2005.

WT/DS183 Brazil – Measures on Import Licensing and Minimum Import Prices – Not pending.

WT/DS182 Ecuador – Definitive Anti-Dumping Measures on Grey Portland Cement from Mexico – Measure expired.

WT/DS181 Colombia – Safeguard Measure on Imports of Plain Polyester Filaments from Thailand – Withdrawal.

WT/DS180 United States – Reclassification of Certain Sugar Syrups – Dead.

WT/DS179 United States – Anti-Dumping Measures on Stainless Steel Plate in Coils and Stainless Steel Sheet and Strip from Korea – Implemented after Panel report.

WT/DS178, WT/DS177 United States – Safeguard Measures on Imports of Fresh, Chilled or Frozen Lamb Meat from New Zealand and Australia – Implemented after Appellate Body Reports.

WT/DS176 United States – Section 211 Omnibus Appropriations Act of 1998 – RPT extended to 30 June 2005.

WT/DS175, WT/DS146 India – Measures Affecting the Automotive Sector – Complied after AB report.

WT/DS173 France – Measures relating to the Development of a Flight Management System – m/ina.

WT/DS172 European Communities – Measures relating to the Development of a Flight Management System – m/ina.

WT/DS170 Canada – Term of Patent Protection – Implemented after AB report.

WT/DS169, WT/DS161 Korea – Measures Affecting Imports of Fresh, Chilled and Frozen Beef – Implemented after AB report.

WT/DS168 South Africa – Anti-dumping Duties on Certain Pharmaceutical Products from India – Inactive.

WT/DS167 United States – Countervailing Duty Investigation with Respect to Live Cattle from Canada – Dead.

WT/DS166 United States – Definitive Safeguard Measure on Imports of Wheat Gluten from the European Communities – Implemented after AB report.

WT/DS165 United States – Import Measures on Certain Products from the European Communities – Appellate Body Report and Panel Report: the measure at issue in this dispute no longer in existence.

WT/DS164 Argentina – Measures Affecting Imports of Footwear – Measure lapsed.

WT/DS163 Korea – Measures Affecting Government Procurement – Panel Report: Korea won.

WT/DS162, WT/DS136 United States – Anti-Dumping Act of 1916 – No retaliation taken yet, US Congress has passed law repealing the 1916 Act.

WT/DS160 United States – Section 110(5) of the US Copyright Act – Mutually satisfactory temporary arrangement and agreement expired on 20 December 2004.

WT/DS159 Hungary – Safeguard Measure on Imports of Steel Products from the Czech Republic – Cancelled.

WT/DS158 European Communities – Regime for the Importation, Sale and Distribution of Bananas – settled.

WT/DS157 Argentina – Definitive Anti-Dumping Measures on Imports of Drill Bits from Italy – Measure lapsed.

WT/DS156 Guatemala – Definitive Anti-dumping Measures on Grey Portland Cement from Mexico – Implemented Panel Report.

WT/DS155 Argentina – Measures Affecting the Export of Bovine Hides and the Import of Finished Leather – Complied after Panel report.

WT/DS154 European Communities – Measures affecting Differential and Favorable Treatment of Coffee – Inactive.

WT/DS153 European Communities – Patent Protection for Pharmaceutical and Agricultural Chemical Products – Dead.

WT/DS152 United States – Sections 301-310 of the Trade Act of 1974 – Panel Report: the US won.

WT/DS151 United States – Measures Affecting Textiles and Apparel Products (II) – MAS.

WT/DS150 India – Measures Affecting Customs Duties – Inactive.

WT/DS149 India – Import Restrictions – Inactive.

WT/DS148 Czech Republic – Measure Affecting Import Duty on Wheat from Hungary – Not pending.

WT/DS147 Japan – Tariff Quotas and Subsidies Affecting Leather – Inactive.

WT/DS145 Argentina – Countervailing Duties on Imports of Wheat Gluten from the European Communities – Inactive.

WT/DS144 United States – Certain Measures Affecting the Import of Cattle, Swine and Grain from Canada – MAS.

WT/DS143 Slovak Republic – Measure Affecting Import Duty on Wheat from Hungary – Withdrew.

WT/DS142, WT/DS139 Canada – Certain Measures Affecting the Automotive Industry – Implemented after AB report.

WT/DS141 European Communities – Anti-Dumping Duties on Imports of Cotton-Type Bed Linen from India – Implemented after AB Reports.

WT/DS140 European Communities – Anti-Dumping Investigations Regarding Unbleached Cotton Fabrics from India – Settled.

WT/DS138 United States – Imposition of Countervailing Duties on Certain Hot-Rolled Lead and Bismuth Carbon Steel Products Originating in the United Kingdom – Implemented after AB Report.

WT/DS137 European Communities – Measures Affecting Imports of Wood of Conifers from Canada – Settled.

WT/DS135 European Communities – Measures Affecting Asbestos and Asbestos-Containing Products – Appellate Body Report: EC won.

WT/DS134 European Communities – Restrictions on Certain Import Duties on Rice – Settled.
WT/DS133 Slovak Republic – Measures concerning the Importation of Dairy Products and the Transit of Cattle – Solved.
WT/DS132, WT/DS101 Mexico – Anti-Dumping Investigation of High Fructose Corn Syrup (HFCS) from the United States – Implemented after AB report.
WT/DS131 France – Certain Income Tax Measures Constituting Subsidies – Settled.
WT/DS130 Ireland – Certain Income Tax Measures Constituting Subsidies – Settled.
WT/DS129 Greece – Certain Income Tax Measures Constituting Subsidies – Settled.
WT/DS128 Netherlands – Certain Income Tax Measures Constituting Subsidies – Settled.
WT/DS127 Belgium – Certain Income Tax Measures Constituting Subsidies – Settled.
WT/DS126 Australia – Subsidies Provided to Producers and Exporters of Automotive Leather – MAS after Recourse to Article 21.5 of the DSU by the United States.
WT/DS125 Greece – Enforcement of Intellectual Property Rights for Motion Pictures and Television Programmes – MAS.
WT/DS124 European Communities – Enforcement of Intellectual Property Rights for Motion Pictures and Television Programmes – MAS.
WT/DS123 Argentina – Safeguard Measures on Imports of Footwear – Withdrawal. WT/DS122 Thailand – Anti-Dumping Duties on Angles, Shapes and Sections of Iron or Non-alloy Steel and H-Beams from Poland – Reached agreement after AB report.
WT/DS121 Argentina – Safeguard Measures on Imports of Footwear – Implemented after AB Report.
WT/DS120 India – Measures Affecting Export of Certain Commodities – Not pending.
WT/DS119 Australia – Anti-Dumping Measures on Imports of Coated Woodfree Paper Sheets – MAS.
WT/DS118 United States – Harbour Maintenance Tax – m/ina.
WT/DS117 Canada – Measures Affecting Film Distribution Services – Lapsed.
WT/DS116 Brazil – Measures Affecting Payment Terms for Imports – Inactive.
WT/DS115, WT/DS82 European Communities, Ireland – Measures Affecting the Grant of Copyright and Neighbouring Rights – MAS.
WT/DS114 Canada – Patent Protection of Pharmaceutical Products – Implemented after Panel report.
WT/DS113, WT/DS103 Canada – Measures Affecting the Importation of Milk and the Exportation of Dairy Products – MAS.
WT/DS112 Peru – Countervailing Duty Investigation Against Imports of Buses from Brazil – Inactive.
WT/DS111 United States – Tariff Rate Quota for Imports of Groundnuts – m/ina.
WT/DS110, WT/DS87 Chile – Taxes on Alcoholic Beverages – Implemented after AB report.
WT/DS109 Chile – Taxes on Alcoholic Beverages – Cancelled.
WT/DS108 United States – Tax Treatment for Foreign Sales Corporations – On Appealing of Article 21.5 Panel Report.
WT/DS107 Pakistan – Export Measures Affecting Hides and Skins – Inactive.

WT/DS106 Australia – Subsidies Provided to Producers and Exporters of Automotive Leather – US withdrawal.

WT/DS105 European Communities – Regime for the Importation, Sale and Distribution of Bananas – Cancelled.

WT/DS104 European Communities – Measures Affecting the Exportation of Processed Cheese – Settled.

WT/DS102, WT/DS74 Philippines – Measures Affecting Pork and Poultry – MAS. WT/DS100 United States – Measures Affecting Imports of Poultry Products – MAS.

WT/DS99 United States – Anti-Dumping Duty on Dynamic Random Access Memory Semiconductors (DRAMs) of One Megabit or Above from Korea – Implemented after Panel report.

WT/DS98 Korea – Definitive Safeguard Measure on Imports of Certain Dairy Products – Implemented after AB report.

WT/DS97 United States – Countervailing Duty Investigation of Imports of Salmon from Chile – Dead.

WT/DS96, WT/DS94, WT/DS93, WT/DS92, WT/DS91 India – Quantitative Restrictions on Imports of Agricultural, Textile and Industrial Products – MAS.

WT/DS95, WT/DS88 United States –Measure Affecting Government Procurement – Lapse of Authority for Establishment of the Panel.

WT/DS90 India – Quantitative Restrictions on Imports of Agricultural, Textile and Industrial Products – Implemented after AB report.

WT/DS89 United States – Imposition of Anti-Dumping Duties on Imports of Colour Television Receivers from Korea – Withdrawal.

WT/DS86 Sweden – Measures Affecting the Enforcement of Intellectual Property Rights – MAS.

WT/DS85 United States – Measures Affecting Textiles Apparel Products – MAS.

WT/DS84, WT/DS75 Korea – Taxes on Alcoholic Beverages – Implemented after AB report.

WT/DS83 Denmark – Measures Affecting the Enforcement of Intellectual Property Rights – MAS.

WT/DS81 Brazil – Certain Measures Affecting Trade and Investment in the Automotive Sector – Not pending.

WT/DS80 Belgium –Measures affecting Commercial Telephone Directory Services – Settled.

WT/DS79, WT/DS50 India – Patent Protection for Pharmaceutical and Agricultural Chemical Products – Complied after AB report.

WT/DS78 United States – Safeguard Measure against Imports of Broom Corn Brooms – MAS.

WT/DS77 Argentina – Measures Affecting Textiles and Clothing – Lapse of Authority for the Establishment of the Panel.

WT/DS76 Japan – Measures Affecting Agricultural Products – MAS after AB report.

WT/DS73 Japan – Procurement of a Navigation Satellite – MAS.

WT/DS72 European Communities – Measures Affecting Butter Products – MAS.

WT/DS71 Canada – Measures Affecting the Export of Civilian Aircraft – No retaliation imposed yet.

WT/DS70 Canada – Measures Affecting the Export of Civilian Aircraft – Recourse by Brazil to Article 21.5 of the DSU – No retaliation imposed yet.

WT/DS69 European Communities – Measures Affecting the Importation of Certain Poultry Products – Implemented after AB report.

WT/DS68, WT/DS67, WT/DS62 European Communities – Customs Classification of Certain Computer Equipment – Appellate Body Report: EC won.

WT/DS66 Japan – Measures Affecting Imports of Pork – Inactive.

WT/DS65 Brazil – Certain Measures Affecting Trade and Investment in the Automotive Sector – MAS.

WT/DS64, WT/DS59, WT/DS55, WT/DS54 Indonesia – Certain Measures Affecting the Automobile Industry – Implemented after Panel report.

WT/DS63 United States – Anti-Dumping Measures on Imports of Solid Urea from the Former German Democratic Republic – MAS.

WT/DS61 United States – Import Prohibition of Certain Shrimp and Shrimp Products – Not pending.

WT/DS60 Guatemala – Anti-Dumping Investigation Regarding Portland Cement from Mexico – Appellate Body Report: Guatemala won.

WT/DS58 United States – Import Prohibition of Certain Shrimp and Shrimp Products – Implemented Report of the Appellate Body.

WT/DS57 Australia – Textile, Clothing and Footwear Import Credit Scheme – Settled.

WT/DS56 Argentina – Measures Affecting Imports of Footwear, Textiles, Apparel and other Items – Implemented after AB report.

WT/DS53 Mexico – Customs Valuation of Imports – Inactive.

WT/DS52 Brazil – Certain Automotive Investment Measures – MAS.

WT/DS51 Brazil – Certain Automotive Investment Measures – Not pending.

WT/DS49 United States – Anti-Dumping Investigation Regarding Imports of Fresh or Chilled Tomatoes from Mexico – Settled.

WT/DS48, WT/DS26 European Communities – Measures Concerning Meat and Meat Products (Hormones) – Retaliation imposed.

WT/DS47 Turkey – Restrictions on Imports of Textile and Clothing Products – Not pending.

WT/DS46 Brazil – Export Financing Programme for Aircraft – No retaliation imposed yet.

WT/DS45 Japan – Measures Affecting Distribution Services – m/ina.

WT/DS44 Japan – Measures Affecting Consumer Photographic Film and Paper – Report of the Panel: Japan won.

WT/DS43 Turkey – Taxation of Foreign Film Revenues – MAS.

WT/DS42 Japan – Measures Concerning Sound Recordings – MAS.

WT/DS41 Korea – Measures concerning Inspection of Agricultural Products – Solved.

WT/DS40 Korea – Laws, Regulations and Practices in the Telecommunications Procurement Sector – MAS.

WT/DS39 United States – Tariff increases on products from the European Communities –US withdrew the measure.

WT/DS38 United States – The Cuban Liberty and Democratic Solidarity Act – Lapse of the Authority for Establishment of the Panel.

WT/DS37 Portugal – Patent Protection under the Industrial Property Act – MAS.
WT/DS36 Pakistan – Patent Protection for Pharmaceutical and Agricultural Chemical Products – MAS.
WT/DS35 Hungary – Export Subsidies in respect of Agricultural Products – MAS.
WT/DS34 Turkey – Restrictions on Imports of Textile and Clothing Products – MAS.
WT/DS33 United States – Measures Affecting Imports of Woven Wool Shirts and Blouses from India – AB-1991-1 – Measure withdrawn after AB report.
WT/DS32 United States – Measures Affecting Imports of Women's and Girls' Wool Coats – Removed the restraint.
WT/DS31 Canada – Certain Measures Concerning Periodicals – Withdrew measure after AB report.
WT/DS30 Brazil – Countervailing Duties on Imports of Desiccated Coconut and Coconut Milk Powder from Sri Lanka – Not pending.
WT/DS29 Turkey – Restrictions on imports of Textile and Clothing Products – Not pending.
WT/DS28 Japan – Measures Concerning Sound Recordings – MAS.
WT/DS27 European Communities – Regime for the Importation, Sale and Distribution of Bananas – Retaliation imposed by US and withdrawn by Ecuador.
WT/DS25 European Communities – Implementation of the Uruguay Round Commitments Concerning Rice – No report but solved.
WT/DS24 United States – Restrictions on Imports of Cotton and Man-made Fibre Underwear – Complied after Report of the Appellate Body.
WT/DS23 Venezuela – Anti-Dumping Investigation in Respect of Imports of Certain Oil Country Tubular Goods (OCTG) – Venezuela decided to close the investigation.
WT/DS22 Brazil – Measures Affecting Desiccated Coconut – AB Report: Brazil won.
WT/DS21 Australia – Measures Affecting the Importation of Salmonids – MAS. WT/DS20 Korea – Measures concerning Bottled Water – MAS.
WT/DS19 Poland – Import Regime for Automobiles – MAS.
WT/DS18 Australia – Measures Affecting Importation of Salmon – Recourse to Article 21.5 by Canada – Complied Report of the Panel.
WT/DS17 European Communities – Duties on Imports of Rice – No report but solved.
WT/DS16 European Communities – Regime for the Importation, Sale and Distribution of Bananas – Cancelled.
WT/DS15 Japan – Measures Affecting the Purchase of Telecommunications Equipment – No official notification but solved.
WT/DS14, WT/DS12 European Communities – Trade Description of Scallops – MAS.
WT/DS13 European Communities – Duties on Imports of Grains – MAS.
WT/DS11, WT/DS10, WT/DS8 Japan – Taxes on Alcoholic Beverages – MAS.
WT/DS9 European Communities – Duties on Imports of Cereals – No Panellists selected.
WT/DS7 European Communities –Trade Description of Scallops – MAS.
WT/DS6 United States – Imposition of Import Duties on Automobiles from Japan under Sections 301 and 304 of the Trade act of 1974 – Notified settlement.
WT/DS5 Korea – Measures Concerning the Shelf-Life of Products – MAS.
WT/DS4 United States – Standards for Reformulated and Conventional Gasoline – Implemented after Report of the Appellate Body.

WT/DS3 Korea – Measures Concerning the Testing and Inspection of Agricultural Products – Solved.
WT/DS2 United States – Standards for Reformulated and Conventional Gasoline – Implemented after AB report.
WT/DS1 Malaysia – Prohibition of Imports of Polyethylene and Polypropylene – Modified the import licensing measure for polypropylene.

Index

C

D

E

F

G

H

I

J

K

L

M

N

T

U

V

W

Z

Studies in Global Economic Law
Studien zum globalen Wirtschaftsrecht
Études en droit économique mondial

Present and future economic, technological and societal changes and evolutions fundamentally affect traditional legal structures of the territorial state system. They increasingly call for global approaches and solutions, transgressing the tools of classical public international law. This trilingual series publishes monographs, studies and collected papers dedicated to these challenges. The contributions examine existing instruments, in particular within the framework of the international trading system. They explore new approaches and search for innovative solutions within the global process of legal integration. Research efforts are dedicated to different walks of life and areas of regulation, and to the quest for adequate constitutional structures of transnational and democratic processes.

Wirtschaftliche, technologische und gesellschaftliche Entwicklungen der Gegenwart und Zukunft bewirken tiefgreifende Änderungen traditioneller Strukturen des Rechts des Territorialstaats und rufen zunehmend nach globalen Vorgehensweisen und Lösungen, die oftmals über das Instrumentarium des klassischen Völkerrechts hinaus weisen. Die dreisprachige Reihe publiziert Monographien, Studien und Tagungsbände, die sich vertieft mit diesen Herausforderungen auseinandersetzen. Die Beiträge untersuchen das bestehende Instrumentarium namentlich im Rahmen des Welthandelssystems und forschen nach neuen An-sätzen und Lösungen im Rahmen des globalen Integrationsprozesses. Dazu gehören Studien zu den Regelungen einzelner Sach- und Lebensbereiche wie auch zu Fragen adäquater transnationaler demokratischer Verfassungs- und Entscheidungsstrukturen.

Les évolutions actuelles et futures sur le plan technique, économique et social ne cesseront d'influencer profondément les structures traditionnelles du droit de l'état territorial. Par conséquent, des approches et des solutions dépassant les instruments du droit international public classique deviennent de plus en plus nécessaires. Cette collection trilingue publie des monographies, études et actes de colloques qui analysent et font face à ces défis. Les contributions examinent les instruments existants, notamment dans la domaine du système commercial mondiale. Elles cherchent à développer des approches nouvelles et des solutions innovatrices dans le contexte du processus d'intégration globale en incluant des études de droit touchant aux différents secteurs et domaines de vie. De plus, les travaux de recherche seront également destinés à trouver les procédures consti-tutionnelles et décisionnelles les plus adéquates et démocratiques au niveau transnational.

Studies in Global Economic Law
Studien zum globalen Wirtschaftsrecht
Études en droit économique mondial

edited by Thomas Cottier

Vol. 1 Martin A. Girsberger – Biodiversity and the Concept of Farmers' Rights in International Law, 1999

Vol. 2 David Wyss – Bankdienstleistungen im Allgemeinen Dienstleistungsabkommen der WTO. Auswirkungen auf das schwiezerische Bankenrecht, 1999

Vol. 3 Benoît Merkt – Harmonisation internationale et entraide administrative internationale en droit de la concurrence. Droit du GATT/OMC, droit européen, accords bilatéraux et perspectives pour le droit suisse, 2000

Vol. 4 Ingo Meitinger – Der Schutz von Geschäftsgeheimnissen im globalen und regionalen Wirtschaftsrecht. Stand und mögliche Entwicklungen der internationalen und regionalen Rechtsharmonisierung, 2001

Vol. 5 Joëlle de Sépibus – Die Umweltschutzsubvention im Gemeinschaftsrecht. Eine umweltrechtliche Kritik der europäischen Beihilfekontrolle, 2003

Vol. 6 Bobjoseph Mathew – The WTO Agreements on Telecommunications,
2003

Vol. 7 Lukas Engelberger – Die Unmittelbare Anwendbarkeit des WTO-Rechts in der Schweiz. Grundlagen und Perspektiven im Kontext internationaler Rechtsentwicklung, 2004

Vol. 8 Thomas M. Fischer – Die Entbündelung der letzten Meile in der Schweiz im Lichte des GATS, 2004

Vol. 9 Dae-Won Kim – Non-Violation Complaints in WTO Law. Theory and Practice, 2006

Vol. 10 Qi Zhang – Consultation within WTO Dispute Settlement: A Chinese Perspective, 2007

FSC
www.fsc.org
MIX
Papier | Fördert
gute Waldnutzung
FSC® C083411

Kolibri 360 GmbH
Ferdinand-Jühlke-Straße 7
99095 Erfurt, Deutschland
produktsicherheit@kolibri360.de

Druck:
CPI Druckdienstleistungen GmbH
im Auftrag der
Kolibri 360 GmbH
Ferdinand-Jühlke-Str. 7
99095 Erfurt